WHY THE ENLIGHTENMENT MATTERS

The shift in our thinking that made the modern world

WHY THE ENLIGHTENMENT MATTERS

*The shift in our thinking
that made the modern world*

ADAM WAKELING

AʃP

© Adam Wakeling 2023

First published 2023 by
Australian Scholarly Publishing Pty Ltd
7 Lt Lothian St North
North Melbourne, Victoria 3051

tel: 61 3 93296963
enquiry@scholarly.info / www.scholarly.com

ISBN: 978-1-922952-06-6

ALL RIGHTS RESERVED

Cover design: Amelia Walker

CONTENTS

Introduction	1
I: The World Before Enlightenment	18
II: The End of Authority	34
III: The Toleration of Dissent and the Enlightenment in the Netherlands	47
IV: Challenging the Divine Right of England's Kings	65
V: Government by Contract and the Enlightenment in England	82
VI: Thinking Scientifically	106
VII: A Heretical Idea	120
VIII: The Science of Man and the Enlightenment in Scotland	133
IX: Free Trade Over Mercantilism	153
X: *Enclyclopédie* and the Enlightenment in France	169
XI: Human Rights	189
XII: Bridging Science and Technology	208
XIII: Enlightenment's End?	220
XIV: Escaping the Malthusian Trap	237
XV: The Divergence	243
Conclusion	255
Notes	262
Index	276

INTRODUCTION

On the morning of 27 October 1553, as the bells of St Pierre Cathedral began to strike eleven, the constabulary of Geneva led a bound man out of the city's south-east gates.[1] The prisoner was in his early forties, a bearded man of medium height and slight build. A nondescript man, in other words, except for one feature—nobody who met him failed to notice the intensity of his dark eyes. He was a Spaniard, and his name was Miguel Serveto. In those days learned men were commonly called by the Latinised version of their names, hence we know him today as Michael Servetus. And he was immensely learned—a polyglot, scholar, theologian, scientist, and Renaissance man in every sense of the word. While studying medicine in Paris, he had written the first book in Europe to give an accurate description of how the blood circulates between the heart and the lungs (Middle Eastern scholar Ibn al-Nafis had previously written on it in Arabic).

It was not his medical knowledge for which Servetus was then famous, however. Or infamous. He was a heretic. This might seem odd to us today, for Servetus was a devout Christian who professed Christ as his saviour. But in reading the Bible and the works of the church fathers, Servetus concluded there was no basis for the concept of the Holy Trinity—one God in three eternal persons—the Father, the Son and the Holy Spirit. Jesus was undoubtedly the son of God, he concluded, but Jesus did not exist until God created him in Mary's womb. Christians would describe Jesus as the 'eternal son of God' when, in fact, they should call him 'son of eternal God'. The placement of the word 'eternal' would prove a matter of life and death.

His anti-Trinitarianism was not Servetus' only heresy, as he also believed there was no support in the Bible for the practice of baptising infants. People should only be baptised if they decided to join the Church of their own volition. On these points, Servetus concluded, all mainstream Christian scholars—Catholic, Calvinist and Lutheran alike—were wrong. But it would be his refusal to call Jesus the 'eternal son of God' which would be his undoing.

Servetus was a very intelligent man but also a fiery and intemperate one. In his writings, he called infant baptism 'a diabolical invention and infernal falsehood destructive of Christianity' and described the Holy Trinity as a three-headed monster which could only be accepted by polytheists. Forced from France and in flight to Italy, he was arrested in Geneva. On 24 October the Council of Geneva found him guilty and pronounced the sentence for heresy, dreaded throughout Medieval Europe: 'We condemn thee, Michael Servetus, to be bound, and led to the place of Champel, there to be fastened to a stake and burnt alive, together with thy book, as well the one written by thy hand as the printed one, even till thy body be reduced to ashes; and thus shalt thou finish thy days to furnish an example to others who might wish to commit the like'.

Servetus would not change his opinion. On the morning of his execution, he was locked in a debate with a Protestant theologian, William Farel, who urged him to repent and save his soul. Servetus asked Farel to produce a Bible verse which described Jesus as 'Son of God' before his incarnation. Farel could not satisfy him. The exchange was interrupted by the arrival of Geneva's *de facto* religious leader, Protestant reformer John Calvin himself.

Calvin's appearance brought an element of human tragedy to the whole episode. Calvin and Servetus had once been friends, before they fell out over the question of the Trinity. The two men were undoubtedly alike in many ways, from the depth of their erudition to the steadfastness of their views. Servetus had been arrested at a sermon Calvin was preaching, and Calvin had been the driving force behind his prosecution.

As Calvin's own followers were then being sent to the flames throughout Catholic Europe, Calvin might have had a reason to sympathise with Servetus. But the irony did not occur to him—his followers were martyrs to the truth, not heretics. His position in Geneva was far from secure; the city was then in the midst of theological strife between Calvin and his followers on one side and a rival Protestant sect on the other. And Calvin needed to show Europe he could be just as tough on heresy as the Catholic Church which he sought to overthrow. And finally, he believed wholeheartedly that heresy deserved death. 'Whoever shall now contend that it is unjust to put heretics and blasphemers to death will knowingly and willingly incur their very guilt' he wrote in his own tract on heresy. Throughout the trial he prayed Servetus would repent, and when he did not, asked as a last mercy for the Council to grant him a faster death by beheading. But he did not doubt either the justice or necessity of putting his old friend to death.

In their final meeting, Calvin insisted he never bore any personal animosity against Servetus.

'Sixteen years ago I spared no pains at Paris to gain you to our Lord' Calvin told him. 'You then shunned the light. I did not cease to exhort you by letters, but all in vain. You have heaped upon me I know not how much fury rather than anger. But as to the rest, I pass by what concerns myself. Think rather of crying for mercy to God whom you have blasphemed.' Servetus remained quiet and humble, but he would not repent. In obedience to St Paul's exhortation in Titus 3:10–11 to shun heretics, Calvin left the room. The kindly Farel stayed with Servetus to the end, and walked with him on the fateful road to Champel. Servetus asked God to forgive him his sins and forgive his accusers, and professed his belief in Christ as his saviour. But he would not repent.

Today, Champel is a leafy suburb of Geneva offering fine views of the rocky massif of the Salève to the south. The constables took Servetus to a spot which now is opposite the University Hospital, a short walk from the street which today bears Servetus' name. There the Lord Lieutenant of the city and his herald were waiting on horseback amidst the drifts of fallen autumn leaves. And next to them, the executioner and the stake, with bundles of wood piled around. Servetus saw that the wood was still green, and knew his death would not be fast. The small procession of spectators which had followed the party from the gates of the city gathered around. Farel called on them to pray for Servetus; Servetus remained silent.

The first person in Europe to write an accurate account of pulmonary circulation was led to his pyre. The executioner secured Servetus to the stake with an iron chain, placed a copy of his heretical book *Cristianismi Restitutio* in his arms, and bound book, man and stake together with a rope. He placed a crown of leaves covered with sulphur on his head, and brought forth the burning torch. 'Misericordias!' ('Mercy!') Servetus cried, falling back into his native tongue as the heat from the fire made his horrifying fate brutally real.

The executioner set the torch to the logs, but green wood burned only slowly. Some of the spectators, either through impatience or a feeling of humanity, threw bundles of dry firewood onto the pyre to hasten Servetus' end. Then the flames began to take him. The spectators were assailed by smoke, and soon afterwards, the smell of burning flesh. The ordeal continued, minute by minute. Then Servetus gave a last cry of 'Jesus Christ, thou Son of the eternal God, have mercy upon me!' Son of the eternal God, not eternal Son of God—Servetus held to his beliefs to the end. He spoke no more, and the fire consumed his body.

Calvin was unrepentant, and throughout Europe, Servetus' fate was unexceptional. But not everyone approved. One of Calvin's critics, Sebastian Castellio, wrote In the book *Contra Libelum Calvinim* (Against Calvin's Booklet):

> To kill a man is not to defend a doctrine: it is to kill a man. If Calvin had killed Servetus for saying what he believed to be true, then Calvin killed him for telling the truth. He should have been taught, not killed, if he was wrong. I believe that on judgment day God will judge morals, not dogmas.

It was, perhaps, a sign of things to come.

***

I write Servetus' story from the living room of my apartment in Melbourne's inner west. And between his life and mine, there is a gulf which can only be crossed with a tremendous leap of imagination. Today is a Sunday, yet I'm not forced to attend any religious ceremony. I am free to write in this book that God is three people, or one, or none at all. The laptop on which I'm writing would seem like an instrument of black magic to people of Servetus' time, or even my great-grandparents. If I want to check something, I can take my phone out of my pocket and use it to access humanity's collective knowledge through the internet. The varied and cheap food at my local supermarket would look like a miracle to the hundreds of generations of humanity living with the threat of starvation. For most of history parasites such as lice and fleas were ubiquitous and often spread dangerous diseases, but as I can have a shower and put on clean clothes every day I have no fear of them. If I get sick, I can go to the local doctor, courtesy of Australia's public health system. Even though I'm in my thirties I still have all my teeth, thanks to modern dentistry—without it I would have lost them by now. When I was twelve I became short-sighted, but can see thanks to modern optometry and affordable mass-produced spectacles. Had I lived any time before the twentieth century, my world would have been a blur. I am neither rich nor poor by the standards of twenty-first century Australia, but compared to the generations of humanity before mine, I am part of a global one per cent.

People who live in western countries today live in the most successful societies in human history. Our civilisation is the only one to have had knowledge of the atom, the cell, the galaxy, evolution through natural selection, the connection between germs and disease, vaccination, how electricity may be harnessed to create motion, general anaesthesia, and birth control. Ours is the only civilisation in which the majority of citizens can read and write, where the death of a woman in childbirth is seen as a freak tragedy rather than a fact of everyday life, and where starvation is almost unknown. We have gone further than anyone before in restraining the exercise of power with the apparatus of law, providing effective means of peaceful dispute resolution, and protecting the rights of individuals to speak and worship as they choose. Anyone who turns on the TV news at night can see that we still have a long way to go, and the struggle against want, injustice and oppression will not be won in our lifetimes, if at all. But we have the potential to keep going.

In this book, I will argue our successes are not simple good fortune or the inevitable progress of history. Rather they are due to a decisive shift in our thinking which took place over the seventeenth and eighteenth centuries. Across the Christian and Islamic worlds in Servetus' time, from the Atlantic coast of Ireland to northern India, conventional thinking on topics from science to politics was defined by a rigid philosophy combining the ideas of Ancient Greece with the scriptures of the Abrahamic religions. China remained similarly restrained by centuries of inflexible Confucianism. Due to some historical and geographical oddities, thinkers in north-western Europe in the early seventeenth century began to tear down this philosophic edifice and come up with replacements. For simplicity, I will refer to this shift in thinking in its entirety as the Enlightenment, although many historians view the Enlightenment as a narrower and more specific period of this time.

This shift in the seventeenth and eighteenth centuries gave us the ideas on which the success of the modern West depends, like freedom of speech, the scientific method, legal restraints on the power of government, a free market economy, and human rights. In short, modernity. These ideas all had origins much further back in time. And nor were they only ever proposed in north-western Europe. For example, the often-overlooked Ethiopian philosopher Zera Yacob (1599–1692) wrote about empirical thinking, freedom of religion and freedom of speech before Baruch Spinoza or John Locke did. Yet it was only in northern and western Europe during the Enlightenment these ideas came together into one cohesive whole, took on the forms we know today, and came to become the dominant ideas of these societies. Theologians across the Christian and Islamic world had affirmed for centuries that man was beloved of God and created in his image, yet this had little effect on the practical brutality of everyday life before the Enlightenment. Antecedents to the Industrial Revolution and the rise of capitalism had been seen in advanced societies from Renaissance Italy to Gujarat in India, but none had taken off. Zera Yacob was a great philosopher, but his principles were not taken up by Ethiopian society in the same way the principles of the Enlightenment thinkers were taken up in their societies (at least eventually). I have set out to explain how this happened and why it mattered.

***

People who live in western countries today live in a civilisation defined by the Enlightenment. We are marinated in it. But the Enlightenment was not inevitable. In Europe in 1600, there was little reason to believe the world would be very different in 1800, and completely unrecognisable in 2000. In retrospect, the unpredictable can look like the unavoidable. For example, think about the global domination of the English language today. We take it for granted that English is the international language of commerce, academia and entertainment. Yet a thousand years ago, English (as it existed then) was a minor language spoken on the fringe of the developed world, no more significant than Finnish, Bulgarian, Armenian, or Vietnamese. Suggesting a businessman or politician in wealthy and populous India would one day need to speak English would be absurd.

It's easy to make the same mistake about the Enlightenment. We can treat the Scientific Revolution, the Declaration of the Rights of Man and the Industrial Revolution as natural and inexorable steps on the pathway from living in a cave to living on the International Space Station. But the Enlightenment was neither natural nor inevitable. Established ideas about science, philosophy and politics had not been proven inadequate, and they had powerful, intelligent and energetic defenders. Today, we think of a modern liberal democracy like Canada as the default human society, and an authoritarian theocracy like Iran as an aberration. But throughout history, human beings have tended to live in societies more like modern Iran than modern Canada.

Nor was the Enlightenment part of a gradual progression towards more knowledge, more wealth, and more freedom. Human history has had periods when life improved, periods when it went backwards and, more commonly than both, periods when it hardly changed. Outside episodes of upheaval, most human beings lived a life almost identical to their great-grandparents. Since the Enlightenment, though, we have been living in the longest and most significant of these periods of upheaval.

Here's one example from science which shows just how fixed and long-lasting ideas can be, even ideas which later turned out to be wrong, and also how quickly they could be overturned. In Ancient Greece, Aristotle taught that the sun, moon and planets orbited the Earth in fixed spheres of aether, each one moved by its own god. In 1600, nearly two millennia later, almost every educated person in Europe still believed Aristotle had been correct, although they had replaced his pagan gods with Christian angels. Likewise with scholars in the Islamic world, although their angels were obviously those referred to in the Qur'an rather than those in the Bible. In China, Jesuit missionaries had introduced Aristotle's model, where it replaced the previously held belief that the world was flat. In 1700, by contrast, most educated people in the Protestant countries in northern Europe knew the Earth and the other planets orbited the Sun, they were held in place by gravity, and their movement was governed by laws of motion as explained in scientific papers. I will describe this particular example in more detail in Chapter VII. It is one example of many; there were more scientific advances in Europe between 1600 and 1800 than in the entire world in the entire course of human history before that point.

The Enlightenment was a time of introspection and challenge. Western society turned its attention in on itself, questioned its fundamental principles, and discarded many of them. It replaced them with new ones, which I will summarise as the recognition of the limits of reason, empirical thinking, the toleration of dissent, universality, and progress. These, in turn, led to the scientific method, constitutional government, human rights, the modern capitalist economy, and the other drivers of high standards of living in the developed world today. Here are the five factors in more detail.

First, the limitation of reason. This sounds odd, as the Enlightenment is often called 'The Age of Reason', after a book by Thomas Paine published between 1794 and 1807. Paine's book is an attack on organised religion and a defence of deism, the belief that there is a God but he does not conform to the dogma of any formal religion. 'I believe in one God, and no more; and I hope for happiness beyond this life' Paine wrote.

> I do not believe in the creed professed by the Jewish church, by the Roman church, by the Greek church, by the Turkish church, by the Protestant church, nor by any church that I know of. My own mind is my own church. All national institutions of churches, whether Jewish, Christian or Turkish, appear to me no other than human inventions, set up to terrify and enslave mankind, and monopolize power and profit.[2] This is the sort of writing typical of the Enlightenment.

Still, calling the Enlightenment 'The Age of Reason' is actually something of a misnomer; it was the age when we recognised the limits to our reason and accounted for them. The ancients and the medieval scholars believed the universe had an innate order which could be figured out. This was particularly true of Christian and Islamic philosophers, who held it had been created by a benevolent God who had given men the gift of reason so they could come to know him through his creation. Into the seventeenth century, it was still seen as necessary for researchers to begin scientific tracts with a discussion on how the discoveries meshed with existing philosophy and theology.[3] Enlightenment philosophers, by contrast, recognised that the world around us was more random and complex than we had thought, and our powers of reason were more limited than we would like to admit. David Hume famously declared that reason could only ever be a slave to the passions, and Immanuel Kant titled his major work on knowledge the *Critique of Pure Reason* (1781). We were like someone looking through an ajar door into a dark room—some objects would be visible, some obscured or in shadow, and some unknown to us in complete darkness.

How, then, could we open the door further? This leads to the second principle of the Enlightenment—empirical thinking. The only way to gain knowledge of the world around us was to go out and observe it. We could then develop hypotheses and see if they fit these observations. And if they did not, they needed to be changed or discarded, no matter how well they fit in with our existing ideas. Empirical thinking led us to inductive reasoning and the scientific method.

Recognising the limits to our reason also gave us the third principle—toleration of dissent. If I don't know everything, then I shouldn't be able to stop you from disagreeing with me. Toleration in early modern Europe began through necessity, once Catholics and Protestants both recognised that neither was strong enough to completely overcome the other. It then developed, through the works of writers such as John Locke, Baruch Spinoza, Voltaire, Adam Smith and Thomas Paine, into an active good. From this principle came rights to freedom of thought, speech, and press, as well as the ability of scientists to freely publish their findings even when they conflicted with religious doctrine.

Modern science assumes the laws of the universe are constant and predictable. This leads onto the fourth principle, universality. The Enlightenment rejected special knowledge, special rules, special privileges and arbitrary divisions. Just as gravity applies everywhere, so too do human rights apply to everyone. The Enlightenment promoted humanism. As Baruch Spinoza wrote, 'the good which everyone who seeks virtue wants for himself, he also desires for other men'.[4]

The final Enlightenment idea is perhaps the one which has had the biggest impact on the world—the idea of progress. In other words, the expectation that things can improve. We can know more, produce more, and learn to treat our fellow human beings better. Science, constitutional government, and market economics all depend on the belief that the present is not perfect. The growth of scientific knowledge, the industrial revolution, political emancipation and the spread of human rights are all manifestations of the idea of progress in our society.

***

The Enlightenment was not the first period of technological, economic and social progress in human history, but it marked the beginning of what is by far the longest and most spectacular. There were other societies which could point to Golden Ages of their own—the Ancient Greek city-states, Medieval Baghdad, Song China, or Renaissance Italy. But none managed to sustain their progress long enough to see the benefits of wealth and innovation spread throughout society and improve the lives of ordinary people. The engineers of the Song Dynasty in China invented the pound lock, marine compass, block printing and gunpower, but the average Chinese peasant still lived the hard and narrow life which has been the lot of almost all human beings before modern times. And for all societies before ours, a step forward was inevitably followed by a step backwards. The mini-Renaissance of the High Middle Ages in Europe, for example, was followed by the Late Medieval Crisis with its famines, plagues and peasant revolts.

Progress which was both widespread and sustained was extremely difficult to achieve—how difficult is hard to see in retrospect. While the Enlightenment came about in the seventeenth and eighteenth centuries, the economic benefits only reached ordinary people in the nineteenth. Likewise, the new political ideas of liberalism, constitutional government and the secular state took time to roll down from the elite. Our society continues to grapple with questions around these institutions and how their benefits might be best-realised by more people today and into the future.

In a sense, the Enlightenment hasn't really ended, as its ideas continue to dominate our society. Conventionally, though, the Enlightenment is usually taken to end sometime between the start of the French Revolution in 1789 and the end of the Napoleonic Wars in 1815.

Obviously the Europe of 1789 is not the world we live in today. Science was far more advanced than it had been two centuries earlier but still rudimentary by our standards—people believed diseases were caused by miasma, or bad air, or supernatural causes. A quick review of the headstones in a nineteenth-century cemetery shows how common infant mortality still was. Slavery was both legal and practiced in the British and French colonial empires and in the United States. Some of the worst atrocities of the colonial era, such as the Belgian administration of the Congo, were still ahead. Women could not vote, nor enter most professions, and married women could not own property. People who committed minor crimes could be hanged in public or transported to penal colonies for life. Laws restricting freedom of religion or political expression were common. Political power was concentrated in the hands of a wealthy minority and poor people were powerless. But the ideas which brought us from 1600 to 1789 are the same ideas which have brought us from 1789 to today. We can—and have—made further progress.

Paradoxically, this can make Enlightenment easy to overlook. Unlike the Renaissance, for example, the Enlightenment has not left us statues or basilicas. We cannot point to something as 'an Enlightenment building' or 'Enlightenment art'. It left us ideas, and those ideas are so embedded in our society we may not give them any thought, in the same way a fish may not be aware of the water it swims in.

Of course, we do need to acknowledge that the legacy of the Enlightenment is not uniformly positive. For example, the Enlightenment did not invent colonialism or racism, but it did facilitate them in new ways. John Locke's treatises provided a justification for seizing land from indigenous peoples. Thomas Jefferson wrote that it was self-evident all men are created equal while living from the labour of his slaves. And according to David Hume, 'there never was any civilized nation of any other complexion than white, nor even any individual eminent in action or speculation'.[5] Tyrants from Maximilien Robespierre to Vladimir Lenin have justified killing on an industrial scale in order to bring the promise of the Enlightenment to fruition more quickly.

We can also fairly blame the Enlightenment for scientific racism. Rejecting religious ideas of mankind's common origin and the promotion of empirical research threw the door open for racial hierarchies. And partly, also, this was simply because of how successful it made European countries. Arguing in favour of the genetic superiority of Europeans in 1600 would have been hard, because Europe was then no more successful than Persia or China. But by 1800, it was much easier, because European countries were so much wealthier and more powerful than their non-European rivals. Attributing the success of European countries and their colonies like the United States to the racial superiority of Europeans has a simplistic appeal even today (hence a reason to write this book) and many Enlightenment thinkers believed it. Immanuel Kant wrote 'Humanity is at its greatest perfection in the race of the whites' and gave anthropology lectures for years on the inherent inferiority of non-whites.[6] It is impossible to consider Kant, including his ideas on democracy, peace and ethics, without also considering this significant body of his work.

In defence of the Enlightenment, though, nobody was going to argue for entirely modern ideas about the rights of women and minorities in seventeenth-century Europe (or seventeenth-century anywhere else) and be taken remotely seriously. Plus, one of the great strengths of Enlightenment ideas is they provide the means of ameliorating the evil they create. Saying 'all men are created equal' and not following through with the principle is still better in the long run than denying that all men are created equal in the first place. Enlightenment science created the atomic bomb, but Enlightenment humanism has made the world's great powers reluctant to use it. Industrialisation has threatened our environment, empirical science lets us understand the nature of these threats and how we might avoid them. The Enlightenment gave us scientific racism, but also provided the universal human rights behind the twentieth century's civil rights movements. And in practical and measurable terms, Enlightenment ideas have still done more good for more people in the long run than any other philosophy a human society has come up with. It is difficult to argue today that anyone, women and people of colour in particular, would be better off had the Enlightenment not happened, or had Enlightenment ideas been abandoned. But the criticisms of the Enlightenment are not baseless, and I will look at them in more detail later in this book.

***

Why write about the Enlightenment now? I am not a catastrophist, even though my books would probably sell more copies if I were. But even the modern optimist has some cause for concern. I finished the first draft of this book towards the end of 2019 and put it aside to work on other projects. Revisiting it in 2022, I find it even more relevant.

The biggest and most obvious event has been the global COVID-19 pandemic, which has cost 3.5 million lives at the time of writing and thrown the global order into chaos. Microbes are one of humanity's oldest and deadliest enemies, and infectious diseases remained the largest single cause of premature death and disability into the twentieth century.[7] The 1918–20 influenza pandemic killed an estimated 50 million people. The SARS-CoV-2 virus behind the pandemic is significantly more infectious than the flu and about ten times as deadly, but in the intervening century our ability to manage pandemics has improved dramatically.[8] We have a far better understanding of how viruses spread, allowing us to control COVID through disinfecting, quarantine and lockdown. Respirators, antiviral drugs and antibiotics to control secondary infections have kept alive huge numbers of people who would otherwise have died. And we now have a vaccine developed using empirical science, mass-produced through industrialisation, and funded through the surplus wealth of advanced capitalist economies.

All through this struggle, thousands of people around the world have committed acts of collective self-harm. They have refused to follow the medical community's guidelines, and have packed themselves together indoors, creating superspreader events. They have rejected centuries of modern science in favour of quack treatments ranging from silver-infused toothpaste to household bleach. American Televangelist Kenneth Copeland claimed he could vanquish the virus by blowing the 'wind of God' on it.[9] Others, without the least knowledge or understanding of epidemiology, have spread bizarre conspiracy theories through social media, some denying that the virus even exists. People who, quite sensibly, would not let anyone except a qualified mechanic work on their car freely credited the uninformed opinions of bloggers and YouTubers over doctors and scientists.

COVID-19 has been our biggest challenge, but it's been far from our only one. On 16 October 2020, teacher Samuel Paty was beheaded by an Islamic extremist outside a suburban Paris school after he showed caricatures of the Prophet Mohammed to a class during a lesson on the 2005 cartoon controversy. Police shot the attacker dead, but a total of seven were arrested in connection with the murder, Paty's students among them.[10] This was not the outburst of a lone madman, but a crime planned for and justified by people who shared John Calvin's belief that those who fail to show due deference to their religious beliefs should be killed. Paty's killers strike us as monsters, but three centuries ago their attitude would have been unexceptional in much of the world. It is easy to forget, living in a pluralistic society, that hundreds of millions of people in non-western countries are still sympathetic to their ideology. Blasphemy remains a capital crime in Iran, Pakistan, Afghanistan, Brunei, Mauritania and Saudi Arabia, a law which enjoys significant public support.[11] It is no accident that free societies are much better places to live than theocratic ones, and French secularism and liberalism is a major reason why there are far more refugees from Middle Eastern countries in France than French refugees in Middle Eastern countries. But people like Paty's murderers are not usually amenable to persuasion.

The year 2020 has been a pandemic year, but it has also been, like its predecessor, an unusually hot one. According to NASA, 2020 is tied with 2016 as the hottest year on record.[12] Individual temperature records don't mean much when we talk about broad trends, but there have been some interesting (and potentially troubling) numbers. The 18.3°C (64.9 °F) recorded at an Argentine research base on the Antarctic Peninsula on 6 February 2020 is the highest temperature recorded on the Antarctic mainland, beating a previous record of 17.5°C (63.5 °F) recorded in March 2015.[13] The 38°C (100.4°F) recorded at Verkhoyansk on 23 June 2020 is likely to be confirmed as the highest temperature recorded north of the Arctic Circle.[14] And the 54.4°C (129.9°F) recorded in Death Valley, California, on 16 August 2020 may be the highest reliably-recorded temperature on Earth, beating by 0.4°C (0.7°F) readings taken in Death Valley in 2013 and Kuwait in 2016.[15] There are a few historical readings worldwide that are slightly higher, such as a reading of 134°F (54.7°C) at Death Valley in 1913, but they are much older and, for various reasons, unlikely to be accurate.[16] The August 2020 temperature is the highest recorded at the time I am writing this using modern equipment and modern methods.

The world's peak scientific bodies are unanimously of the view that the world is warming at a rate unprecedented in historical times, and much of this warming is driven by the burning of fossil fuels.[17] My city of Melbourne spent much of January 2020 wrapped in smoke from devastating fires throughout south-eastern Australia, while Californians had a similar experience in September. Severe bushfires in Australia are nothing new, but it is very likely that climate change has made the conditions which lead to dangerous fires more common. Eighteen scientists estimated that the probability of a high Fire Weather Index has increased by at least 30% since 1900, while the report of the Royal Commission into the Australian bushfires concluded that 'climate change has already increased the frequency and intensity of extreme weather and climate systems that influence natural hazards'.[18] The industrial civilisation which has given us so many advantages also carries its own risks, and a good understanding of science is critical to managing them. As with the debate over our collective response to COVID-19, many of the loudest voices are also the least informed. I am not a climatologist, but I don't claim to know more about climatology than the authors of the reports of the Intergovernmental Panel for Climate Change (IPCC) or any of the scientific papers on the world's climate.

And, of course, we've seen the spread of online conspiracy theories leading to a deranged attack on the United States Capitol, the cheerleading of Vladimir Putin's indefensible invasion of Ukraine by extremists of the far left and far right, and the rise of new forms of anti-Enlightenment thinking and the resurgence of old ones, all of which led to me to believe there is still a place for this book.

I am grateful for the assistance of Richard Allsop, Harry Redner, Denis White, David Kemp, and Brian Hurlock in bringing it to completion. The success of our societies is not an accident, nor is it guaranteed to continue. This is the story of how we bridged the gap between Michael Servetus' life and mine.

CHAPTER I

THE WORLD BEFORE ENLIGHTENMENT

On All Saints' Day, 1512, the newly-renovated Sistine Chapel re-opened its doors to the public. For the first time, curious residents of Rome were able to come in and see for themselves the frescos which Michelangelo had painted on the ceiling. The Florentine artist was already famous for the statue of David he had given his native city. Standing seventeen feet tall, the young Israelite warrior looked southwards towards Rome with warning in his eyes, his sling over his shoulder and a rock clasped in his right hand. Not only a remarkable capture of the human anatomy in marble, but a clear symbol of Florence's desire to defend its independence. And Michelangelo had finished it before he was thirty. The artist then went south to Rome, attracted by the patronage of the 'Warrior Pope', Julius II. Appreciating the value of beautiful imagery in buttressing the authority of the Church, Julius had put the Florentine to work in the Sistine Chapel. Michelangelo, even though he viewed painting as a lesser medium than sculpture, had laboured diligently over four years to make the ceiling a masterpiece of Renaissance art.

Visitors would have marvelled at the entire ceiling, with its various scenes from the Book of Genesis. But one panel stood out; one in the very centre. The most striking scene of all—God giving Adam the spark of life.

Michelangelo's God would have left a strong impression on anyone who saw it; even today the centrepiece of the Sistine Chapel's ceiling is one of the most famous paintings in history, instantly recognisable and widely-parodied. When God appeared in Medieval art, he was a two-dimensional, regal figure, wearing a crown and seated on a heavenly throne, at the top of a hierarchy of angels and men and distant from everyday people. But Michelangelo had painted a real, physical, corporeal God. In the place of a crown and ermine robe he wore a simple white tunic, flowing over his muscular limbs, and instead of a throne he was seated on a cloud, surrounded by childlike angels. With God and Adam facing each other, and seeming to mirror each other, Michelangelo had put into fresco an embodiment of Genesis 1:27: 'So God created man in his own image, in the image of God created he him'.

The influence of Ancient Greece and Rome on the image is also clear. Michelangelo's God could be Zeus or Jupiter, the entire brightly lit scene reminiscent of the Mediterranean in times gone by. This was the Renaissance, the era of the rebirth of the ancient world. In Florence, the Medici Family had used some of the vast wealth they had accumulated in wool and banking to collect ancient manuscripts, the works of Plato were being republished, and fine marble buildings with rows of Doric columns and lofty domes were rising over Italy's cities. Construction on Saint Peter's Basilica had begun, Botticelli had painted Venus, and in the year before the Sistine Chapel opened, Rafael finished *The School of Athens*, showcasing the philosophers of Ancient Greece whose books had found a new audience. At the same time, Michelangelo had confirmed the simple truth for every Christian in Europe—the only connection with God lay through communion with the Catholic Church. Smoke rising from the pyres of burning heretics reinforced this idea to any who doubted it.

But even then, seemingly at its brightest, the Renaissance was petering out. In 1494, after half a century of peace, the riches of Florence and the other cities of northern Italy attracted foreign armies. True, the city-states had fought each other with *Condottieri* mercenaries, but those mercenaries had found it more profitable to simply let themselves be paid off, sometimes fighting theatrical but largely bloodless battles to give the impression to their employers they were getting value for money. The city-states, in turn, found it easier to keep paying rather than risk defeat and plunder. But this came to an end with the invasion of northern Italy by France, then the Holy Roman Empire. The *Condottieri* crumbled before the French *Gendarmie* and Imperial *Landsknecht*, and one by one, the centres of Renaissance culture were sacked.

In 1494, threatened by the French, the people of Florence expelled the Medici Family, bankers and patrons of the arts, and installed the theocratic monk Girolamo Savonarola as the leader of a new republic. Condemning the excessive adoration of the pagan ancient world, Savonarola ordered much of the city's art to be destroyed in 'bonfires of the vanities'. A precursor to the Protestant reformers challenging the authority of the corrupt church—or a book-burning fanatic. Tiring of his quest to establish a new Jerusalem, the people of Florence turned against him, and in 1498 he was hanged and burned in the town square on the order of Church authorities, his views having become too unorthodox for comfort.

Northern Italy had recently suffered another blow; the opening of sea routes across the Atlantic by the Spanish (in 1492) and around Africa to India by the Portuguese (in 1498). No longer would Europe's trade need to flow through the hands of the merchants of Venice and Genoa. The beginning of the Age of Discovery was a mammoth change, a culmination of both steady technological improvement in shipbuilding and navigation beginning in the High Middle Ages and a growing desire to bypass middlemen in trade. But while it would vastly increase the wealth and power of Spain and Portugal it would not change them significantly from their early Renaissance mindset. At least not yet. Other changes were harder to find. At Frombork beside the Vistula Lagoon, Nicolaus Copernicus laboured on a book proposing that the Earth orbited the Sun, but nobody knew who he was yet.

This was the world of 1512, revolutionary in some ways, but unchanged from antiquity in many. It was then home to about five hundred million people. The world's population had grown, but slowly, probably surpassing

200 million during the time of the Roman Empire and Han Dynasty in China and 300 million and 400 million during the High Middle Ages before collapsing during the Black Death of 1347–1351. About a quarter of the world's people lived in China, and the majority of the rest in the kingdoms and empires stretching across Europe, North Africa and Asia, from Japan to Portugal. In the nation-states and empires, around 90% of people lived in the country and made a living, such as it was, through farming. Beijing, the world's largest metropolis, had between 500,000 and 1,000,000 residents; most of the rest of the world's cities were far smaller. The world's most populous, advanced and powerful states were still found where an observer from fifteen hundred years ago would expect to find them—Ming China, Safavid Persia, the Ottoman Empire in the Middle East, and the Holy Roman Empire and the Kingdom of France in Europe. Throughout Africa, the Americas, south-east Asia and Polynesia, there were many smaller kingdoms and chiefdoms, built around staple crops and local domesticated animals. The steppes of Asia, the Sahara and the deserts of the Middle East remained home to nomadic herdsmen. And in Australia, the Arctic, and large parts of the Americas, people continued to live as hunter-gatherers just as they had done for tens of thousands of years.

In all these societies, human life was hard, and had always been hard. In pre-modern times, about 40% of all children died before their fifth birthday.[19] There was no medical science, no anaesthetic, no antibiotics, no understanding of sterilisation, and so what we would consider to be minor injuries or illnesses were disfiguring or often fatal. The economy was based in subsistence, so most people only had to eat what they could grow, hunt or gather themselves. And when they ran out, there was little to protect them from starvation. The world's richest countries had rates of per-capita GDP (Gross Domestic Product) similar to the poorest parts of sub-Saharan Africa today. Death from war, capital punishment, or other forms of violence was troublingly common. Among hunter-gatherers or people living in troubled societies, violent death rates of one in ten were not unusual.[20]

Life for most people was oppressive. In parts of West Africa, such as Dahomey, up to one-third of the population was enslaved. People were condemned to slavery for minor offences, real or imagined, and many were worked to death or used for human sacrifice to show off the wealth and power of their masters. Entire families were sold into slavery for the transgression of one member. Slave trade routes ran across the Sahara, the Red Sea, and the Indian Ocean. 'The Arabs have pillaged our land, the land of Bornu, and continue doing so' wrote the King of Bornu in modern-day Nigeria and Chad in 1391–1392. 'They have taken as slaves free men and our fathers, the Muslims, and they are selling them to the slave-dealers of Egypt, Syria and elsewhere, and keep some for themselves.'[21] He was lamenting that the Arabs had not honoured the Islamic prohibition against taking other Muslims as slaves. These established slave trading routes would soon be joined on a titanic scale by new routes across the Atlantic Ocean. In almost all societies, women were subservient to men at best and their property at worst, and violence against women was treated as a property crime. Or often not prosecuted at all. Only three rapists were convicted in Frankfurt between 1562 and 1695.[22]

All this was true of Europe, the future home of the Enlightenment. The continent may have been in the midst of the Renaissance, but its effects were difficult to find outside the cities, and outside northern Italy in particular. The peasants continued to live in much the way they had done for centuries, rebuilding their wattle-and-daub huts when they fell into disrepair or were destroyed in warfare, planting their fields, and attending mass every Sunday.

True, Feudalism had broken down, and most of the people of Britain, France and the Holy Roman Empire were no longer serfs bound by law to serve a lord. Those who survived the Black Death had been able to demand higher wages and better conditions. Some had bought their freedom, while others successfully demanded it in the face of civil unrest. A few had even prospered. The Wealden houses of Kent, frequently double-storeyed and with many rooms, are examples of the types of homes well-off peasants could afford in the fifteenth and sixteenth centuries.

But life remained extremely difficult for the majority. The staple food of Europe was still pottage, a soup of grains and vegetables, served where possible with thick and heavy bread of rye or barley. Potatoes had not yet made their way into Europe from the New World, and people still mostly ate what they could grow themselves—like onions, turnips, cabbage, or peas. Meat was still rare. The economy was still mostly based on subsistence farming and barter. Peasants could make a little extra money by working for someone else or through cottage industries like weaving, but they produced little surplus. And crop failure and famine were constant threats.

In Spain, excessive rains over the winter of 1504–1505 and then droughts in 1506 and 1507 led to failures of the harvest three years in a row. Andrés Benáldez, the parish priest of Los Palacois in Seville, wrote in 1506:

> The countryside and villages were emptied of people, and leaving behind their homes men and women went in search from one place to the next, with their children on their shoulders, by road, in search of bread, and holding other children by the hand, starving, asking help from those who had some for God's sake, which was very painful to see. And many died of starvation …[23]

'And many died.' This was not unusual. The famine was followed immediately by a plague, an even more serious threat. From when it first appeared in 1346 until 1671, there was an outbreak of the Bubonic Plague virtually every year somewhere in northern or western Europe.[24] A bacterial infection of the lymphatic system spread through the stomach of fleas, the plague would cause swellings in the armpits, groin and neck of its victims, which would quickly turn black and gangrenous. They would suffer from fever and chills, cough up black blood, and usually die. There was no known prevention or cure. Doctors at the time thought the disease was carried through 'bad air', and so lit bonfires, waved around bags of herbs, or decked rooms in flowers. Desperate for any cure, people washed themselves in urine or drank arsenic. Frenzied persecutions of Jews and foreigners often followed outbreaks.

The old diseases were joined by new ones. In June 1517 there was an outbreak of the 'Sweating Sickness' in southern England. 'More deadly than the sword' according to Sir Thomas More, it went in a few hours from initial chills and tremors to an intense fever which left the body covered in perspiration. Mortality was 30% to 50%, and many died within hours of showing symptoms.[25] The mysterious summer illness was, according to *Holinshed's Chronicles of England, Scotland and Ireland*, 'so sharp and deadly that the lyke was never hearde of to any manne's remembrance before that tyme'.[26] And as summer turned to autumn, the outbreak of the Sweating Sickness was followed by another of the bubonic plague.

While some physicians such as Ibn Al-Khatib in the Arab world had proposed some sort of theory of infection, conventional medical knowledge held that diseases were caused by bad air, or an imbalance of bodily humours, or black magic. Nobody knew what we now take for granted—most diseases are caused by microscopic organisms. Most medicine, even in the most advanced societies such as China, was based in pseudoscience. Unsurprisingly, infant and child mortality rates around 50% were common, and minor infections frequently fatal. Cheshire lawyer and gentleman Humphrey Newton (1466–1536) kept a 'commonplace book'; a sort of diary. He and his wife Ellen were fortunate enough to have eleven children born live between 1495 and 1507 without killing their mother in childbirth. But as was normal, four died in childhood. The names Robert, Ranulph, Matilda and Petronella are crossed out with 'mortus est' written next to them—a simple and stark image of the harsh reality of being a parent in the pre-modern world, even a wealthy landowner.

Then there was the ever-present threat of violence. For a start, the law was violent. Any who turned to stealing could expect little mercy. In the reign of Henry VIII in England, from 1509 to 1547, there were 72,000 hangings—a huge number for a country of around 3 million people.[27] Gallows abounded throughout Europe, in cities, towns and villages, and public hangings were a normal part of life's routine. Everyone, at some point, would have seen a condemned man or woman kicking at the end of a rope; it was not a quick death. Human life was cheap, and most executions were for small property crimes. In England, a life was worth five shillings—the amount for which a thief could hang. Institutions of social welfare were limited, so desperation would drive some to thievery regardless.

Hanging was not fast, but it was positively humane compared to some of the alternatives. We've already seen an example of burning alive, a common penalty for heresy, witchcraft and homosexuality. There was impalement and breaking on the wheel. Between 1531 and 1547, boiling alive was a legal punishment in English law. Richard Roose, a cook who killed two people with poisoned porridge, was tortured into confessing and then boiled alive in 1531. 'He roared mighty loud, and divers women who were big with child did feel sick at the sight of what they saw, and were carried away half dead' one eyewitness recalled. But the rest of the crowd found the spectacle less entertaining than beheading: 'other men and women did not seem frightened by the boiling alive, but would prefer to see the headsman at his work'.[28]

With the breakdown of feudalism, the nine-tenths of Europe's population who made a living by farming were at least no longer tied to the land and bound to serve whomever owned it. But they had few civil or political rights. No country was a democracy, and people commonly found themselves through marriage or civil war owing their loyalty and paying their taxes to a ruler they had nothing in common with. The people of the Netherlands became the subjects of the Duke of Burgundy through marriage in 1384, then the French Crown after the last Duke was killed in battle in 1477, then the House of Hapsburg through marriage.

Peasant rebellions were another source of violence. In the chaotic years after the Black Death and into the sixteenth century, they had been common, but generally ended badly. The 'Poor Conrad' peasant rebellion in Württemberg in 1514 went as expected, with the defeated peasants being tortured and executed. Given the sheer number of peasants and the threat to the existing social order their rebellion could pose, the treatment of defeated peasant rebels was often luridly brutal. In 1514, after a bloody rebellion in Hungary where particularly hated nobles were crucified or impaled, the rebel leader György Dózsa was defeated and captured. Forced to sit on a red-hot iron throne, a red-hot iron sceptre was placed in his hand and a red-hot iron crown forced onto his head in an intentional mockery of a coronation. The executioners tore his charred flesh from his still-living body with hot pincers and his followers, starved for a week beforehand, were forced to eat it.

Weak and ineffective political institutions were another source of violence. Most kings were absolute monarchs, but their power was tempered by weak central states and ambitious nobles. In England, Henry VIII had come to the throne peacefully on his father's death in 1509, but his father, Henry VII, had won his crown in battle in 1485. The Wars of the Roses, the dynastic struggle which had consumed England in the thirty years before then, were still a living memory. In France, King Louis XII had fought against his predecessor, Charles VIII, in the *Guerre Folle* or 'Mad War'. Holy Roman Emperor Maximilian I had spent part of his childhood besieged in Vienna during a war between his father and his uncle. The death of a monarch was a perilous occasion, frequently seeing rival claimants to the vacant throne mustering their armies. And for ordinary people, this meant the risk of plunder and rape, often from the troops of both sides. These weak states struggled to maintain a monopoly on violence, and brigandry was common. Villagers on the Scottish border were under constant threat from raids by the Border Reivers. Those living around the Mediterranean faced the ever-present danger of being seized by Barbary Pirates and sold in the slave markets of North Africa.

Warfare between states, or quasi-states, was seemingly incessant. In 1512, not an unusual year, the Ottoman Empire was undertaking the conquest of Egypt, having won Mesopotamia from the Safavids, and would surely turn its attention west sooner or later. The Duke of Burgundy and Duke of Guelders were fighting a decades-long low-level irregular war in the Netherlands. Peace had only just been concluded between Denmark and Sweden, Venice was fighting a rebellion in Croatia, Spain and Portugal were fighting to expand their colonial empires, the Bengal Sultanate had invaded Chittagong, and Spain was conquering Navarre. And since 1508, Western Europe had been embroiled in the War of the League of Cambrai, fought up and down the continent from Scotland to southern Italy. In the age of feudalism, Europe's kings had relied on their knights and peasant levies to fight for them. Now, more and more, they found it quicker and easier to hire mercenaries from the free companies who wandered the continent, fighting for whomever paid them and plundering the countryside in the brief times of peace.

Italy had the worst of it. French and Gascon troops sacked Brescia with unusual brutality in February 1512, even as the Sistine Chapel was being brought to completion. And the savagery of sixteenth-century warfare can easily be seen in a letter from Niccolò Machiavelli to Isabella d'Este, describing the Sack of Prato by Spanish troops of the Holy League in August 1512:

> ... the Spaniards took possession of the city, put it to sack, and massacred the city's population in a pitiable spectacle of calamity. In order to spare Your Ladyship cause for worry in your spirit, I shall not report on the details. I shall merely say that better than four thousand died; the remainder were captured and, through various means, were obliged to pay ransom. Nor did they spare the virgins cloistered in holy sites, which were all filled with acts of rape and pillage.[29]

It is unsurprising that the Italian wars provided Machiavelli with the background to write *The Prince*, the definitive manual of cynical politics.

The expansion of the Spanish and Portuguese Empires overseas went in much the same way. As the Sistine Chapel opened, with its promise of man's brotherhood and divine origin, Spanish Conquistador Diego Velázquez de Cuéllar was completing the conquest of Cuba. 'I saw here cruelty on a scale no living being has ever seen or expects to see' wrote humanist friar Bartolomé de las Casas of the massacre of three thousand of the indigenous Taíno people at Caonao who had peacefully come out to greet the Spanish with gifts of food.[30] Before Taíno chieftain Hatuey was burned at the stake, a priest asked him if he would become a Christian and so be allowed to enter heaven. He asked if Christians went to heaven, and when answered in the affirmative, said he didn't want to go there, as he wanted to spend no more time around such cruel people. His surviving people were enslaved and forced onto plantations to work for their new Spanish masters. As they died from mistreatment and European diseases, Cuéllar would be compelled to look further afield for his workforce. Within a decade, the slave ships would be sailing from Africa. From his home in the newly-founded city of Havana, Cuéllar would become staggeringly rich.

This is not to condemn the Spanish for being unusually barbaric by the standards of the time.

Hernán Cortés, then working for Cuéllar in Havana, was already thinking of taking the Conquistadores further west, in search of gold in Mexico. When he arrived, he would find the vast Aztec empire, practising human sacrifice on a colossal scale. The Aztecs believed the world would end if the Gods were not given a steady stream of human blood. Or more like a torrent—the blood of tens of thousands, or even hundreds of thousands of people per year. The need for new victims drove wars, just as the demand for slaves led to continuous fighting in Africa. Much of the limited surplus the global economy of 1512 was able to produce was sunk into warfare.

To modern eyes, the world of 1512 looks like a dystopia, something we would expect to see in a benighted African country or a Syrian province under the control of Islamic State. But it was a day-to-day reality for almost all the world's people. In Shakespeare's *Measure for Measure*, the brothel owner Mistress Overdone makes a dark joke which would have rang true to people with personal experience of the sixteenth century: 'thus, what with the war, what with the sweat [sweating sickness], what with the gallows, and what with poverty, I am custom-shrunk [have no customers left]'. It is hardly surprising that the *Dance Macabre*, a performance of dancing skeletons, is such a common theme in late Medieval and early Renaissance Art, particularly in the wake of the Black Death.

Most Christians would have appreciated the sentiment of Job 14:1: 'Man that is born of a woman is of few days and full of trouble'. But few would have actually recognised the quote, even if they were devout. Peasants generally could not read, and even if they could, the Bible was written in Latin, not their own language. Books of any sort were rare and expensive. A Bible, painstakingly hand-copied by monks, cost as much as a warhorse, or a year's income for a labourer. By 1450 German goldsmith Johannes Gutenberg in Strasbourg had built a working movable-type printing press, a truly revolutionary invention, but by the early sixteenth century the number of books printed was still miniscule.[31]

This made the Church all the more critical—as a repository of knowledge, as a moral authority, and as a source of solace. People crowded into churches to beg God in his mercy to spare them from the myriad of punishments their sins deserved. Feudalism had been based in a rigid social and economic system where peasants worked for all, knights fought for all, and the clergy prayed for all. By 1512, only the last was still true. The Catholic Church was, in the Middle Ages and Renaissance, the custodian of not just theology but philosophy. Fields which today we would consider unrelated to religion, like science and economics, were therefore bound up with the Church's teachings. By the fourteenth century, this bundle of ideas, the official position of the Church on most important matters, was referred to as Scholastic philosophy. Based in the preserved wisdom of the Ancient Greeks, most significantly Aristotle, it had been made harmonious with Christianity and applied across almost every field of human knowledge.

***

The foremost Scholastic philosopher was Thomas Aquinas. He had learned of Aristotle's books from Islamic sources, and like the Islamic writers whose commentaries he read, sought to reconcile Aristotle's ideas with holy scripture. Reading Aquinas is a good way to understand Scholastic thinking, not only because he was very influential, but because his books are still very readable. In his most famous work, *Summa Theologica*, he makes his case through a series of questions and responses, like a modern FAQ. Aquinas was both very erudite and very devout, and in his study of the works of Aristotle came to the conclusion that the Ancient Greek (whom he referred to as *the* Philosopher) had discovered important truths about the universe even though he was a pagan bereft of the guidance of the Bible. Clearly, God had not left his creations with no capacity to distinguish virtue from vice outside of the scriptures, which many of them would never come across.

Aquinas' explanation was a concept called natural law. The idea came from the Greeks, but it was Aquinas who explained it rigorously and with reference to Christianity. In the treatise on the law in *Summa Theologica*, he recognised four types of law—eternal, divine, natural and man-made.[32] Eternal law was made up of the unchanging principles through which God directed the universe and was unknowable to humans. Divine law was God's direct revelation through scripture, such as the Ten Commandments and the sayings of Christ in the Gospels. Skilled and practiced reading of the scriptures could interpret divine law, although Aquinas acknowledged Christians could have different views on its interpretation.

Natural law was also of divine origin, but it was not written down. Instead, all people could figure it out through reason, even if they were not Christians. God created humans for a purpose, and by identifying our purpose and acting in a way consistent with it we would follow the laws of nature and be happy. By nature, all humans had the desire to do things consistent with natural law—to feed ourselves, to reproduce, to live in society with others, and to seek God. By using our reason, we could better-understand how to live in accordance with the laws of nature, show virtue, and be happy. Finally, according to Aquinas, there was man-made law, which societies needed to function. To use a modern example, there is nothing in either divine or natural law telling us what side of the road to drive on. However, it is necessary for us to pick one and have the government enforce it.

The laws formed a hierarchy. Man-made law could not contradict natural law, as following such a law would be immoral. Likewise any reasoning which interpreted natural law as being contrary to scripture would be invalid. A man could not through reason decide that the Pope should have no authority, there was no Purgatory, or God did not exist at all. Or if he did reach such conclusions, he would keep them to himself if he did not fancy death by burning. And furthermore, as God was taken to be the source of all reason, concluding that he did not exist would be, by definition, irrational. There must be a flaw in such an argument.

Aquinas' philosophy assumed, as did Aristotle's, a natural order to the universe comprehensible through reason. And it was a universal law, explaining everything from the rotation of the Sun around the Earth to the sinful nature of usury. He also followed Aristotle's views on natural philosophy, modified to mesh with Christian doctrines. The Greeks believed the universe to be eternal, for example, whereas Aquinas and the Scholastics maintained it was created by God as recounted in the Book of Genesis. But on the whole, Scholastic philosophy was Aristotelian. As the Jesuit *Ratio Studorium* (*Plan of Studies*) of 1586 put it: 'In logic, natural philosophy, morals and metaphysics, the doctrine of Aristotle is to be followed'.[33]

None of this was of particular concern to most Catholics. Their interaction with the Church was through mass with their parish priest, celebrated every Sunday and on other occasions as well. It bound them as a community of believers, brought them comfort, and kept them within the Church and on the difficult path towards salvation. Prior to the introduction of the Tridentine Mass in 1570, there wasn't a uniform liturgy across the Catholic world. The lack of education of many priests and the scarcity of books made regulating the service difficult. Still, there were commonalities in Mass as it was held from Austria to Iceland, and any modern Catholic familiar with the Latin mass would probably be able to follow a Medieval service.

It's easy to imagine the scene in a small church somewhere in Europe in 1512. The parishioners, seated in pews, their heads hooded, their hands clasped in prayer. The priest, the only one wearing white, facing the altar, chanting or singing a melodious stream of Latin liturgy. One of the psalms, the *Kyrie Elesion* in its mixture of Latin and Greek, and then *Gloria in Excelsis Deo*. The parishioners may have joined in with the *Amens* or repeating the confession of their sins while striking their chests with their fists—*mea culpa, mea culpa, mea maxima culpa*. The mass was not meant to impart information, so understanding was not the goal. The highlight of each service was the Eucharist, the point where the priest would hold aloft first the communion wafer and then the chalice of wine and repeat the words the Gospels reported Jesus saying to his disciples at the last supper. Those who had attended mass often might recognise the words *mysterium fidei*, the mystery of the faith, the miracle of transubstantiation where the bread and wine actually became the body and blood of Christ. They looked, felt and tasted no different from ordinary bread and wine, but through a process the Church said was inexplicable, would transform their substance. At this point, the parishioners would cross themselves, and after the dismissal, leave the service. Medieval Catholics only actually took communion rarely; to be in the presence of Christ's body and blood was enough.

There was nothing outwardly special about the Europe of 1512; nothing to indicate it would dominate the world over the next four centuries and make itself completely unrecognisable to any person who had ever lived. England and Scotland were unimportant in world affairs, the modern Netherlands and the northern German states were fringe provinces of the Holy Roman Empire, and Denmark and Scandinavia had been mostly ignored since the decline of Vikings four and a half centuries earlier. There was the Renaissance, but then, there had been something of a Renaissance in the High Middle Ages, and another before that in the days of Charlemagne. Each had burned out and ended in crisis, and it looked like the Renaissance of the fifteenth century was going the same way.

But one radical change was coming. Hardly unsurprising, given the corrupt state of the papacy and the Church, but not easily anticipated. In the autumn of 1517, almost five years exactly after the Sistine Chapel reopened, we might find a stocky black-clad man in his mid-thirties nailing a document to the door of a church. I say might, because it's possible that

Martin Luther did not actually nail his Ninety-Five Theses to the door of the All Saints' Church as legend has it. He might have, though, as it was a custom of the University of Wittenberg where Luther was a professor of theology to make announcements in this manner. He did certainly mail them to the Archbishop of Mainz, and within a few months they were being reprinted and widely distributed throughout Germany. The Catholic Church was about to face the first serious challenge to its theological and philosophical monopoly in western Europe in over a millennium.

CHAPTER II

THE END OF AUTHORITY

In the long centuries in which human beings have lived in cities and had governments, writing, scholarship and all the trappings of what we call civilisation, the Enlightenment only happened fairly recently and in a particular place—northern Europe in the seventeenth century. Why then and there, and not in Ancient Greece or Rome, or Islamic Spain, Mughal India, or China in the Song Dynasty? Or even more simply, why did it happen at all?

For the Enlightenment to happen, there had to first be a breakdown of the existing system of ideas. This was a necessary—but not sufficient—condition. As the Enlightenment philosopher Immanuel Kant wrote in 1784, 'This enlightenment requires nothing but *freedom*—and the most innocent of all that may be called "freedom": freedom to make public use of one's reason in all matters. Now I hear the cry from all sides: "Do not argue!" The officer says: "Do not argue—drill!" The tax collector: "Do not argue—pay!" The pastor: "Do not argue—believe!"'[34] The first step towards Enlightenment was to make it possible for people to argue.

Since the Fall of the Roman Empire, Europe had been split into rival states. Among the centres of civilisation in the old world, this made it unusual. This may be an accident of Europe's geography, and if it was, it would prove a critically important one. Europe is naturally divided, and the Alps, the Pyrenees, the English Channel, and the seas ringing the continent led to distinct nation-states with natural geographic borders. Or independent city-states, as in the case of Renaissance Italy.

In contrast, geographically-compact China had been unified in the Qin Dynasty (221–206 BC) and despite periods of breakdown, had generally remained unified since then. Persia, the Arab world, and India had likewise tended to support centralised Empires over independent countries. In Europe, however, no one nation managed to become powerful enough to overwhelm all of its neighbours at once, despite the efforts of some very determined conquerors.

This created competition between independent states. An idea which was suppressed in one country could still survive in another. And those which proved successful inevitably spread. A classic example is maritime exploration and the building of colonial empires. Portugal, a small, poor country looking out to the Atlantic, began seeking a sea route around Africa to the East Indies in the early fifteenth century in order to avoid paying high prices to various middlemen for spices shipped across the Mediterranean. Spain followed, and once those two countries became rich from their newfound colonies, so did others.

Consider that China, too, easily had the wealth and technological knowledge to found overseas colonies of its own. And for the first three decades of the fifteenth century, the Ming Dynasty sent fleets of ships throughout the Pacific and Indian Oceans from East Africa to Sumatra. In 1436, the Dynasty changed its policy, banned the construction of seagoing ships and suppressed records of the voyages. Had a European king done so, his country would have found itself at a disadvantage if everyone else took a different view. But all Chinese civilisation was united under one throne, so the Ming Dynasty's change in policy had no immediate consequences. When Jorje Álvares of Portugal reached China in 1513 the country had no deep-water fleet to speak of. So it was small and not particularly wealthy Portugal that sent a ship to China rather than rich and populous China sending a ship to Portugal.

There had been previous examples of the advantages of geographical division. Ancient Greece and Renaissance Italy, two of Europe's previous centres of creativity and innovation, were both divided into city-states able to support themselves independently through trade. These city-states proved more dynamic than sprawling agrarian kingdoms or empires.

Europe's political division made the Church all the more important. Secular authority in Europe was divided from the fall of the Western Roman Empire onwards, but religious authority remained centralised in the Catholic Church and the Pope. The Great Schism of 1054 had seen the Roman Catholic and Eastern Orthodox Church split, but in western Europe, the Roman Catholic Church remained a monopoly. But while everyone (except heretics) accepted the principle of the Church's authority in religious matters, not everyone agreed where the division between religious and non-religious matters should be. This resulted in friction and sometimes open conflict between the Church and the State, particularly the most powerful secular authority in Europe, the Holy Roman Emperor. Ruling over a loose confederation of German and Italian states, he was nominally the successor of the Western Roman Emperor, although his authority never stretched anywhere near as far. As Voltaire put it with his characteristic wit, the Holy Roman Empire was not holy, nor Roman, nor an empire.

Of course, there was nothing we could consider today to be a separation of church and state in medieval Europe. On unequivocally religious matters, the State would enforce the Church's teachings. Contrary to popular belief, the Papal Inquisition never actually had the power to burn people at the stake for heresy. However, it could hand them over to the secular authorities for execution. To someone sentenced to death by burning, this would have been small comfort. But in the long run, it would matter.

This division of religious and secular authority was also unusual. Historically, in most societies, religious leadership has been seen as part of political leadership. The Caliphs of the Islamic Caliphate claimed to be the successors of the Prophet Mohammed, and exercised both religious and political authority just as he had. There was never an Islamic Pope as a potential rival to Islamic sovereigns. Likewise, in pre-modern China the emperor was both a religious and a political leader.

An explanation for Europe's difference can probably be found in the early history of the Christian religion. Christianity was never designed as a state religion, and until the Edict of Toleration in 313 AD, it was a persecuted sect within the Roman Empire. The Jesus of the Gospels is little-concerned with political philosophy. 'My kingdom is not of this world' he tells Pontius Pilate in John 18:36, making it clear he is not posing a direct challenge to the secular authority of the Roman Empire in Judea. He also appears to explicitly endorse a form of a separation of church and state when asked whether his followers should pay their taxes. 'Render unto Caesar the things that are Caesar's, and unto God the things that are God's' was his famous response as quoted by Matthew, Mark and Luke.[35]

The Romans were willing to tolerate a diversity of religions throughout their Empire provided all their adherents were equally willing to participate in national rites based on the Roman pagan faith. Christians refused to do this, and so suffered from bouts of persecution. This shifted during the reign of Constantine the Great (306–337), the first Emperor to convert to Christianity.

A religion which taught its adherents to obey the government and pay their taxes was naturally appealing to the Emperors, and after they legalised Christianity they moved fairly quickly to make it compulsory. With the Edict of Thessalonica in 380, Catholic Christianity was established as the state religion of the Roman Empire and all other forms of worship banned. The Pope and the Church would advise the Emperor on what was correct regarding spiritual matters, and he would enforce their teachings among his subjects. Over the fourth and fifth centuries, Catholic Christianity was standardised and rival forms, such as the Arian Heresy, were suppressed. The collapse of the Western Roman Empire in the fifth century left secular authority in Europe fractured, but the barbarians who established new kingdoms in its former territory nonetheless converted to Catholic Christianity and (more or less) recognised the authority of the Church and the Pope. Even while Europe was divided politically, a single established set of ideas dominated across the continent.

***

Which leads us back to Dr Luther and the possibly-apocryphal story of the church door. Luther was a pious and passionate man who had abandoned his legal studies to pursue theology in an effort to find the truth, but had become disillusioned with the Catholic Church. The issue which finally compelled him to make his disillusionment public was the practice of selling indulgences, where the Church would forgive sin or lessen time in Purgatory in exchange for money. Unsurprisingly, it had been widely abused. More broadly, Luther challenged the authority of the Catholic Church on divine matters. Instead, he argued the Bible was the only divinely-inspired source of truth, and the Church had no spiritual power. Attending mass and doing good works were futile on their own—faith was what mattered. Luther taught that people were saved by God's grace alone, through faith alone, on the basis of scripture alone. *Sola Gratia, Sola Fide, Sola Scriptura.*

After he refused to repent, Luther was excommunicated by the Church, declared an outlaw by the authorities of the Holy Roman Empire, and driven into hiding. In that time, he translated the Bible into German, so ordinary people could read it and decide for themselves who was right. In his view, the Scholastic philosophers with their long texts in Latin were unnecessary, even harmful, to a proper understanding of God's intent.

Luther was not the first person to challenge the authority of the Church. There had been organised heresies before, particularly following the late Medieval crisis. The Lollards of England and the Hussites of Bohemia are both examples. But Luther's challenge succeeded where others had failed. The printing press was undoubtedly one reason for his success. The growth of an educated merchant class in the cities of northern Europe was another. General dissatisfaction with the corrupt sixteenth-century papacy, where the Holy See was won through intrigue or bought with gold and then used as an instrument to advance the worldly interests of its backers was another.

In the 1520s, cities and states in the Holy Roman Empire began to break with the Catholic Church and adopt Lutheranism as their new religion. Rulers who converted to Protestantism knew they risked being targeted by a crusade. But they also knew they could stop paying to support the Church and seize its assets for themselves, creating an economic incentive to break away. Luther returned to Wittenberg and established a new church there, and his ideas spread through Germany and Scandinavia. The Protestant Reformation had begun.

It didn't end with Luther and Lutheranism, though. In the 1540s, new reformers began to call for a more radical overhaul of the Christian religion. Luther had been content to keep many of the features of the Catholic Church, modified to suit his new theology. There would still be clergy, but they would be permitted to marry (Luther set an example himself by marrying a former nun). There would still be a mass said before an altar, but it would be in German, not Latin. And while Luther rejected transubstantiation, the principle that the bread and wine actually became the body and blood of Christ, he held that Christ was still present in the Eucharist in some form. And he didn't particularly care if the priest held up the bread and wine during the mass, or the people in a village wanted to begin their Sunday morning service by marching in a procession through the churchyard holding aloft a cross and singing hymns as they had done for centuries. He was committed to his principles, but could be pragmatic on how they were applied.

To the second generation of reformers, though, this could all look too much like a compromise with Popery. The foremost of these was John Calvin (1509–1564), the Priest from Picardy in northern France who ended up as the spiritual leader of Geneva. He became a Protestant around 1530, and in 1536 he published the *Institutes of the Christian Religion*, where he outlined the new set of principles which he put into practice in Switzerland.

Luther accepted that all humans were corrupted by the original sin of Adam and Eve, and could therefore only be saved through faith in Christ. But Calvin went further. He argued that all people were not just naturally inclined to sin but totally depraved, unable to take any conscious effort to save themselves from damnation. Salvation was only available through God's own actions, a doctrine called unconditional election. Once God picked you for salvation, you were saved for all time and counted among his elect. Calvinism gained a following in Germany, France, Hungary, the Netherlands, and Scotland, in the last under the auspices of reformer John Knox (1513–1572). The Reformed Dutch Church, the Reformed French Church, and other churches with 'Reformed' in their names are generally Calvinist. An example of Calvinist theology can be seen in the liturgy which Knox wrote for the Kirk, as the Reformed Church in Scotland came to be known:

> Honour and praise be given unto thee, O Lord God Almightie, most deare father of heaven for all thy mercies and loveing kindnesse shewed unto us in that it hath pleased thy gratious goodnesse freely and of thine owne accord to elect and choose us to salvation before the begynning of the world; and even lyke continuall thanks be given to thee for creating us after thine owne image; for redeeming us with the pretious blood of thy deare Sonne when wee were utterly lost ...[36]

The Calvinists took seriously the prohibition in the Ten Commandments against worshipping idols. They overturned altars, smashed stained glass windows, and tore down crucifixes from church walls. They celebrated mass, but made it clear it was purely symbolic—there was nothing supernatural about the bread and wine.

The Lutherans and Calvinists were joined by others. When the Pope refused to permit him a divorce, English King Henry VIII made himself the head of the Church in England, and Protestant bishops such as Thomas Cranmer reformed the new Anglican Church along Protestant lines. Then there were Anabaptists, who believed only those who actually professed faith should be baptised, as Michael Servetus did. In other words, it was idolatrous to baptise infants. They rejected taking oaths and fighting in the Army, and so were persecuted by the others. Unsurprisingly, the Anabaptists failed to win any rulers over to their theology, but the modern Amish and Mennonites are their descendants. Even more unorthodox were the Libertines, who believed being saved by grace meant they could now do whatever they wanted, much to the chagrin of civil and religious authorities. And as the Reformation continued, more and more sects joined the throng—Puritans, Quakers, Baptists, and Unitarians like Servetus who rejected the idea of the Trinity.

The Catholic Church had no intention of giving up. At the Council of Trent in 1545 it resolved to make some necessary reforms to reduce the appeal of Protestantism, but otherwise expressed its determination to drive the new ideology from the continent. It was backed by Charles V, Holy Roman Emperor and King of Spain, whose lands in southern Europe remained loyal to the Church.

The Protestant Reformation is sometimes mistakenly viewed as a softening of Christianity, and the replacement of dogma and force with tolerance and reason. In reality, it unleashed intolerance and violence like nothing else before it. The Catholic powers, from the start, naturally turned on Protestants with the same fury they had dealt with other heretics. Protestants, for their part, often turned on Catholics or Protestants from rival sects with the same violence. Europe was convulsed by wars of religion. Medieval warfare had been brutal, but now all restraints were removed as the different sides could commit any atrocity with the excuse that their victims were idolaters and heretics. They were no longer just fighting the enemies of their king; they were fighting the enemies of God. If their enemies were successful, humanity would be denied the benefit of Christ's sacrifice on the cross and damned to hell for eternity. As the Protestant King of Sweden, Gustavus Adolphus, wrote to his brother-in-law, the Elector of Brandenburg, before his invasion of Europe in the Thirty Years' War: 'This is a fight between God and the Devil. If His Grace is with God, he must join me. If he is for the Devil, he must fight me. There is no third way.'[37]

The fruits of the Renaissance were consumed by fire as rapacious mercenary armies raged across Europe, burning villages and towns and putting their populations to the sword.

Wars of Religion in France from 1562 to 1598 killed between 2,000,000 and 4,000,000 people, more in that country in absolute and far more in relative terms than the First World War did. In the Netherlands during the Eighty Years' War of 1568 to 1648, Dutch towns which fell victim to the 'Spanish Fury' were left in ruin. At least 200,000 of Ireland's 1.5 million people perished between 1641 and 1653 as Oliver Cromwell's Puritan army conquered the country. The conflicts reached their crescendo with the Thirty Years' War of 1618 to 1648. Practically every country in Europe had fought at one point on one side or another, or both. Catholic France, for example, supported Protestant princes in Germany to undermine the power of the Holy Roman Empire, its chief rival. Atrocities became the norm, often described using the black humour of the times. The Protestant armies of Sweden became known for the *Schwedentrunk*, or 'Swedish drink', where victims would have their stomachs pumped full of boiling mixtures of water, animal manure, or sewerage. After the brutal sacking of the Protestant German city of Magdeburg in 1631 and the massacre of its population by the army of the Holy Roman Empire, Protestant soldiers began to jokingly describe massacring the population of Catholic towns as granting 'Magdeburg Mercy'.

By modern estimates, the population of Europe declined by 15–20%.[38] Even at the low end of this range, this would make the Thirty Years' War the most destructive conflict in European history. By comparison, the Soviet Union lost 12% of its population during the Second World War between 1941 and 1945. In the worst-affected areas, the death rate was even higher. According to census data, the German state of Württemberg lost 57% of its population from 1634 to 1655.[39] An analysis by historian Max Roser estimated that the Thirty Years' War killed a larger proportion of the world's population than any conflict outside the two World Wars, a staggering number given it was confined to central Europe.[40] The cultural memory of the conflict was long-lasting. In a radio broadcast of 4 May 1945, Albert Speer warned the German people that they were now facing destruction not seen since the Thirty Years' War. Facing destruction, even though he was speaking after the Allied fire-bombing of German cities and the devastating invasion of eastern Germany by the Red Army. And this was only one of the wars to blight Europe in the sixteenth and seventeenth centuries.

Eventually, the two sides came to a series of compromises. The 1555 Peace of Augsburg was an early but unsuccessful attempt—it permitted both Lutheranism and Catholicism to co-exist in the Holy Roman Empire, but provided no protection to religious minorities within Catholic or Lutheran states and left Calvinism illegal. The 1573 Warsaw Confederation permitted both Catholicism and Protestantism in the Polish-Lithuanian Commonwealth. Catholics and Protestants in Hungary made various agreements. In France, the 1598 Edict of Nantes legalised Protestantism and permitted both Catholics and Protestants to participate in French public life. And in 1648 the representatives of the exhausted warring powers agreed to the Peace of Westphalia, ending the Thirty Years' War and the Eighty Years' War in the Netherlands. The independence of the Dutch Republic and the Swiss Confederation were recognised, and the various parties agreed to stop interfering in each other's religious affairs. Rulers of different nations and city-states within the Holy Roman Empire could choose Catholicism, Lutheranism or Calvinism as their state religion, and religious minorities would be permitted to practise their faith in private and in allocated times in public. A brittle and uneasy peace settled briefly over continental Europe.

With the Peace of Westphalia, any attempt to impose religious uniformity across Europe by force ended. With it ended also much of the temporal power of the Catholic Church. Pope Innocent X called the Treaty of Westphalia 'null, void, invalid, iniquitous, unjust, damnable, reprobate, inane, empty of meaning and effect for all times' but he was ignored by the signing parties, including the Catholic ones.[41]

***

Europe in the immediate aftermath of the Peace of Westphalia was still far from a modern, tolerant or enlightened society. To the Catholic powers, the Protestants were still heretics, and outside of the Holy Roman Empire they continued to persecute them. Many of the early Protestants were what we today would call fundamentalists, and had little tolerance for those with differing opinions. Luther and Calvin were not thinkers of the Enlightenment, as the fate of Michael Servetus shows. In England, radical Anabaptist Edward Wightman was burned at the stake for heresy in 1612 when he, like Servetus, rejected the Holy Trinity. And in the Massachusetts Bay Colony, controlled by hardline Protestant reformers, there were executions of Quakers in 1659, 1660 and 1661. Many Protestants still looked on the Catholic Church as the Synagogue of Satan foretold in the Book of Revelation, and in Protestant England, Catholic priests were hanged, drawn and quartered throughout the seventeenth century.

But in the long run, the Protestant Reformation laid some of the groundwork for the Enlightenment. Because Protestant churches encouraged their adherents to read the Bible and the teachings of their founders, they promoted literacy. Scotland provides a good example of the long-term effects of this. John Knox's 1560 *Book of Discipline* called for schools to be founded, and in 1696, with the religious violence of the seventeenth century largely out of the way, the Scottish Parliament passed an act to establish a school in every parish. By some estimates, adult male literacy in Scotland reached 55% by 1720 and 75% by 1750.[42] Every sizeable Scottish town had a lending library by 1750, and their surviving records show blacksmiths, bakers and domestic servants borrowing books, including the works of Enlightenment thinkers such as John Locke. And as the public became more literate, steadily more books were printed to meet their demand. Books were still expensive into the nineteenth century—a copy of Jane Austen's *Pride and Prejudice* cost 18 shillings when it came out in January 1813, at least £55 in 2021 currency and possibly more.[43] But they were within the reach of the middle classes and were available more broadly through subscription libraries.

The Reformation also had an effect on the economy. Many of the world's religions, the Medieval Catholic Church among them, had viewed asceticism and monasticism as the ethical ideal and looked down on making wealth in the physical world as something of a necessary evil. When Franceso Datini (*c*.1355–1410), a self-made merchant in the Italian city of Prato, amassed a fortune of 70,000 Florins, he found himself haunted by a constant fear of damnation. He finally found peace by leaving his money to the Church in his will.[44]

The Protestants took a more pragmatic view. There were no Protestant monasteries, and the more hardline Protestants disliked the idea of any sort of religious iconography, so Protestant Churches didn't need vast sums of money for massive buildings, ornate statues, gold crucifixes and stained-glass windows. Protestantism was most enthusiastically adopted by commercial cities in northern Europe, and the merchants in those cities further developed Protestant theology to suit their needs. For all these reasons, Protestantism promoted hard work as a form of devotion and material prosperity as a sign of God's favour. As Scots Calvinist Minister John Castairs preached, 'There is a notable consistence betwixt fervour in spirit in serving the Lord, and not being slothfull in business ... as they are both enjoyned by the Holy Ghost'.[45]

This idea was most famously developed by German sociologist Max Weber in his 1905 book, *The Protestant Ethic and the Spirit of Capitalism*. According to Weber, Protestantism—specifically Calvinism—was a necessary, although not sufficient, pre-condition for the development of modern capitalism. You had no way of proving you were one of the elect, and your salvation was entirely out of your own hands, but following your calling and doing well in the world was a way of showing God's favour. In Weber's view, this mindset was critical to capitalism's development.

Additionally, the Protestant Reformation promoted the challenging of authority, favoured anti-absolutist governments which were more predictable and less inclined to seize property, undermined the traditional social structure, dismantled the monasteries and forced learning out into the secular realm, left Scholastic philosophy open to criticism, and removed some of the impediments to economic growth like the strong prohibition against usury (lending money for interest).

Its most significant effect, though, was the shattering of central authority. For the first time since Christianity became the official religion of the Roman Empire, there was no one authority in Europe, either religious or secular. Had the Reformation succeeded completely and Lutheranism swiftly replaced Catholicism across the continent, there might not have been an Enlightenment. Had there been a clean break between Lutheran and Catholic Europe, as happened between the Roman Catholic and Eastern Orthodox Church in 1054, there might not have been an Enlightenment either, although it is likely Lutheran Europe would have pulled ahead of Catholic Europe given the greater attraction of Protestantism in commercial cities and its promotion of literacy. But the Reformation left a patchwork quilt, with Lutherans and Calvinists living in the same countries, often alongside Catholics and small minorities like Anabaptists. There were no longer simple answers to the biggest questions in life, like how to achieve salvation and escape hell. National and religious differences had led to mass killing. Old ideas had been discredited, and the future looked uncertain. In the countries where Protestantism had become established, there was no one alternative to the Catholic Church and its Scholastic philosophy. What, then, would replace it?

CHAPTER III

THE TOLERATION OF DISSENT AND THE ENLIGHTENMENT IN THE NETHERLANDS

The Enlightenment succeeded in overcoming the natural tendency of human societies to enforce conformity of thinking on their members, a habit which can be observed in communities from hunter-gatherer bands all the way to large empires. Certain ideas were off-limits, and their spread needed to be prevented to preserve society and prevent social collapse. The crime of heresy is as old as religion itself. In one famous example, Socrates was accused by Meletus before a jury of 500 Athenians of being 'a doer of evil, and corrupter of the youth, and he does not believe in the gods of the state, and has other new divinities of his own'.[46] The jury accepted this was a crime against the city-state of Athens, and convicted him. Given a choice between death and exile, Socrates chose suicide.

In *Summa Theologica*, Thomas Aquinas considered whether heresy should be tolerated, but rejected the idea. Forgers were executed, and the case for executing heretics was stronger than the case for executing forgers, he concluded, as 'it is a much graver matter to corrupt the faith which quickens the soul, than to forge money, which supports temporal life'. A heretic should be given an opportunity to repent, but:

> ... if he is yet stubborn, the Church no longer hoping for his conversion, looks to the salvation of others, by excommunicating him and separating him from the Church, and furthermore delivers him to the secular tribunal to be exterminated thereby from the world by death. For Jerome commenting on Galatians 5:9, 'A little leaven,' says: 'Cut off the decayed flesh, expel the mangy sheep from the fold, lest the whole house, the whole paste, the whole body, the whole flock, burn, perish, rot, die. Arius was but one spark in Alexandria, but as that spark was not at once put out, the whole earth was laid waste by its flame.'[47]

This was a reference to the Arian Heresy, an early variant of the Christian religion which denied the divinity of Christ and brought disorder to the Christian community.

The closest term to heretic in Islam is *zindīq*, from the Persian *zand* ('free interpretation'). Most Islamic societies have suppressed *zinādiqa* to a greater or lesser degree. 'Tolerance is laudable' Abbasid Caliph Abu al-'Abbās is quoted in one history as saying, 'except in matters dangerous to religious belief, or to the sovereign's dignity'.[48] While medieval and early modern Islamic societies would generally permit Christians and Jews to live within them as *dhīmmis* subject to legal restrictions, they would try to stamp out heretical interpretations of Islamic doctrines. At different times, Sunni Islamic states would suppress Shi'a Islam and visa-versa. Jews did not have their own state, and so could not enforce criminal law against heretics, but still had the doctrine of *Herem*, or excommunication from the community, as a means of dealing with the unorthodox.

The suppression of heresy existed in China throughout its history, with the Government of the Empire permitting or prohibiting various religious traditions in the interest of maintaining social harmony.[49] Confucianism was suppressed in the Qin and early Han Dynasties and then made the effective philosophy of the Empire. Buddhism was suppressed during the Tang Dynasty, with Emperor Wuzong issuing an edict in 845 AD condemning the religion for disrupting social order and economic production by isolating monks and nuns in wastefully-expensive monasteries:

> Buddhist monasteries daily grew higher. Men's strength was used up in work with plaster and wood. Men's gain was taken up in ornaments of gold and precious stones. Imperial and family relationships were forsaken for obedience to the fees of the priests. The marital relationship was opposed by the ascetic restraints. Destructive of law, injurious to mankind, nothing is worse than this way.[50]

He confirmed he had completed the destruction of 4,600 monasteries and compelled 265,000 monks and nuns to return to secular life, and 'with simplified and regulated government we will achieve a unification of our manners, that in future all our youth may together return to the royal culture'. By the time of the Ming and Qing Dynasties Confucianism, Buddhism and Taoism were all accepted, but early Jesuit missionaries to China still needed to persuade the Emperor they were preaching a proper religion and not a dangerous cult which needed to be suppressed. In the Confucian tradition, it is the role of the national leader to maintain social harmony, which includes deciding which faiths should be permitted.

Of course, there have always been exceptions. At different times the Achaemenid Persian Empire, the Roman Empire, Moorish Spain during the Umayyad Caliphate (756–1031), the Mughal Empire, and the Mongol Empire permitted pluralism of religious belief. But many communities within those empires did not. The link between being a member of a society and holding the religious or philosophical beliefs common to that society remained a strong one. Likewise, religions generally make a virtue out of accepting their doctrines on faith, although there have been exceptions here as well. 'Just as the experts test gold by burning it, cutting it, and applying it on a touchstone, my statements should be accepted only after critical examination and not out of respect for me' the Buddha is quoted as saying.[51] His followers, though, have not always followed this principle.

To modern minds, even devoutly-religious modern minds, making it illegal to have incorrect ideas about religion is bizarre. If someone believes something which will land them in hell for eternity, it is profoundly unfortunate for them but not really a problem for the government. But the suppressors of heresy had two arguments—one from social cohesion, the other from the need to protect society from divine wrath. The God of the Old Testament destroys humanity except for Noah and his family in a flood, he rains down fire on Sodom and Gomorrah, and he punishes the Israelites for their wickedness by allowing their enemies to defeat and enslave them. There was no reason to assume he had ceased this practice, and Christian (and Islamic) theologians often viewed the Mongol Conquests and the Black Death as evidence of God's judgement. To the medieval mind, not just the individual but society as a whole needed to be righteous, and to be righteous it needed to take it on itself to weed out those who preached evil. Burning heretics was horrifying, everyone knew, but having Christendom itself perish in conquest or epidemic like the society before the Great Flood would be far worse.

***

With the end of the Thirty Years' War in 1648, both Catholics and Protestants had been forced to accept neither could drive the other from Europe by force. No doubt the Catholic Church would have stamped out the Protestant heresy if it could, and no doubt the Protestants would have torn down and destroyed the Catholic Church if they could, but neither was strong enough. Both were left eyeing each other warily. In some cases, within the same country. The Polish-Lithuanian Commonwealth, the first country in Europe to allow free practise of religion to Catholic and Protestants alike, is one such example. But in most of Europe, if there was toleration, it was toleration under compulsion. And a number of countries continued to enforce laws against heresy. Spain, for example, carried out its last execution for heresy in 1826.[52] Europe was still a long way from viewing toleration of dissenting ideas as a virtue rather than an uncomfortable state of affairs which had been forced onto it.

One country in Europe, which formally gained its independence in

1648, was a leader in the tolerance of dissenting views, political liberty and Enlightenment thinking. Originally from necessity, but later, as a matter of national pride. This was the Dutch Republic. It was, according to English ambassador Sir William Temple in 1672, a place of: '... general liberty and ease, not only in point of conscience, but all others that serve to commodiousness and quiet of life, every man following his own way, minding his own business, and little enquiring into other men's'.[53] One German observer in 1694 noted it was impossible to tell servant girls from their mistresses because they spoke, dressed and acted so similarly.[54] Travellers from the gentry were often surprised to find themselves addressed casually by commoners on passenger barges. Women had more rights than in the rest of Europe.

The success of the Dutch Republic was a testament to the advantages of political, religious and economic freedom. A freedom very limited by modern standards, but striking for the seventeenth century. The Netherlands had historically been something of a backwater, being both poor and considered difficult to manage due to its patchwork of civil and religious authorities. Divided by two large rivers, the Rhine and the Meuse, and numerous smaller waterways, the Dutch had resisted the establishment of central authority. Individual cities and provinces had their own systems of government.

From the late Middle Ages onwards, an extensive program of land reclamation was undertaken where dykes and windmill-driven pumps were used to drain the shallow waterways and create new farmland. Peasants needed to be incentivised to move onto reclaimed land, breaking down the feudal system of serfdom. By 1500, most of the land in the Netherlands was owned outright by the people who farmed it, not by feudal lords.[55] At the same time, a shortage of farmland and ready access to the Rhine and the North Sea made sea-trade attractive to the Dutch, and Amsterdam and the other coastal cities were developed into major ports. This made the society increasingly urbanised.

The Church in the Netherlands was naturally weak and fractured, with its authority undermined by political disputes. For example, part of the region fell within the jurisdiction of the bishopric of Cambrai, yet the Bishop of Cambrai was a subject of the King of France, the arch-enemy of the Habsburgs. Ecclesiastical law was often flouted, and a significant number of priests openly lived in concubinage. This meant the Reformation took hold quickly, and the response from civil authorities was often lacklustre.

Unlike England, the Netherlands had an entirely bottom-up Reformation. Without any central guiding authority, the various Protestant sects all became established and were soon at each other's throats. It was not until the 1550s that Calvinism became the dominant denomination, and not until 1571 that an official Dutch Reformed Church was founded.

The Netherlands had originally been part of the holdings of the Dukes of Burgundy, but were added to the lands of the House of Habsburg in 1482. And when the Habsburgs inherited the Spanish Crown in 1556, the Netherlands passed under Spanish rule. Charles V and his son, Phillip II, sought to increase their control over the provinces. Their attempts to suppress Protestantism, impose heavier taxes, and curtail the powers of the local nobility and merchant guilds met with increasing resentment. In 1568, the Netherlands rose in revolt.

The Dutch Revolt, or the Eighty Years' War, notionally lasted until 1648, when the Netherlands was formally recognised as an independent country. In practice the Seven Provinces had won their independence by 1581, becoming modern Europe's first republic.

Government arrangements in the Dutch Republic were complex. The country was a confederation of seven provinces, each of which retained a high degree of autonomy. Holland was the largest and richest, and dominated the federation. The main federal institution of government was a legislature of representatives from each province, the States-General. Each province also vested executive power in a *Stadtholder* or steward, a role which descended from the feudal stewards who managed the provinces on behalf of their distant rulers. In practice, a number of provinces appointed the same *Stadtholder* and the position was hereditary, being held by the princes of the House of Orange. Politics in the Republic was therefore defined by divisions—province verses province, the small provinces against Holland, and supporters of the House of Orange versus republicans. For these reasons, Dutch political institutions were not widely admired. American founding father James Madison, in considering whether the Netherlands could provide a model for the United States, rejected the idea on the basis that the Dutch Republic was marred by 'imbecility in the Government; discord among the provinces; foreign influence and indignities; a precarious existence in peace, and peculiar calamities from war'.[56] Still, this fractured and semi-autonomous character had its advantages as well as its disadvantages.

Stadtholders were much weaker than European kings, and partially absent. *Stadtholder* William II of Orange died in 1650, leaving an unborn son. The Government was effectively taken over by liberal republicans under Johan de Witt, himself a mathematician from the merchant class. Many of the earlier restrictions on freedom of thought and expression were allowed to lapse or left unenforced, and the Republic entered two decades of unusual freedom. After the year of disasters (1672), de Witt was lynched by an angry mob in the Hague and William of Orange made *Stadtholder*, but many of the policies of the previous two decades continued.

The Dutch had rebelled against the Spanish in the name of freedom (*Vryheid*), but their own attitudes to religious liberty and the tolerance of dissent were mixed. Religious tolerance in the Netherlands was originally driven by necessity—the country could not function if the Catholics and the members of the different Protestant Churches were locked in conflict. But they quickly learned something else about tolerance, though, which made it seem even more attractive; it could be extremely profitable. The coastline, waterways and central location between Britain, France and Germany made trade highly appealing. All the United Provinces needed were the skilled artisans to manufacture, refine and distribute the goods. As it turned out, they were readily available, thanks to the intolerance of Europe's monarchs. In 1492, Spain expelled its Jews. Many more who had notionally converted to Catholicism left both Spain and Portugal over the next century in search of somewhere they could return to practising their faith. Then there was the steady stream of Protestants fleeing Hapsburg-controlled lands throughout the sixteenth and seventeenth centuries. And finally, the flight of the French Huguenots (Protestants) through the seventeenth century, which reached its peak when Louis XIV issued the Edict of Fontainebleau in 1685, revoking the Edict of Nantes and ending their religious freedom in their own country.

Many of these refugees ended up in the Netherlands. The population of Amsterdam went from 10,000 in 1514, to 30,000 in 1562, 60,000 in 1600, and then 140,000 in 1647.[57] The city was full of bustle, from the cargoes being loaded and unloaded from tall ships in the harbour, to the crowds getting on and off the barges, to the dock workers withdrawing to the taverns at lunchtime to eat hearty dishes of Dutch *Hutspot* with rye bread and wheat beer.

This increase in population was driven almost entirely by immigration. By 1600, one-third of Amsterdam's population and one-tenth of the total population of the Dutch Republic were immigrants.[58] These immigrants tended to be wealthier and more educated than average Europeans, as poor people did not have the resources to flee hundreds of miles and had less-incentive to prioritise religious and economic freedom over the necessities of life. The Jewish and Protestant refugees brought their money and skills to the Netherlands, triggering an economic revolution.

Amsterdam in the Dutch Golden Age was a vibrant city, and the stage of an equally-vibrant theological debate. The Churches dominated the skyline—the Oude Kerk and Nieuwe Kerk, converted from Catholicism, and the newly-built Oosterkerk and Westerkerk specially-consecrated for the Dutch Reformed Church. Those familiar with the city could find their way around by the different sounds of the bells, even if they were blind. Within them were both devout Calvinists who viewed the city's prosperity as being entirely down to God's will and more humanist thinkers who believed they could take matters into their own hands. More prosaically, there was an ongoing debate on whether the Westerkerk should have a church organ. The most hardline Calvinists denounced the idea as Popish, but the church finally commissioned one in 1681.

The Netherlands also retained a large Catholic minority—up to 30% in some provinces. This would make attempting to suppress Catholicism a losing proposition from the start. Being tolerated, the Catholics were often willing to participate fully in public life. Catholics in Leiden even raised money to help Huguenots fleeing France in 1685, a truly remarkable act of ecumenism by seventeenth-century standards.[59]

There were definite limits to Dutch tolerance. Only members of the Dutch Reformed Church could participate in politics, for example. And while the Dutch were more tolerant of unorthodox views in religion, philosophy and science, they were much less tolerant than their southern neighbours of pornography, prostitution and other practices considered to be immoral by the social mores of the time. Dutch society remained, at its heart, disciplined and conservative.[60]

Perhaps the strongest link between the Enlightenment and Dutch commerce was in the publishing industry. Dutch is not a widely-spoken language, so the printers who set themselves up in the Netherlands needed to continue to publish in French and Latin. Combined with the Republic's internal diversity, this made the Netherlands the most natural place for books to be translated. The Netherlands became a halfway-house for ideas as well as goods. Isaac Newton's science reached the European continent through the Netherlands, for example. There were efforts to censor especially controversial books, but none were particularly successful. Books were expensive in those days, and if one province cracked down on the publishing industry, another could let the presses keep working and tax the profit.

The Netherlands was critical for the Enlightenment. Dutch printers freely published their books, which were then carried around Europe on Dutch merchant ships. The little low-lying country became an incubator of new ideas, republican government and free trade. And it also sheltered some of the Enlightenment's most important figures.

***

French philosopher René Descartes (1596–1650) was one Enlightenment thinker who found a home in the Netherlands. Sometimes called the founder of modern philosophy, he became the most prominent advocate of new ideas. Descartes came from a wealthy family in the Touraine province of Central France, and received a conventional Catholic education. He became adept at mathematics, and is known today for inventing co-ordinate geometry, which is called Cartesian geometry after him. He remained an observant Catholic his whole life, although found himself asking questions which the Church did not have ready answers for. He had a lifelong distaste for the cold and a love of sleeping in late, and was fortunate enough to early on in life inherit enough money to live in simple comfort in rural France. However, desiring to see more of the world, he enlisted in the Dutch Army in 1617. In 1619 he moved to the Bavarian Army, and was present at the Battle of White Mountain, an early and critical Catholic victory in the Thirty Years' War. While in Bavaria in the winter of 1619–1620, he sought shelter from the cold by crawling into a large oven which was still warm. He remained there all day, and according to him, his new system of philosophy was half-formed by the time he emerged.

How can we know that something is true? In the Europe of Descartes' time, the simple answer was that God had revealed the truth in scriptures, his words were interpreted for us by the divinely-guided Church, and we could use our reason to build on this foundation and know everything we needed to know to live a moral and productive life. But Descartes, as devout as he was, was not entirely satisfied with this explanation, and came up with something novel. Descartes' new philosophy, which he explained in *Discourse on the Method* (1637) and *Principles of Philosophy* (1644), works something like this.

I know I am sitting in my living room typing this book on my laptop. Or am I? Sometimes I have had dreams which are so lucid I would have sworn at the time they were real, so I could be asleep and dreaming. Or I could be insane, and what I think is real could be a delusion. King Charles VI of France believed he was made of glass and lived in fear of being shattered. Or I could be under the spell of some sort of demon who makes an illusion seem like reality. My laptop, my living room, and even my body itself might not exist. This idea has been a popular subject for science fiction in our time. For example, it is the premise of the Wachowskis' 1999 film *The Matrix*, where computers have taken over the world and humans are kept enslaved in an artificial reality which they believe to be real.

There is one thing, though, which I can be absolutely sure of, no matter what. Because I ask these questions, I must exist in some form. The evil demon might make me believe any number of things which aren't true, but he can't make me believe that I exist if I don't. Triumphantly, Descartes had hit on his first truth, which he expressed in the famous phrase *Cogito Ergo Sum*: I think, therefore, I am.

From this starting point, Descartes was able to work forward and put all of his experiences back in their proper place. He was satisfied that the material world existed, God existed and his Catholic beliefs were fundamentally sound. Descartes' subsequent thinking is less original than the sceptical starting-point for which he is known. His approach of assuming everything is an illusion and reasoning your way out of the logical darkness is called Cartesian scepticism.

After his experiences in the War, Descartes returned to Paris, then lived and worked in the Netherlands from 1628 to 1649, where he published his books. Queen Christina of Sweden began a correspondence with him, and she brought him to her court as her personal tutor. It was not a good idea. She could only spare time for lessons at 5am, and so throughout the Scandinavian winter, Descartes needed to get up in the cold and dark castle to give them. Neither person seemed to have benefitted all that much from the arrangement, and Descartes fell ill and died in February 1650.

Descartes is commonly seen today as the founder of a system of thought called Continental Rationalism. Continental, because most of its leading proponents lived in continental Europe, and rationalism, because they believed the truth could be identified through reason. Like Descartes, they were sceptical of sensation and experience, believing it could be more readily-corrupted than logic. The alternative school of thought, which also came out of the Enlightenment, is called British Empiricism—we will come to it later. Both schools of thought had the effect of pushing learning out of religious institutions and into the secular world.

Descartes' books attracted the ire of religious authorities when they were published. His thought experiment where the world was under the control of an evil demon hints at a belief system called Gnosticism, which had inspired heresy in the Christian and Islamic worlds since ancient times. Descartes didn't believe it, but proposing it even as an idea was questionable. Still, by the 1660s Cartesian philosophy had become accepted in Dutch academic circles. Despite his own robust Catholicism, his books were added to the Catholic Church's index of banned books in 1663 and suppressed in his native France on the order of King Louis XIV. But in the Netherlands, Cartesianism was safe.

***

If Descartes was controversial, he was nothing compared to Baruch Spinoza (1632–1677), a philosopher on whom he had a great influence. Spinoza came from a Portuguese Jewish family who had fled the inquisition, and was born and grew up in the Jewish community of Amsterdam. He had a conventional Jewish education and became a star pupil, but as he grew into adulthood his teachers increasingly found his ideas less and less palatable. In 1656, at age twenty-three, he was expelled from the community. In their now-famous document of censure, Amsterdam's Jewish leaders forbade any member of the community from associating with him or reading anything written by him:

> By the decree of the angels, and by the command of the holy men, we excommunicate, expel, curse and damn Baruch de Espinoza, with the consent of God, Blessed be He, and with the consent of all the Holy Congregation, in front of these holy Scrolls with the six-hundred-and-thirteen precepts which are written therein, with the excommunication with which Joshua banned Jericho, with the curse with which Elisha cursed the boys and with all the curses which are written in the Book of the Law. Cursed be he by day and

cursed be he by night; cursed be he when he lies down, and cursed be he when he rises up; cursed be he when he goes out, and cursed be he when he comes in. The Lord will not spare him; the anger and wrath of the Lord will rage against this man, and bring upon him all the curses which are written in this book, and the Lord will blot out his name from under heaven, and the Lord will separate him to his injury from all the tribes of Israel with all the curses of the covenant, which are written in the Book of the Law.[61]

This all seems rather extreme to us, but it's important to remember that Jewish communities in Europe lived in constant fear of persecution, and they had every incentive to clamp down on anything which could be seen by wider society as unorthodox or atheistic. We don't know exactly what the youthful Spinoza had said or written to bring down such harsh censure on himself, but based on his later works, we can guess. He remained in the Netherlands and spent the rest of his life making a modest living as a lens grinder. None of the curses foretold by the leaders of his former community came to pass, but he did die at the disappointingly early age of forty-four.

Spinoza was influenced by Descartes, and followed him into the continental rationalist tradition. He wrote two particularly significant works, the *Theologico-Political Treatise* (1670) and the *Ethics*, published posthumously. The second is more famous, but the first represented one of the most significant challenges to the existing intellectual order ever seen in the western world.

Spinoza clearly wanted to write more broadly on the topics which had seen him thrown out of the Amsterdam Jewish community, but knew he would need to tread very cautiously. In 1668, his friend Adriaan Koerbagh published a book called *Een Bloemhof van allerley lieflijkheyd* (A Flower Garden of all Kinds of Loveliness). Koerbagh argued that God was synonymous with nature, Jesus was not divine and miracles were impossible. Koerbagh made the questionable decision to publish in Dutch rather than Latin, so everyone could read the book. As a result, he was convicted of blasphemy and died in squalid conditions in prison. Spinoza took careful note of this, and published the *Theologico-Political Treatise* anonymously in Latin. He took the same approach, later, with *Ethics*, writing it in a-deliberately-obtuse style resembling a mathematical dissertation in order to throw off casual readers.

Theologico-Political Treatise had an awkwardly-descriptive title, but an even more awkwardly-descriptive subtitle. It was 'a critical inquiry into the history, purpose, and authenticity of the Hebrew scriptures; with the right to free thought and free discussion asserted, and shown to be not only consistent but necessarily bound up with true piety and good government'.[62]

Spinoza's ideas were radical—no one person could prove his or her religion to be correct so a person's morality could only be judged by his or her behaviour, miracles were nothing more than natural phenomena with a yet-unknown cause, the Bible was a book of many authors with ambiguous and sometimes-contradictory meaning (here Spinoza had the advantage of being able to read the Old Testament in the original Hebrew), denying religious freedom to a community would damage its peace and well-being, and a good society would have freedom of speech and thought and mutual respect. He did not reject religion entirely, but argued that having a religion, and indeed, having one religion, would make society more coherent and promote good behaviour among citizens. Amsterdam in the de Witt era was his model:

> In this most flourishing republic and noble city, men of every nation, and creed, and sect live together in the utmost harmony, and, in their transactions with one another, the only questions asked are whether the parties be rich or poor, and whether they are wont to act with good faith or not; there is never a question of religion or creed, for in presence of the judge these have no part in the proceedings, and neither justify nor condemn a man; and here there is no sect, however odious and despised, whose ministers, provided they do injury to none, but give every one his

due and live respectably, do not find countenance and protection from the magistrate [...] there is nothing safer for the common weal than that piety and religion should be wholly comprehended in the practice of charity and justice, and that the authority of the ruling power in the state, both as regards sacred and lay affairs, should be restricted to actions; for the rest, that liberty of thinking as they list, and of saying what they think, should be conceded to all without restriction.

The book complete, Spinoza then set out to find a publisher. Amsterdam then had over a hundred of them, and while they needed to be licensed, they were not required to submit books to the government for censorship before publication. Spinoza's Treatise was taken on by his friend, the radical publisher Jan Rieuwertsz. Rieuwertsz was used to handling controversial topics, but both he and Spinoza recognised just how inflammatory the Treatise was and just how much care they would need to take. When it was published, the title page gave its place of publication as Hamburg, and it did not name the author.

These precautions were justified. Even in the Republic of the de Witt era, the Treatise crossed the line, and the reactions against it seem absurdly violent by today's standards. Between 1677 and 1680, there were more than fifty edicts against Spinoza's books issued by religious and secular authorities, from the Synods of the Dutch Reformed Church down to the City Council of Leiden. The South Holland synod of the Dutch Reformed Church called the Treatise 'as obscene and blasphemous a book as, to our knowledge, the world had ever seen'.[63] The Catholic Church described the *Theologico-Political Treatise* as a book 'forged in hell by a renegade Jew and the devil' (once Spinoza was outed as the author by the end of 1671), and Spinoza's works remained on the Catholic Church's index of banned books into the twentieth century.[64] For the next century, Spinoza's name remained synonymous with immorality.

The Synods lobbied the Estates of Holland, the Parliament of the Province of Holland, to ban the book. But the Estates dithered, referring the matter to a committee. Their motivation is unclear—they may have decided that censorship would lead to more public disorder than the ready availability of an obscene book, or they might not have wanted to draw attention to the Treatise for much the same reason. With de Witt's murder and the restoration of the House of Orange in 1672, Spinoza's enemies began to gain a little more traction, and the Dutch Republic finally imposed a nation-wide ban on the Treatise in 1674. But it was then readily-available throughout the country in clandestine editions, and sympathetic city councillors may have tipped off booksellers to give them advance warning of raids. And from the docks of Amsterdam, the Treatise spread throughout Europe.

Spinoza's influence remains debated to this day. Because of his dark reputation, none of his contemporaries would admit to being influenced by him. But his work does seem to have been widely-known in educated circles. Voltaire, for example, refers to him in his 1764 *Philosophical Dictionary* in a way that suggests he assumes his readers know of him.[65] Today, Spinoza is widely-seen as a symbol of moderation in religion. 'I believe in Spinoza's God, who reveals Himself in the lawful harmony of the world, not in a God who concerns Himself with the fate and the doings of mankind ...' wrote Albert Einstein in a letter.[66]

Spinoza's books demonstrate that the Dutch Republic was not a paradise of free thought, but at the same time, it was ineffective at censorship—it was difficult to ensure that one book would be banned in every town and province at the same time. So controversial books continued to roll off Dutch presses, and from there, to the holds of ships destined for ports around Europe.

***

This fractured society where all attempts to impose uniformity of thought quickly failed rapidly became the most successful in the world. Despite never having had more than 0.3% of the world's population through the seventeenth century, the Dutch Republic was operating the largest fleet of merchant ships by 1602. While estimating Gross Domestic Product

(GDP) in societies hundreds of years ago is difficult, it seems certain that sometime between 1500 and 1600 the Netherlands surpassed northern Italy to become Europe's richest region, and soon after, became the richest region by GDP per capita of all time.[67]

The fractured nature of the Dutch state may have led to the creation of another major Dutch innovation—the modern corporation. In those days, international trade was a high-risk high-reward business. Outfitting a ship and sending it to the other side of the world was expensive, and the threat of accident, warfare or piracy meant the investors could lose everything. However, if the ship made it back to Europe, the voyage could be enormously profitable. Generally such voyages had royal backing. For example, Vasco da Gama's original voyage to India in 1498 was a project of the Portuguese crown. However, in the Dutch Republic, many of the provinces had their own small trading companies. This led, in 1602, to the creation of the *Vereenigde Oostindische Compagnie*, or Dutch East India Company. The Company was created by the Estates-General, but enjoyed a high degree of independence. It could enter into treaties with the Estates-General's approval, it was required to report to the Estates-General on its activities, and its naval and military commanders needed to swear a dual oath of loyalty to the Company and the Republic. Otherwise it could operate largely on its own. It was not a particularly liberal institution, enjoying a monopoly granted to it by the government and expanding its commercial activities through conquest and violence. But it also created a way for private investors to share the risks and rewards of major projects. A private investor or partnership of investors who could only afford to outfit one ship risked bankruptcy. But by joining with hundreds of other merchants, they could all have a stake in many, and the losses from some would be made good from the gains from others. The Company became the first institution in the world to have shares bought and sold on a stock exchange. And with the corporate structure, there was for the first time a way of funding large-scale projects without the government.

It would be tempting to attribute the Dutch miracle to the Dutch colonial empire and the plundering of the East Indies by the Dutch East

India Company. But the rapid economic growth of the second half of the sixteenth century preceded both—the Dutch East India Company was not founded until 1602 and the Dutch conquest of the East Indies did not begin until 1605. The average Dutchman was far richer than the average Spaniard in 1600, even though Spain had a vast colonial empire rich in gold and silver.

Of course, the growth of the Dutch economy was not only due to the toleration of dissent. It benefitted from urbanisation, the strength of the merchant classes, its seas and waterways, and its central position in Europe. But its restrained government which was forced to act within its own rules was a key factor in its success.

In military power the Republic far exceeded its size. It resisted reconquest by Spain, Europe's superpower, defended its border against Louis XIV's France, and held its own in a series of trade wars with England. The Second Anglo-Dutch War (1665–1667) came to an end when Dutch Admiral Michel de Ruyter sailed up the Medway and destroyed the English fleet at anchor, forcing King Charles II to sue for peace. Charles sought an alliance with Louis XIV, but in the Third Anglo-Dutch War (1672–1674) the little Republic fought off both France and England together. Contrary to previous opinion, a society did not need to enforce uniformity of thinking in order to be strong.

Aside from being a leader in wealth and power, the Dutch Republic also became a leader in ideas. Dutch scientists like physicist and astronomer Christiaan Huygens and biologist Antonie Philips van Leeuwenhoek were premier in their fields. The pendulum clock, Mercator map projection, and mercury thermometer all came out of the Dutch Golden Age. The first explorers to chart the coasts of Australia and New Zealand were Dutch. The Dutch Enlightenment made a small and previously-insignificant country great. Others would take note.

CHAPTER IV

CHALLENGING THE DIVINE RIGHT OF ENGLAND'S KINGS

Why should a subject obey his or her king? To the Scholastic philosophers of the Middle Ages, the answer was simple—a legitimate king was placed on the throne by God, and just as the king answered to God so too must his subjects answer to him. God appointed Saul as King of the Israelites, but then withdrew his support after Saul disobeyed him. In *Summa Theologica*, Thomas Aquinas argued that it was natural for human beings to form societies as one person could not meet all of their wants and needs alone, and this meant that it was also natural for there to be a form of authority: 'Now obedience to a superior is due in accordance with the divinely established order of things ... the order of justice requires that subjects obey their superiors, else the stability of human affairs would cease'.[68] Determining when authority was legitimate was harder, and Aquinas allowed that an illegitimate king would not have divine authority and therefore could be overthrown or even killed.

The Ancient Greeks considered the merits of various systems of government. Plato (in *The Republic*) and Aristotle (in *Politics*) had proposed various constitutions with their own pros and cons. In *The Republic*, Plato describes the four unjust constitutions—timocracy (rule by the wealthy), oligarchy (rule by a clique), democracy (rule by the mob) and tyranny (rule by a single tyrant). As a counter to these, Plato proposed an aristocracy of philosopher-kings who would be without property but learned in the ways of justice. It is not clear how practical Plato thought this system would be in practice.

Aristotle was more inclined to empirical research than his teacher had been, and after analysing various forms of government in and around Greece he settled on six constitutions. Three were 'just', where those in government worked for the common good, and three were 'unjust', where those in government worked only for themselves. Where government was by one person, the just form was monarchy and the unjust tyranny. Where it was by a few, the just form was aristocracy and the unjust oligarchy. And where it was by many, the just form was a republic and the unjust form a democracy. Like Plato, Aristotle used 'democracy' (or rather, the Greek *dēmokratía*) to mean unrestrained mob rule. Aristotle, therefore, recognised that three different types of constitution could be just. He was critical of Plato's ideal system of government, but rather vague on what he was proposing in its place. In *Politics*, he described an ideal state where power would be shared between all property-holding citizens who would be properly educated for the task of government—perhaps falling somewhere between an aristocracy and a republic.

Nonetheless, from the days of the Roman Empire and through the Middle Ages, monarchy was the normal form of government in Europe. According to the Church and the Scholastic philosophers, a just monarchy could not be absolute, as a Christian king would rule within the bounds of natural and divine law. However, on purely secular matters, it was considered normal for a king to hold ultimate authority. Aquinas thought monarchy the best system of government as it left the least room for internal conflict. This is the opposite position to the modern liberal view, where we consider it a good thing that power be split between different institutions. England had a parliament of nobles, knights and burghers (representatives of the towns) since the thirteenth century, meeting in a separate House of Lords and House of Commons since 1341. It imposed a restraint on English kings which most of their continental counterparts did not have, although its power was never fixed.

In practice, medieval monarchy offered little of the promised stability. Take the English monarchy, the subject of this chapter (along with the Scottish one, with which it merged in 1603). Since the Norman Conquest in 1066, transitions of power had been violent more often than not. William I won his crown at the Battle of Hastings, where his predecessor, Harold II, was slain. Following his death there was a civil war between his sons, which was won by his successor, William II. He, in turn, was killed in a hunting accident which looked curiously like an assassination, leading to another civil war among William's surviving brothers, which was won by the new king, Henry I. Henry's death was followed by a long period of civil war known as the Anarchy, finally ending in 1154 with the coronation of a French nobleman as Henry II. Henry II ended his reign fighting a civil war against his sons, and he was succeeded by his son Richard. Richard's reign began in 1189 and ended in 1199 when he was mortally wounded fighting a rebellious nobleman in France. Richard was succeeded by his brother John, who spent his reign fighting his barons in a series of civil wars. He died of illness on campaign in 1216, and was succeeded by his son, Henry III. And so it went on, with rebellions, fratricidal conflict and kings dying in battle or in dungeons being common for the rest of the Middle Ages. Henry VII, the first Tudor monarch, won his crown at the Battle of Bosworth in 1485, ending the Wars of the Roses. He passed it onto his son, Henry VIII, who faced the Reformation.

***

England had not been devastated by wars of religion like the countries of the European continent, but questions of religion and politics had caused a massive headache for successive monarchs and parliaments. Henry VIII had separated the English Church from Rome in 1534 and then dissolved the monasteries, but these changes were more political than doctrinal. The reformation of the English Church did not begin in earnest until the reign of his son, Edward VI, which began in 1547. Under the leadership of Protestant reformers like Archbishop Thomas Cranmer, religious icons in churches were destroyed, the Latin mass replaced with English services from the Book of Common Prayer, and the practice of saying prayers for the dead discontinued. These changes met with both support and opposition, and bloody rebellions broke out in parts of the country where loyalty to Catholicism remained strong.

Edward VI died at the age of fifteen in 1553, bringing his reign to an unexpectedly early end and leading to the succession of his devoutly Catholic half-sister, Mary I. She applied herself with vigour to reversing the Reformation. Laws against heresy were re-instated, and hundreds of Protestants, including Cranmer, were burned at the stake. Attempts were made to re-Catholicise the churches, and Protestant worship was driven underground. The Marian persecutions, as they were called, left long and bitter memories. But Mary did not live long enough to see the reforms of her half-brother's reign undone, dying childless in 1558. The throne now passed to her Protestant half-sister, Elizabeth, the third monarch of the decade.

By this stage a range of religious opinions existed in England, varying from conventional Catholics who still acknowledged the authority of the Pope to hardline Protestants who felt the church needed to be completely stripped of any Roman veneer, leaving nothing not plainly spelled out in the Bible. Elizabeth and her ministers sought to create a broad-based English Protestant (Anglican) Church which would include as many people across the middle of this spectrum as possible. The 1558 Acts of Supremacy and Uniformity established the Church of England as once again independent from Rome with the sovereign as its supreme governor, and made it compulsory for all English people to attend its services on a Sunday. As the Pope did not recognise Elizabeth I as the rightful queen, Catholics were forced to choose between their faith and their country. Those who remained within the Roman Church and continued to recognise the Pope's authority risked being prosecuted for treason.

At the same time, the government also tried to silence Protestant hardliners who argued that the Church of England was still too Catholic in its structure and doctrine and had not been fully reformed. These were called non-Conformists, as they would not conform to the teachings of the Anglican Church. The most fundamentalist and anti-Catholic of these were the Puritans, who are famous today for their refusal to celebrate Christmas. Non-Conformists criticised the continued authority of bishops, the wearing of vestments by priests, and the imposition of the Book of Common Prayer. Opposition to the Church of England by Catholics and non-Conformists continued, in some cases, in open rebellion. But the Act of Uniformity was only loosely-enforced, and most people in England were content to attend Anglican services, so it seemed some sort of compromise had been reached.

***

Like her half-brother and half-sister, Elizabeth was childless when she died in 1603. The crown passed to king James VI of Scotland, the next in line for the throne, who became the first of England's kings from the House of Stuart. Scotland had gone through a reformation of its own in the 1560s, led by Calvinist clergyman John Knox. James was, therefore, a Protestant, although he disliked the austere Calvinism of the English Puritans and Scottish Presbyterians. But he was now faced with a problem.

The Anglican Church in England is Episcopalian, meaning it is governed by bishops. The Scottish church, or Kirk, is Presbyterian, meaning it has no bishops and is governed by church elders. When he was in England, the King needed to believe that bishops were the rightful successors to Saint Peter and an indispensable part of the church. But when he crossed the Tweed River into Scotland, he had to believe they were a Papist hinderance to a truly reformed church. Needless to say, this was impossible.

The Stuart Kings were Scottish, so it's easy to assume they would have come down on the Calvinist side of the debate. However, they found bishops to be their natural allies and so began to wish that the Kirk would become more like the Anglican Church.

James was far from fanatical on religious matters, leaving many lay Catholics alone. He gave his name to the King James Bible, an official English translation of the scriptures commissioned during his reign to promote greater uniformity in the Church. Still, discontent continued. From 1630, increasing numbers of Puritans left England for new colonies in North America. After the failed Gunpowder Plot of 1605, an attempt by a group of Catholics led by Guy Fawkes to blow up the Parliament while the King was opening it, James demanded that Catholics take an oath of allegiance.

In contrast to his good relationship with the Anglican Church, James' dealings with Parliament were troubled. James had written a steadfast defence of the divine right of kings when he was still James VI of Scotland, describing monarchy as the 'form of government, as resembling the divinity, approacheth nearest to perfection, as all the learned and wise men from the beginning have agreed upon, unity being the perfection of all things'.[69] He pointed out that Paul had called upon the Romans to obey even Nero, a tyrant who persecuted Christians.[70] For subjects to rebel against their king would be, according to James, as unnatural as a body turning on its head. But even when James wrote his tract, these ideas were no longer as simple as they once had been. Protestants and Catholics could often not agree on who actually was legitimate, for a start. Pope Pius V had excommunicated Elizabeth I in 1570, declaring that she was a heretic and so not a legitimate sovereign. Parliament was not persuaded by James' arguments in favour of absolute monarchy and refused to grant him all the money he requested. James therefore dissolved it and ruled without it from 1614 to 1621, before he was forced to recall it. The relationship between the two remained stormy until James' death in 1625.

James' son Charles inherited with his father's crown his belief in absolute monarchy and the conflict with Parliament which accompanied it. Further religious differences intensified it; Parliament remained anti-Catholic and sympathetic to Puritanism, whereas Charles was married to a Catholic and opposed any further reformation of the Anglican Church.

When Charles attempted to impose an Anglican-style liturgy on the Scots, there was widespread discontent. On 28 February 1638, a large crowd assembled in the churchyard of the Greyfriars Church in Edinburgh and signed a document professing loyalty to the King but allegiance to a fully-reformed Kirk. The document was called the National Covenant, and so its supporters became known as Covenanters. Copies of the Covenant were spread throughout Scotland, and in the Bishops' War of 1639–1640, the Covenanters took control of the entire country outside the Northern and Western Highlands. The Covenanters were not liberal. Once they seized power in an area, adhering to the National Covenant was not a choice—everyone had to do it or risk being run out of town, or worse. But they were a popular, even democratic, movement, challenging the authority of the King and the nobility.

By then, Charles had even more serious problems with his Parliament. By mid-1642, matters had become so bad both sides had begun to muster armies. In October, war broke out between King and Parliament. The English Civil War, the collective name for a series of conflicts which consumed Britain between 1642 and 1651, brought devastation on a scale not seen for centuries. Battles were fought across Britain, cities were plundered, civilians massacred, and all told some two hundred thousand of England's five million people died. Charles was captured by the Parliamentary side in 1647, temporarily halting the war, but when a second Royalist uprising broke out he was implicated in plotting it and charged by the Parliament with treason at the urging of the Parliamentary Army. At his trial before a court established by Parliament in January 1649, Charles reiterated the divine right of kings and refused to accept the authority of any worldly court to try him. Unpersuaded, the court convicted him of treason and sentenced him to death. He was beheaded in Whitehall on 30 January.

The Civil War tore out the existing political order by the roots. Men had fought wars for England's crown, but not to have no king at all. During the war and in its aftermath, various popular movements flourished. The Levellers, active throughout the country, pushed for democracy, equality before the law, and religious tolerance. They had some temporary success, gaining enough support within the Parliamentary Army to have their views aired at the Putney Debates in 1647. However, following Charles' execution, they were sidelined by Cromwell and his generals. More radical still were the Diggers, early socialists who tried to establish the common ownership of property—they too had been suppressed by 1650. John Milton published a potent challenge to government censorship, *Areopagitica*, in 1644. But it too failed to sway Parliament.

Britain was a republic, but the power of Parliament was increasingly curtailed by the Parliamentary Army. In 1653 a Protectorate was established under Oliver Cromwell, essentially creating a military dictatorship. Puritanism became England's national religion, and the celebration of Christmas and anything resembling idolatry was banned. This arrangement did not last. The English tired of their authoritarian fundamentalist republic very quickly, and after Cromwell's death in 1658 they began to make plans to restore the monarchy. Charles' son returned from exile and resumed the throne as Charles II in May 1660. In Scotland, the Covenanters were suppressed, first by Cromwell, then more decisively by Charles II. It seemed things were back where they started.

***

One person on whom these events had a major impact was Thomas Hobbes. After witnessing the Civil War and the Restoration, he set out to propose an entirely new justification for political power, one which did not depend on the religious arguments King James had made.

Hobbes was born prematurely in Wiltshire on 5 April 1588; according to legend his mother's labour was induced by the news of the approach of the Spanish Armada. His father, also called Thomas Hobbes, was a vicar with a reputation for pugnacity. In 1604, the family was compelled to leave their native village of Malmesbury after the elder Thomas Hobbes got into a fistfight with another clergyman outside the village church. It is sometimes suggested that the father's belligerence contributed to the son's distaste for violence; this is plausible but unknowable. Hobbes studied Scholastic philosophy at Oxford but found it held little appeal for him, and spent most of his adult life engaged in various literary, philosophical and scientific pursuits of his own. He might have faded into obscurity save for the English Civil War.

Hobbes did not witness the War first-hand as he was then living in Paris. However, he was horrified by the wanton violence which consumed his native country. Over the 1640s, as tens of thousands of his fellow countrymen perished, Hobbes composed his most significant work, *Leviathan or The Matter, Forme and Power of a Common-Wealth Ecclesiasticall and Civil*. Published in 1651, it proposed a radically different idea of the origin, purpose and correct form of government than had previously been accepted.

Philosophically, Hobbes was an empiricist, a sceptic and a cynic. He began the *Leviathan* with an entirely naturalistic account of humans and human nature, comparing people to machines:

> For seeing life is but a motion of Limbs, the begining whereof is in some principall part within; why may we not say, that all Automata (Engines that move themselves by springs and wheeles as doth a watch) have an artificiall life? For what is the Heart, but a Spring; and the Nerves, but so many Strings; and the Joynts, but so many Wheeles, giving motion to the whole Body, such as was intended by the Artificer?

He accepted the existence of God, but apparently doubted whether men have immortal souls. Furthermore, he argued that religion arose naturally in human societies, and it is impossible to verify the accuracy of miracles. These unconventional views were not received with pleasure by the Church when the book was published.

Hobbes began his analysis by considering how people would act in a state of nature. He asks us to undertake a thought experiment—if there was no government, no social institutions like the church, no education, and nothing to restrain people's behaviour, what would they do? Asking this question is a sensible way of starting our quest to find a good system of government, because such a system must be compatible with human nature.

As it turned out, Hobbes had a fairly grim view of human nature, and his state of nature was a state of constant violence. In his view, men are naturally inclined to inflict violence on one another for gain, safety and glory. Without a government and the institutions of civil society, this would lead to his famous 'war of all against all':

> In such condition, there is no place for Industry; because the fruit thereof is uncertain; and consequently no Culture of the Earth; no Navigation, nor use of the commodities that may be imported by Sea; no commodious Building; no Instruments of moving, and removing such things as require much force; no Knowledge of the face of the Earth; no account of Time; no Arts; no Letters; no Society; and which is worst of all, continuall feare, and danger of violent death; And the life of man, solitary, poore, nasty, brutish, and short.

In such a war nothing would be unjust: 'The notions of Right and Wrong, Justice and Injustice have there no place. Where there is no common Power, there is no Law: where no Law, no Injustice.' In other words, he glibly dismissed centuries of Scholastic thought on natural law.

Man did, however, have one innate passion which inclined him to peace—fear of death. In Hobbes' rather dismal view, fear of death provides the basis for civil society. Plato and Aristotle saw civil society as a means to achieving and promoting virtue, but to Hobbes, it was purely for self-preservation.

From the foundation of self-preservation, Hobbes constructed his moral framework, plank by plank. He posited a series of nineteen natural laws. Firstly, everyone ought to work for peace, because in a state of peace people are less-likely to be killed. But if peace is not possible, everyone may use any advantage to win a war. But to achieve peace, people would need to give up some of their absolute freedom to do anything, and make agreements with others to do the same. This led to the second law of nature, that people should do what they agree to. The other seventeen laws followed in similar fashion.

Hobbes rejected the idea of natural rights. In his view, a right and a law were at opposites. In a state of nature, people had a right to do anything. In accepting laws, they gave up their rights.

The solution to the problem of the war of all against all was for people to form a society under a government, or as he calls it, a commonwealth. The citizens of a commonwealth would hand over their right to inflict violence on one another to one individual, who would be their sovereign. A commonwealth was like a person composed of many people, and the cover image of the book depicted a King composed of a multitude of his subjects.

What sort of government is best for a commonwealth? Hobbes considered the types posited by Plato and Aristotle, but decided, in the end, there were only three. Monarchy, rule by one; Aristocracy, rule by a few; and democracy, rule by many. Hobbes concluded monarchy was best:

> Now in Monarchy, the private interest is the same with the publique. The riches, power, and honour of a Monarch arise onely from the riches, strength and reputation of his Subjects. For no King can be rich, nor glorious, nor secure; whose Subjects are either poore, or contemptible, or too weak through want, or dissention, to maintain a war against their enemies: Whereas in a Democracy, or Aristocracy, the publique prosperity conferres not so much to the private fortune of one that is corrupt, or ambitious, as doth many times a perfidious advice, a treacherous action, or a Civill warre.

Hobbes' monarchy is absolute. Once a commonwealth is formed and a king appointed, he has total power and cannot be removed or punished by his subjects. His subjects would need to obey in order to prevent a return to anarchy and civil war. With one exception, that is—self-preservation. The commonwealth was formed to preserve life, so anyone was free to disobey or resist the sovereign if it was a matter of life or death, otherwise there was no point to having the commonwealth in the first place: 'If the Soveraign command a man (though justly condemned,) to kill, wound, or mayme himselfe; or not to resist those that assault him; or to abstain from the use of food, ayre, medicine, or any other thing, without which he cannot live; yet hath that man the Liberty to disobey'. So if the king sentences you to death, you can disobey him.

Hobbes then moved onto questions of religion. Scandalously, he argued that there was no way of assessing whether the teachings of one Christian sect were better than those of any other, therefore the sovereign would be free to pick one and compel his subjects to follow its doctrines: 'And therefore Christian Kings are still the Supreme Pastors of their people, and have power to ordain what Pastors they please, to teach the Church, that is, to teach the People committed to their charge'. This position scandalised the leaders of every Church. The rest of *The Leviathan* is devoted to melancholy attacks on Scholastic philosophy and the Catholic Church.

Unsurprisingly, *The Leviathan* met with a mixed reaction when it was published, and Hobbes became one of the most quoted and criticised figures in Europe. Widely-accused of atheism, he fled back to England and lived as quietly as he could. Descartes admitted his ability but thought his ideas wicked.[71] Even authorities in the Netherlands added the *Leviathan* to the works of Spinoza on their lists of dangerous books, although as with the works of Spinoza, they were unable to suppress it completely. In 1666 the House of Commons launched an investigation into 'books as tend to Atheism, Blasphemy, or Profaneness, or against the Essence or Attributes of God; and, in particular, the Book published in the Name of one White; and the Book of Mr. Hobbs [sic], called The Leviathan'.[72] Nothing concrete came of it, and Hobbes was not prosecuted, but he needed to print his future books in Amsterdam. These he continued to write until the age of eighty-seven. He finally died in 1679 at the remarkably (by the standards of the time) advanced age of ninety-one.

Hobbes is obviously not a liberal philosopher. His argument that we should accept any government as better than no government leads to accepting the authority of a Hitler or a Stalin. I certainly should not like to live in a society run on Hobbesian principles. But we shouldn't just dismiss Hobbes as an apologist for totalitarianism. A few of his ideas have gone on to become significant in liberal thinking. Rather than simply accept the divine right of kings or an explanation for monarchy in natural law, Hobbes argued that authority needed to have a secular and worldly basis. He created the modern idea of the social contract, although he differed from the liberal thinkers by rejecting any right of dissolving a government once it was formed. His system does not assume any innate superiority on the part of kings, but is based in the assumption that all men are equal and therefore a reason is needed for one to submit to the authority of another. And he accepts that anything not prohibited is permitted, and so nobody should be punished by the state unless they have broken an existing law. 'In cases where the Soveraign has prescribed no rule, there the Subject hath the liberty to do, or forbeare, according to his own discretion' he wrote. Modern liberalism has incorporated all these principles.

***

There was peace and quiet after the Restoration, for a while, but Britain's troubles with religion and the relations between king and parliament were not over yet. Charles II had many mistresses but no legitimate children. And as he got older, it seemed increasingly likely that he would be succeeded by his younger brother James.

James was alike to his brother in some ways, but his total opposite in others. Where Charles was warm, outgoing and popular, James was cold, reserved and naturally mistrusted. And while Charles could be pragmatic, James was inflexible. But most significantly, James was a Catholic. He had converted to Catholicism secretly, but his views became public when he refused to take an oath which excluded Catholics.

Parliament was generally hostile to Catholicism, and one group argued that allowing a Catholic to become king would lead to the establishment of an absolute monarchy in Britain similar to those in France and Spain. They introduced a bill to exclude James from the succession. Parliament divided into two factions—those supporting the bill, who subsequently became known as Whigs, and those opposing it, who subsequently became known as Tories. The Whigs favoured Parliament, toleration of Protestant dissenters, and the commercial classes, while the Tories backed the monarchy, landowners and high church Anglicanism.

In the end, the bill did not pass, and when Charles died in 1685 his brother became King James II (or, more accurately, James II of England and James VII of Scotland, but to the chagrin of some Scots, the English numbering system is the one which almost always gets used).

James was unpopular, and in fairness to him, quite a lot of the opposition he faced stemmed from simple anti-Catholic bigotry. He might not be the great villain of English history which the Whigs have liked to paint him as, but at the same time, it's hard to view him as having the temperament and character to have made a successful English or Scottish king.

Shortly after James' ascension he faced a rebellion in the West Country led by the Duke of Monmouth, one of Charles II's illegitimate sons (and hence James' own nephew) and another among the Campbells in Scotland lead by the Earl of Argyll. Both rebellions were defeated and Monmouth and Argyll beheaded, but it was a sharp reminder to James of the opposition he faced as a Catholic king in a Protestant kingdom. In the wake of Monmouth's Rebellion, Lord Chief Justice Judge Jeffrys descended on Somerset in a fury, sending hundreds of actual or suspected rebels to the gallows or convict transports bound for the West Indies. The trials, held throughout the West Country, became known as the Bloody Assizes, giving Jeffrys the nickname of 'the Hanging Judge'. At the time, those charged with the treason had no right to legal counsel, and Jeffrys freely berated suspects from the bench before sending them to exile or death. The Assizes left such a cultural memory that for centuries afterwards mothers in Somerset and Devon would warn unruly children that Judge Jeffrys would come and get them if they did not behave.

James seemed determined to repeat his father's mistakes, only more quickly. He sought from courts power to dispense with acts of parliament and built up and maintained a standing army which he quartered in his subjects' homes. The Whigs were naturally his implacable enemies, but even the Tories turned against him, not least of all because they felt their loyalty to the Stuarts had been betrayed. So he prorogued Parliament. France's absolute monarch, Louis XIV, seemed to be his role model. When seven Anglican bishops wrote to him to ask him to reconsider his policies, he had them arrested for seditious libel (although all were acquitted). In Scotland, the religious violence became so bad the 1680s became known simply as 'The Killing Time'. It is reasonable that James wanted to remove the barriers his fellow Catholics faced in Britain, but he had no general commitment to tolerance, and remained as hostile to non-Conformism as his father and brother.

James was intent on restoring a Catholic dynasty to the British throne. But while he had mistresses and illegitimate children like his brother, his only legitimate children were daughters, and they were Protestant. His enemies, therefore, felt they could wait. But in June 1688 the Queen gave birth to a son, also named James Stuart. The Catholic Stuart succession was now assured.

At this point, a small circle of Protestant nobles decided to act. In France, Louis XIV had revoked the Edict of Nantes which granted toleration to Protestants, and they feared a similar counter-reformation was now underway in England. They also feared a return to Marian Persecutions of the previous century. But it was no small thing to remove the king. They had seen the executions which had followed the previous uprisings. At worst, any attempt to overthrow James would see a return to the bloody civil war which was still a living memory. The utmost caution was needed, and the right candidate.

Luckily for them, they had a candidate. He was just across the North Sea in the Netherlands. William of Orange was born in 1650 in the Hague. His father was *Stadtholder* William II, his mother the daughter of English King Charles I. His father died before he was born and his mother died when he was ten, and she was distant towards him even when she was alive. From his childhood he became the object of a tug-of-war between the Orangists and the Republicans, but through a series of compromises he was granted a role in government through the period when there was no *Stadtholder*. He was brought up in the Dutch Reformed Church and remained a Calvinist with a firm belief in predestination, but he had no desire to fight others based on his religion. Perhaps because of his difficult early life he was, like James, cold and reserved. But even if he wasn't an easy man to like, he was an easy one to respect. He had intellect and courage, and his education and experiences tempered him into an effective leader.

His great moment came in 1672, the year of disasters. With the Netherlands facing destruction from the combined strength of France and England, the mob lynched the leaders of the Republic and called on him to be returned as *Stadtholder*. At the age of twenty-three, he became the leader of the Republic and the commander of its armies. He fought bravely, showing no regard for his own safety as he led his men again and again out to battle against vastly superior French armies commanded by able and experienced generals. By 1678, peace had returned and the crisis had passed—the Dutch Republic had survived.

In 1677 he married his cousin Mary, daughter of James II. It was not an ideal match—she was a bubbly fifteen-year-old who, despite being ostensibly second-in-line to the thrones of England and Scotland, had been given little education in the affairs of state, and he was twenty-seven, serious, and hardened by experience. William initially found his wife tiresome and involved himself with other women. But over time, the partnership strengthened. Their differences, perhaps, proved to be complimentary. Mary could be popular in the way William never could.

It is easy to see why James' enemies in England looked favourably on the Prince of Orange. He was half-English, a grandson of Charles I, and married to James' daughter, so he was not a complete stranger. He could speak English, albeit with a heavy accent. He was a Protestant, he was accustomed to government within the constraints of a constitution and in co-operation with a legislature, and was a proven military and political leader. The nobles approached him and asked him to invade England, promising he would face little resistance and the country would quickly go over to him.

William knew how perilous this proposal was—he was experienced enough as a soldier to appreciate what a vast and risky undertaking an invasion of England would be. But it also presented him with an opportunity he could not let pass. James II and Louis XIV were close, and for sixteen years he had lived under the fear of another combined English and French attack on the Dutch Republic. It had only just survived in 1672, and there was no guarantee it would survive again. If William could overthrow the Stuarts, he could establish a Protestant and pro-Dutch government in London and bring England and Scotland into a Europe-wide alliance to contain Louis XIV, who was preparing busily for another war.

It was then already summer, so William had little time. He told the Estates-General of his decision, and while they permitted him to proceed they made it clear he was acting alone rather than on behalf of the Republic. He then raised the money he needed through a loan from Amsterdam's bankers. He gathered a strong fleet and thirty thousand men, including the elite Dutch Blue Guards who had served him so faithfully against the French. It was then October, and the autumn gales kept his fleet bottled in harbour. Finally the 'Popish' west wind changed to a 'Protestant' east wind, and taking advantage of a narrow window of good weather he crossed the Channel in November. He landed at Torbay, in the west, where the last rebellion against James had happened and the people had little love for the Stuarts. He then unfurled a banner bearing the words *Pro Religione et Libertate* (for religion and freedom); the same slogan his ancestor William the Silent had used in the revolt against Spain. He issued a declaration stating he had come to restore England to her traditional liberties and began his march on London. He moved slowly, in the hope James' regime would collapse from the inside and he could avoid battle.

If James was more decisive, he might have kept his crown. But instead, he dithered. Over November and December, more and more of his erstwhile subjects declared for William. In the end, he threw the great seal of the realm in the Thames and fled to France with his wife and baby son. England and Scotland had no king. Fearing a deterioration into anarchy, the local government in London recognised William's authority. But what would happen next? This was unexplored ground.

CHAPTER V

GOVERNMENT BY CONTRACT AND THE ENLIGHTENMENT IN ENGLAND

On Monday 28 January 1689, the members of the House of Commons assembled in Westminster. The body represented the will of the English people, although it was elected on a very narrow franchise—only about 2% of the population met the property qualifications to vote. The 1689 Parliament included Isaac Newton, as a Whig member of Cambridge University, although he made no contribution to the weighty debates of that year beyond complaining of the cold and asking for the window to be shut. Rarely had the honourable gentlemen met to discuss matters of such gravity. Was James still their king? And if not, who would replace him? And on what terms would England be governed into the future?

The House quickly concluded that, by throwing the seal of the realm into the Thames, James had abandoned his throne. This saved it from needing to consider whether it had the authority to remove him had he not done so. Some of the Tories had written to James asking him if he would consent to return on conditions, and so a settlement could be brokered. But as committed to the divine right of kings as his father, he wrote back in a way which made it clear even to the most devoted admirer of the House of Stuart that he would simply undertake another and even more extensive round of persecutions. So they accepted he was gone for good. The House then split into two broad factions. One, made up mostly of Tories, maintained that the king had abandoned his throne by fleeing the country, and while they wanted a means of ridding the country of one bad king they did not want to risk creating anarchy by establishing a state of affairs where kings could be freely dispatched by Parliament on whatever grounds it fancied. The other, made up of the bolder Whigs, wanted a recognition of some sort of social contract, where James' misgovernment gave them the right to get rid of him and any other king who treated the constitution with disdain. Others fell somewhere in the middle. In the end, the House came to a compromise, where it issued a statement condemning James for his misrule but ultimately held that he had abandoned the throne.

> Resolution that the Throne is vacant. Resolved, That King James the Second, having endeavoured to subvert the Constitution of this Kingdom, by breaking the Original Contract between King and People; and, by the Advice of Jesuits, and other wicked Persons, having violated the fundamental Laws; and having withdrawn himself out of the Kingdom; has abdicated the Government; and that the Throne is thereby vacant.[73]

Who would replace him? The Tories generally favoured allowing the rules of succession to take their course, which would see the crown pass to Mary. Some of the more radical Whigs thought this a good opportunity to re-establish a republic. But most of the Whigs, and most of the House, once again fell somewhere in the middle.

On 29 January, the House resolved that no Catholic nor anyone married to a Catholic could become king, establishing the rule which held until the twenty-first century. They considered offering the crown to Mary, but she made it clear she could only accept it jointly with her husband. They considered offering it to William, but felt Mary should be rewarded for her loyalty, plus she was James' daughter and so would provide continuity. So the House of Commons issued a Declaration of Right, listing the crimes of James II and making a formal offer of the crown of England to William and Mary jointly. It was not strictly an offer on conditions, but it was implied to be one. The House of Lords, which was dominated by Tories, went through the same debates but often came to different conclusions. Eventually, though, the Commons brought the Lords around and the Parliament collectively made its formal offer. On 13 February, William and Mary accepted the Crown and promised to uphold the constitution. They were crowned together on 11 April, as William III (William II of Scotland) and Mary II.

In Scotland there was a similar convention. The Revolution in Scotland was both easier and harder than in England. Easier, because William was a Calvinist and the Scots were unlikely to get another chance to crown a king of their own faith. But harder, because loyalty to the House of Stuart was deeper. This was not because the Stuarts were originally Scottish, nor because Scotland was more Catholic than England (there were Catholic holdouts in the Highlands, but they were a small minority). Rather the Highland clans had deep subterranean networks of loyalty and enmity, and held closely to the old dictum that the enemy of my enemy is my friend. The Campbells were the enemies of the Stuarts, and the enemies of the Campbells became supporters of the Stuarts. Throughout England and Scotland the supporters of the House of Stuart became known as Jacobites, from *Jacobus*, the Latinised form of James.

The Parliament of Scotland proved bolder than its English counterpart, openly declaring James had forfeited his throne through misrule and so rejecting the divine right of kings once and for all. They offered the Crown of Scotland jointly to William and Mary, who accepted it on 11 May. Then the Jacobites rose in rebellion. At Killiecrankie in July the Williamite forces were routed by a Highland charge, but the rebels were finally defeated and the revolt crushed at Dunkeld in August. Peace settled over Scotland.

But peace in Ireland was still years away. The mostly-Catholic country stayed loyal to the Stuarts and could only be brought over to the House of Orange by force. Louis XIV treated the Dutch invasion of England as an act of war, and the long-anticipated Europe-wide conflict broke out in the spring of 1689. William became the effective leader of the league of countries opposed to Louis XIV. Called the Grand Alliance or the League of Augsburg, it included Catholic Spain and Austria, the German states, and Sweden, as well as England and Scotland. With French support, James landed in Ireland with an army. William crossed the Irish Sea.

William proved a better general than James. In July 1690 the long-awaited battle between the two rivals was fought across the Boyne River north of Dublin, and William emerged triumphant—some Protestants in Northern Ireland still commemorate the battle even today. James was once again forced into exile, and by the end of 1691, William had completed the reconquest of Ireland.

This was the Glorious Revolution. Called glorious by the Whigs, because it established a lasting model of government. The people of Britain haven't felt the need to overthrow their king (or queen) again. As Whig historian Thomas Babington Macaulay wrote 'the highest eulogy which can be pronounced on the revolution of 1688 is this, that it was our last revolution'.[74] To the Whigs, the Glorious Revolution didn't establish a new constitution; it merely enforced the existing one. The Tories came to accept it on these grounds, and William showed himself willing to work with both parties. Little blood was spilled in England and the Scottish Lowlands, but the Revolution was violent in the Scottish Highlands and brought two years of bloodshed to Ireland. It was Glorious for Protestants but not Catholics, who were left isolated and subjugated. It established a lasting settlement in England but repression continued in Ireland.

On a practical level, the Glorious Revolution restrained the capricious and arbitrary government which had held back progress in England and Scotland up to that point. In the words of economic historian Joel Mokyr, government becoming less predatory and more predictable was critical to the development of the economy. Long-term investment needed certainty, and this certainty could not exist where the King had the power to seize money or property whenever it suited him. In 1627, Charles I in England had set out to raise money through a forced loan, a tax without Parliamentary consent, and imprisoned without trial those who refused to pay it. The Glorious Revolution had seen the landed gentry take control of the Governments of England and Scotland, and they compelled the Government to acknowledge their right to property. With internal peace and a Government which could only raise taxes through the consent of Parliament, there was enough stability for them to risk steady investment in their businesses, growing them over time.

***

The religious question remained unsolved. Should the Parliaments of England and Scotland once again try to establish a single nation-wide church? One devout English Protestant rejected this idea resoundingly. This was John Locke, generally considered as the founding father of modern liberalism and the British school of empirical philosophy. His three major works touch on almost all areas of Enlightenment thinking. In his *Letter Concerning Toleration*, he argued for religious freedom and a separation of church and state. Over the next year, he brought out *Two Treatises on Government*, which explained his basis for private property, constitutional government and political liberalism; and *An Essay on Human Understanding*, which described his empirical philosophy.

Locke was not a radical, and many of his ideas were becoming increasingly common among forward-thinking people of his time. But he put them together into a coherent system and argued for them cogently and persuasively. Unlike many other modern philosophers, Locke is quite readable. His three major works are all quite short, and his prose is clear and forceful without being fervent. He is adept at argument through analogy, and grounds his ideas in the real world. It's possible to become familiar with his ideas in an afternoon and explain them coherently to others at a dinner party that same evening. If you go to dinner parties with people interested in philosophy, that is.

John Locke was born in 1632, the son of a Somerset solicitor. He kept something of a provincial mindset his whole life. His father served as a cavalry officer in the Parliamentary army during the Civil War. He showed enough academic promise to earn himself a place at London's elite Westminster School in 1647. There, it is likely he heard the crowds assembling for Charles I's execution in 1649—something to persuade him of the benefit of sound constitutional government even at an early age. He went on to Oxford, where he studied science and medicine. His significant career break came when he befriended the Earl of Shaftesbury, who appointed him as his personal physician. Locke performed a difficult and dangerous but ultimately successful operation to save Shaftesbury from a liver cyst by using a small silver tap to drain the cyst, earning his lifelong gratitude. From 1667, Locke became a member of Shaftesbury's household, essentially as his personal physician but in reality as a collaborator on his various projects. Locke was thrown into Shaftesbury's world of high politics.

Shaftesbury was behind the push for the bill to exclude James from inheriting the throne.

As the House of Commons was strongly in favour of the bill, Charles kept dissolving it, calling new elections in March 1679, October 1679, and March 1681. Finally, Charles dismissed the Parliament altogether and borrowed the money his government needed from Louis XIV of France. The Tories reacted violently against this Whig obstructionism, and in July 1681 Shaftesbury was arrested for treason and imprisoned in the Tower of London. The charges were dropped, but Shaftesbury decided not to risk facing another trial, particularly given he was continuing to plot against James. He left England for the Netherlands in 1682, and died the next year in Amsterdam. Locke remained in England, still closely tied to the Whigs.

Hardline Protestants continued to scheme against Charles and James. In June 1683, a major plot was uncovered. A dozen prominent Whigs were executed, and many more imprisoned or forced into exile. It is not known if Locke had any connection to the Rye House Plot, as it became known, but he was one of those who fled to the Netherlands. He lost his place at Oxford, although he was able to continue to receive rent from his properties in Somerset, keeping himself from poverty.

***

Locke long had an interest in liberal ideas; now his experiences had given him a personal interest in toleration. Over 1685 and 1686 he wrote *A Letter Concerning Toleration*.[75]

Locke made three broad arguments against the idea that a government should impose religious uniformity on its population.

Firstly, Locke denied that any earthly authority had the knowledge or wisdom to judge spiritual disputes: 'So that the controversy between these churches about the truth of their doctrines and the purity of their worship is on both sides equal; nor is there any judge ... by whose sentence it can be determined. The decision of that question belongs only to the Supreme judge of all men, to whom also alone belongs the punishment of the erroneous.' This is interesting, because there's no evidence that Locke doubted his own Anglican Protestant views. It's also illustrative of one of the key principles of Enlightenment thinking: the recognition of the limits of human reason. According to Thomas Aquinas, reason can lead right-thinking people to the truth on spiritual matters. Locke accepted Aquinas' position on natural law, but disputed that reason was an entirely sound guide.

Secondly, Locke pointed out that it is impossible to change what someone actually believes by force. Someone may be coerced into saying they believe in Catholic or Protestant doctrine, or they reject it, but they cannot be made to actually believe or disbelieve it.

> The care of souls cannot belong to the civil magistrate, because his power consists only in outward force; but true and saving religion consists in the inward persuasion of the mind, without which nothing can be acceptable to God ... I may grow rich by an art that I take not delight in; I may be cured of some disease by remedies that I have not faith

in; but I cannot be saved by a religion that I distrust and by a worship that I abhor.

This seems like such an obvious point to us today that it hardly needs to be said, but was a novel and controversial idea at the time. In addition to the ineffectiveness of violent persuasion (if that is not a contradiction), Locke also wrote disparagingly of the hypocrisy (or absurdity) of those who claimed to be Christian yet tortured and killed other Christians allegedly out of a desire to save their souls. In his view, they did nothing except discredit Christianity.

This leads onto Locke's third point, directed at those who appealed to social harmony as a reason for imposing religious uniformity: 'It is not the diversity of opinions (which cannot be avoided), but the refusal of toleration to those that are of different opinions (which might have been granted), that has produced all the bustles and wars that have been in the Christian world upon account of religion'.

Can the government ban any religious practice? Yes, if there are secular reasons for doing so. As Locke explained:

> You will say, by this rule, if some congregations should have a mind to sacrifice infants, or (as the primitive Christians were falsely accused) lustfully pollute themselves in promiscuous uncleanness, or practise any other such heinous enormities, is the magistrate obliged to tolerate them, because they are committed in a religious assembly? I answer: No. These things are not lawful in the ordinary course of life, nor in any private house; and therefore neither are they so in the worship of God, or in any religious meeting. But, indeed, if any people congregated upon account of religion should be desirous to sacrifice a calf, I deny that that ought to be prohibited by a law. Meliboeus [a character from a poem by the Roman poet Virgil], whose calf it is, may lawfully kill his calf at home, and burn any part of it that he thinks fit. For no injury is thereby done to any one, no prejudice to another man's goods. And for the same reason he may kill

his calf also in a religious meeting. Whether the doing so be well-pleasing to God or no, it is their part to consider that do it. The part of the magistrate is only to take care that the commonwealth receive no prejudice, and that there be no injury done to any man, either in life or estate. And thus what may be spent on a feast may be spent on a sacrifice.

Locke's arguments in favour of toleration remained limited, however. He was, at best, ambivalent about Catholics. On one hand, if a man could dress in a black robe, drink wine and speak in Latin in his own house, Locke said he should be able to do so before a church congregation. But like many of his contemporaries, he saw non-religious grounds for suppressing Catholicism—the divided loyalty between sovereign and Pope, and the belief that Catholics would not permit freedom of religion to others. Locke drew a definite and much stronger line at tolerating atheists. 'Promises, covenants, and oaths, which are the bonds of human society, can have no hold upon an atheist' he wrote, explaining the secular justification for excluding them. Of course, he does not explain how atheists could be compelled to believe in God, nor how suppression of atheism would not lead to social disharmony, falling foul of his own argument. But his position is understandable.

Locke returned to England in the wake of the Glorious Revolution. The winter journey and sea crossing nearly killed him; fortunately for the progress of the Enlightenment, he survived. *A Letter Concerning Toleration* was published in early 1689 and became immediately popular. In May 1689, Parliament took a step towards taking the same view with the *Act of Toleration*. It was not a large step, as the only change it made to existing law was to allow non-Conformist Protestants freedom of worship provided they accepted the Holy Trinity. Unitarians (who rejected the Holy Trinity) and Catholics were still not permitted to hold services, attendance at religious services on Sundays remained compulsory, and only Anglicans could hold political office. Over the next few years yet more laws were passed to bar Catholics from public life and force them into hiding. But the enforcement of these laws weakened over time. There were certainly political considerations behind the Act as well as philosophical ones, as immediately following the Revolution the new King and Queen were trying to gain as much support as possible, and emancipating non-Conformists was an easy way of winning them over. But it meant that religious uniformity would no longer be a national objective—this was a significant change.

Many prominent Catholics had fled the country with James II. There was still a sizeable Catholic presence in England—some 10–20% of the population in the northern counties—but those which remained tended to go underground. Religious violence was significantly lessened. Catholics were finally emancipated with a series of laws between 1778 and 1829, and Unitarians emancipated with the *Doctrine of the Trinity Act* of 1813. The Jews had been expelled from England in 1290, but they were re-admitted in 1655 and allowed to integrate into the community and freely practice their religion from 1753. By the nineteenth century, the practice of imposing fines for failing to attend religious service had become rare, and the Acts of Uniformity were gradually repealed.

In Scotland, the troubles were finally ended. In 1690, William and Mary approved a religious settlement where the Kirk could continue to do as it wished. The religious violence of the last half-century was over. But while the Kirk was free, it took more time to become tolerant, as University of Edinburgh student Thomas Aikenhead learned to his cost.[76] He began to publicly claim that the Bible was invented by the Prophet Ezra, the Apostles were 'a company of silly witless fishermen', and Jesus was a second-rate magician. Instead of conventional Christianity, he professed some sort of Pantheism, where God and the universe were one and eternal. These were unnecessarily provocative things to say, but in his defence, he was only eighteen.

Finally, in August 1696, he went too far. Walking with a group of friends past the Tron Church and complaining of the unusually cold and wet summer, he remarked that 'I wish right now I were in the place Ezra called hell, to warm myself there'. The authorities decided to grant him his wish. He was prosecuted for blasphemy, convicted, and sentenced to death. His sentence was upheld by the Scottish Privy Council. When it went before King William and Queen Mary, the Kirk petitioned them not to show clemency. They allowed it to stand. Locke took an interest in the case, but could do nothing to help the young defendant. In the afternoon of 8 January 1697, Aikenhead was hanged. 'It is a principle innate and co-natural to every man to have an insatiable inclination to the truth, and to seek for it as for hid treasure' he announced from the scaffold. 'So I proceeded until the more I thought thereon, the further I was from finding the verity I desired ...' Repentant of his blasphemy, he died with a Bible in his hand. It would have been little comfort to Aikenhead, but he was the last person to be executed for blasphemy in Britain. Toleration of dissent began to take hold in Scotland as well.

The modern argument for the toleration of dissenting views is little-changed from the Enlightenment. We certainly still face challenges as a society—how far, for example, do we tolerate intolerance? But Locke's three points from *A Letter Concerning Toleration*—it is difficult for the government to be certain which claims are right and wrong, it is not possible to force someone to adopt a different opinion, and suppressing dissenting viewpoints can be more harmful to social cohesion than allowing them to be put forth and debated—remain perfectly valid today. And behind their protection, the ideas of the Enlightenment grew and spread.

***

In his *Two Treatises on Government* (1689), Locke addressed the social contract and the basis for political power. Locke arrived at a different destination to Hobbes, but then his starting-point was different too. Whereas Hobbes' thinking was shaped by the violence of the Civil War, Locke had lived through the Protectorate, been compelled to leave the country during the reign of James II, and then been able to return following the Glorious Revolution. Locke was less-concerned with anarchy than Hobbes and more-concerned with tyranny.

Locke felt compelled to weigh into the debate on political philosophy to respond to the arguments by the ultra-Tory lawyer and baronet

Sir Robert Filmer (1588–1653). Filmer's most significant work was *Patriarcha*, a staunch defence of the divine right of kings, published posthumously in 1680 but probably written between the 1620s and 1640s. The authority of the king, Filmer argued, was analogous to the authority of a father over his children. God had granted Adam dominion over the world, and this power had been passed down to Noah, and then to Noah's sons, and then their patrilineal descendants in each part of the world. Just as a child is subject to the authority of his or her father from the moment of birth, so too is a person subject to the authority of his or her king. Unsurprisingly, Filmer's essay found sympathetic argument with the Stuart Kings of England.

But even if you accept the divine right of kings (and very few people do these days) it's hard to find Filmer's argument persuasive. Locke had little trouble refuting it, which he did in his *First Treatise on Government*. The authority of a king, Locke pointed out, was not the same as the authority of a father. A father could not sentence his children to death, for example. And once someone reached the age of twenty-one or married and left home, they did not need to obey their father anymore. Even if Adam ever had the authority Filmer gave him, there is nothing to suggest that it must have passed onto heirs. And even if it did, the laws of succession were not fixed and certain, and succession could often be disputed. And finally, even if Filmer's argument was sound in principle, it would be impossible to apply in practice as no one could figure out who Adam's heir was anyway. At the very least, Filmer would struggle to explain how there could be multiple legitimate kings in the world.

So if the divine right of kings provided no basis for government authority, what did? Locke considered Hobbes' argument in *The Leviathan*, but did not accept it. So he created a new model, which he outlined in his *Second Treatise on Government*. If the *First Treatise* was directed at Filmer, the *Second Treatise* was arguably (although much less openly) directed at Hobbes. Like Hobbes, Locke began with a state of nature. However, Locke's state of nature is radically different to Hobbes'. Primarily, Locke did not believe that a state of nature would inevitably be a state of war.

People would live together like the world's nations, sometimes fighting, but frequently at peace and engaged in trade.

Unlike Hobbes, Locke did not believe that a state of nature was a state of license. Locke believed in a natural law, which is apparent to us through our conscience. Locke's natural law is not arbitrary, but flows from all people being created by God to achieve his purpose. Therefore nobody could take the life, liberty or property of another unless it be to do justice to an offender. Likewise, under Locke's moral code, suicide and selling yourself into slavery would both be immoral, as 'no body can give more power than he has himself; and he that cannot take away his own life, cannot give another power over it'.

Locke's argument for natural law is, therefore, almost an argument from property. People are created by God to achieve his purposes, and so to kill them without the justification of the natural law is, to put it crudely, stealing from God.

In a state of nature, everyone would be allowed to enforce the laws of nature, which would be apparent to sane men through reason (a similar position to Aquinas'). Under the laws of nature, everyone would also be able to gather property to themselves from nature, which God had given to all people in common. The securing of property and the need for the better enforcement of the laws of nature would eventually lead to the rise of civil society.

Locke illustrates this process through a parable. Suppose I'm walking along in the state of nature and I see an apple hanging on a tree. Can I pick it and eat it? Yes, because everything in nature is given by God to mankind in common. When does the apple actually become mine? Is it when I see it, when I pick it, or when I eat it? According to Locke, it is when I pick it. I can make something from nature my property by mixing it with my labour. In the case of the apple, this is by picking it. However, if I were to cultivate an acre of land, I would make the land my property, and anything I grow on it would be mine even before I pick it. Locke accepts one proviso to this. If I pick so many apples that I can't eat them all and they begin to spoil, it would acceptable for someone else to come along and eat them. This, according to Locke, conforms to reason—God has given us the applies to eat, not to waste.

So if I have more apples than I can eat, it makes sense for me to trade them with others. In Locke's state of nature, individuals would trade with each other in the same way countries do. Property rights come from the laws of nature, so no government or other authority is required. But what if I have a lot of apples, and I want to buy your bananas, but the bananas are not yet ripe? This isn't a problem, said Locke. We can agree that something rare and imperishable will stand in for goods or labour and can be exchanged for them. Like gold, or silver. You can give me gold or silver now in exchange for the apples, and I can give you gold or silver back at some future date in exchange for the bananas. The gold or silver won't spoil, so it doesn't matter when the bananas are ready. Hence Locke believes currency could exist in a state of nature without needing to form a government.

Eventually, of course, this will all become too complex to manage among ourselves and we will all form a government through social contract. This will give us the advantages of settled law, an impartial judge, and the power of a state which can enforce the law. Locke was not thinking of a professional police force, as one did not exist in his time, but of institutions like the courts, the county sheriff, and the constabulary. The social contract, though, does not replace the laws of nature. We will still retain our rights to life, liberty, and property, and may disobey the government if it does not respect them. This is another difference between Locke and Hobbes. Of course, most people in Locke's England did not actively consent to join the society—they were the King's subjects from birth. How, then, could the social contract be a basis for government authority? Locke argued that by relying on the protection of the government, someone gave tacit consent to obeying its laws.

Locke then considers the three forms of government, which he calls democracy, oligarchy, and monarchy—the rule by many, few, and one. He accepts that all three may work, provided they adhere to his principle that the role of government is to protect the natural rights of the citizens.

One of Locke's most important innovations, and one which separates him decisively from Hobbes and most of the thinkers who had gone before, was the separation of powers. Rather than lead to a weak and factitious government, Locke argued that such a separation of powers, properly defined, would lead to liberty and justice.

Locke identified three types of power—legislative, executive and federative. The legislative power is the power to make new laws, and Locke considered it the most important. Making laws was best done, Locke argued, by a parliament of many legislators, all subject to the laws they make. The executive power is the power to enforce the laws. By making sure that the people who make the laws are not the same people as those who enforce them, Locke felt there would be the best chance that the laws would be just and enforced justly. Locke argued that the executive should be subordinate to the legislature, but it would need to continue permanently whereas the legislature would only need to meet periodically to make new laws, and the executive would also need to have some discretionary powers of its own (prerogatives). The final type of power, federative, was the power to form alliances and unite different societies into a federation, like the Dutch Republic. This was not really any different to executive power in practice, though, and has fallen out of use. Baron de Montesquieu (1689–1755) argued that the third type of power was the judicial power to interpret laws, and Montesquieu's interpretation is the accepted one today. Unlike Hobbes, Locke believed that unjust governments could rightly be overthrown and replaced. This had happened, in his view, in the Glorious Revolution.

Over 1689, the English Parliament came around to the same view as John Locke. It passed a Bill of Rights, confirming the idea that English people had natural rights which it was the job of government to protect, and the executive and legislative power should be split. Reiterating the crimes of James II and expressing gratitude to William 'whome it hath pleased Almighty God to make the glorious Instrument of Delivering this Kingdome from Popery and Arbitrary Power' it declared:

- the pretended power of suspending the laws and dispensing with laws by regal authority without consent of Parliament is illegal;
- the commission for ecclesiastical causes is illegal;
- levying taxes without grant of Parliament is illegal;
- it is the right of the subjects to petition the king, and prosecutions for such petitioning are illegal;
- keeping a standing army in time of peace, unless it be with consent of Parliament, is against law;
- Protestants may have arms for their defence suitable to their conditions and as allowed by law;
- election of members of Parliament ought to be free;
- the freedom of speech and debates or proceedings in Parliament ought not to be impeached or questioned in any court or place out of Parliament;
- excessive bail ought not to be required, nor excessive fines imposed, nor cruel and unusual punishments inflicted;
- jurors in trials for high treason ought to be freeholders;
- promises of fines and forfeitures before conviction are illegal and void;
- for redress of all grievances, and for the amending, strengthening and preserving of the laws, Parliaments ought to be held frequently.[77]

The American Bill of Rights is based on the same principles, and any American familiar with their country's constitution will easily be able to map many of the amendments to an English precedent.

***

How good does Locke's theory of government look over three centuries later? The basic premises of the *Second Treatise* are now widely-accepted in western democracies. People have human rights which pre-date the formation of governments, governments should protect those rights, governments may only exercise their authority within the law, people within government should be bound by the law themselves, and the powers of government should be divided between institutions. Countries whose governments operate according to these principles are generally wealthier and more stable than those which reject them.

Let's look at Locke's theory in detail, starting with his state of nature. Some readers might question whether Locke's idea of a mostly-peaceful state of nature is realistic. In societies where government has collapsed, as in Afghanistan after the Afghan-Soviet War or Somalia today, violent anarchy usually ensues. However, this is not a true state of nature where people have never known central authority. A better model for the state of nature are the world's nations, which have never known central authority. They do fight at times, but also live in peace and trade with each other.

But have human beings ever lived in such a state? At the time Locke was writing, archaeology was in its infancy and palaeontology was not yet established as a science, and so he knew much less of early human societies than we do today. In fact, it isn't clear from Locke's writings if he believed the state of nature had ever existed, or if he is only proposing it as a hypothetical situation to better understand human nature (the same can be said of Hobbes). Today, knowing what we know about human evolution, we can assume modern humans lived in groups from the start. Prior to the discovery of agriculture around 11,500 years ago all humans were hunter-gatherers, and every hunter-gatherer society observed in modern times has consisted of nomadic bands of a dozen to over a hundred individuals. Chimpanzees and bonobos, our nearest relatives in the animal kingdom, have a similar social structure, so it is likely our common ancestors had one as well. So there would never have been a time when a single person lived alone in a state of nature. However, competing human societies, from rival bands of hunter-gatherers to rival nations, do act as Locke described, sometimes fighting, and at other times living in peace or trading.

There are examples of smaller communities peacefully amalgamating into larger ones, such as the Old Swiss Confederation formed in the late

Middle Ages. So Locke's model is not completely fanciful, although it is probably more of a thought experiment than an actual explanation of world history. The question is how well its ideas work in practice, not whether it's describing something which actually happened.

Locke's justification for private property makes sense to us intuitively. Suppose you and I live in a share house where all the food in the fridge is held in common. We pay equally into the weekly grocery bill, and share everything we buy. If you take some of the food out of the fridge and make a sandwich, and I come along and eat it, you'll probably be annoyed. And if I point out that the food in the fridge is held in common, you'll probably retort that you made the sandwich, and if I wanted a sandwich I should have made one myself. In other words, you're asserting your property rights over the sandwich as you mixed your labour with the ingredients.

But Locke's entire model of civil society is sometimes criticised for his dependence on property. It's worth noting at the outset that Locke uses the word 'property' more broadly than we do, as he considers our property to include our own person. Our land and possessions he refers to as our 'estate'. Each man 'hath by nature a power, not only to preserve his property, that is, his life, liberty and estate, against the injuries and attempts of other men'.[78] Therefore, not every reference to 'property' in the Second Treatise is a reference to things we own. Still, Locke undoubtedly does place a high value on things we own. If there was no private property, a government would still be needed to protect our rights to life, liberty and person, but Locke's complete story wouldn't work. And Locke's idea of gaining property through cultivating land certainly privileges the Somerset farmer or Virginia planter over the native American. And additionally, Locke himself would have known that many great aristocratic estates in England and Scotland were won originally by conquest rather than labour. After all, Locke lived on the patronage of one such aristocrat, Lord Shaftesbury, who was rich because his ancestors were favoured by kings, not because he tilled so much as a single furrow himself.

Today, our major political debates tend to be about how much of a role the government should play in providing services like healthcare and education, and how it should levy taxes to pay for these services. Locke doesn't have too much to say on this point (unlike Adam Smith, whose argument we will consider in due course). Locke recognises that the legislature has a right to levy taxes, but also recognises a right to private property, presumably limiting the government's power to appropriate property. Locke was writing at a time when most goods were produced by small farmers and small tradesmen, and so doesn't foresee the huge corporations and industrial fortunes of modern times. It's not clear from his writings whether he believes the law of nature should place a limit on how much private property one person can accumulate. He does state that the earth is given to mankind in common, and accumulating more food than you can eat or leaving another person to starve is contrary to the laws of nature. But he isn't any more specific. Modern philosophers are often critical of Locke because of the contradictions he leaves unresolved and the questions he leaves unanswered.

Still, the Enlightenment has shown us that human reason is imperfect, and systems of knowledge do not need to be complete and consistent to be valuable. Entirely-consistent systems are more likely to be consistently wrong than consistently right. This point was made by one of Locke's critics, Bertrand Russell, in his hugely-influential *History of Western Philosophy* (1945). Russell thought Locke's philosophy mediocre and, as a socialist, believed his idea of acquiring property through mixing labour with it was of little use in the age of the factory, the assembly-line, and the corporation. Still, Russell's overall view was that Locke's philosophy of government, even if inadequate to the demands of the twentieth century, was much better than any which came before. He acknowledged that 'on the whole, the school which owed its origin to Locke, and which preached enlightened self-interest, did more to increase human happiness, and less to increase human misery, than was done by the schools which despised it in the name of heroism and self-sacrifice'.[79] We cannot look to Locke for answers to all of our political questions, but we shouldn't overlook the value in the model of government which he proposed.

***

Locke's *Second Treatise* was not immediately popular in the way *The Leviathan* had been, but it took off in the second half of the eighteenth century. Locke was one of those most fortunate writers who put forward an idea whose time had come. Locke had some involvement in practical politics, co-authoring in 1669 fundamental constitutions for the Carolinas, which established religious freedom but also permitted slavery and serfdom. But as the eighteenth century progressed, his ideas found their way into more and more documents.

Like the Netherlands, Britain became extremely successful. Once the Government abandoned religious uniformity as a goal and made its parliament supreme, the country became wealthy, stable and powerful. As in the Netherlands, this was not solely due to the tolerance of dissent, but it was a necessary starting point. The French philosopher Voltaire, who lived in England from 1726 to 1729, was left with a lasting and positive impression of British religious pluralism. 'If one religion only were allowed in England, the Government would very possibly become arbitrary; if there were but two, the people would cut one another's throats; but as there are such a multitude, they all live happy and in peace' he wrote.[80] Voltaire overstates the religious harmony given the ongoing suppression of Catholicism and non-Christian groups, but they were at least living together in peace, if not yet in happiness. Voltaire is best-known today for the aphorism 'I disagree with what you say, but I will defend to the death your right to say it'. There's no evidence he actually wrote it, but given the rest of his writings, he probably wouldn't mind having the sentiment attributed to him.

As the eighteenth century continued, toleration and religious pluralism went from being seen as merely necessary to actively beneficial. In *The Wealth of Nations*, published in 1776, Adam Smith argued that the benefits of the free market applied just as much to ideas as it did to goods and services. State religions, he argued, would naturally ossify over time and become hostile to innovation. Just like state-imposed economic monopolies, in fact. But a multitude of churches would compel everyone to learn tolerance and seek new converts:

> The interested and active zeal of religious teachers can be dangerous and troublesome only where there is either but one sect tolerated in the society, or where the whole of a large society is divided into two or three great sects; the teachers of each acting by concert, and under a regular discipline and subordination. But that zeal must be altogether innocent where the society is divided into two or three hundred, or perhaps into as many as a thousand small sects, of which no one could be considerable enough to disturb the public tranquillity.[81]

Smith goes further, suggesting that this state of affairs:

> [M]ight in time probably reduce the doctrine of the greater part of them to that pure and rational religion, free from every mixture of absurdity, imposture, or fanaticism, such as wise men have in all ages of the world wished to see established; but such as positive law has perhaps never yet established, and probably never will establish, in any country.

In this, he was over-optimistic, not taking into account that people are often attracted to extreme sects not because they are rational but because they are mystical. But his basic point stands.

Limiting the power of government and forcing it to adhere to its own rules was, perhaps, the most significant reform to come out of the Glorious Revolution. The *Treason Act* of 1695 provided that people should only be prosecuted for treason based on evidence in the indictment, should be allowed a copy of the indictment at their expense, and be defended by counsel. Judge Jeffrys, the Hanging Judge, was stripped of his power and locked in the Tower of London, where he soon died. From the 1730s, defence counsel began to appear in the Old Bailey to defend those accused of crimes both great and small. The criminal justice system remained harsh, and if anything, more statutes imposing capital punishment were added to the books. But some of the more extreme penalties, such as hanging, drawing and quartering, began to fall into disuse. It was a start.

***

John Locke's most significant legacy is outside Britain, in the founding documents of a country established on Enlightenment principles and with a system of government based in his ideas. *A Letter Concerning Toleration* and *The Second Treatise on Government* were not the only books which influenced the American Founding Fathers, but their influence was huge. Benjamin Franklin, John Adams and James Madison referred to and praised Locke in different writings.[82] Thomas Jefferson, the principal author of the Declaration of Independence, was heavily-influenced by Locke, including the 'Locke on government' in a list of recommended books to a young friend eager to get a well-rounded understanding of the world.[83] The text of the Declaration itself reflects a Lockean view where the government is formed by citizens to protect their rights, and they can remove it if it fails to do so:

> We hold these Truths to be self-evident, that all Men are created equal, that they are endowed by their Creator with certain unalienable Rights, that among these are Life, Liberty, and the pursuit of Happiness—That to secure these Rights, Governments are instituted among Men, deriving their just Powers from the Consent of the Governed, that whenever any Form of Government becomes destructive of these Ends, it is the Right of the People to alter or abolish it, and to institute a new Government, laying its Foundation on such Principles, and organizing its Powers in such Form, as to them shall seem most likely to effect their Safety and Happiness.

Parts of the Declaration follow the *Second Treatise* even more closely. On revolutions to overthrow unjust governments, Locke wrote:

> ... such revolutions happen not upon every little mismanagement in public affairs. Great mistakes in the ruling part, many wrong and inconvenient laws, and all the slips of human frailty, will be born by the people without mutiny or murmur. But if a long train of abuses, prevarications and artifices, all tending the same way, make the design visible to the people, and they cannot but feel what they lie under, and see whither they are going; it is not to be wondered, that they should then rouze themselves, and endeavour to put the rule into such hands which may secure to them the ends for which government was at first erected;

While Jefferson put the same idea like this:

> Prudence, indeed, will dictate that Governments long established should not be changed for light and transient Causes; and accordingly all Experience hath shewn, that Mankind are more disposed to suffer, while Evils are sufferable, than to right themselves by abolishing the Forms to which they are accustomed. But when a long Train of Abuses and Usurpations, pursuing invariably the same Object, evinces a Design to reduce them under absolute Despotism, it is their Right, it is their Duty, to throw off such Government, and to provide new Guards for their future Security.

Commenting on the charge that he copied the Declaration from Locke, Jefferson wrote that he 'turned to neither book or pamphlet while writing it' but 'did not consider it as any part of my charge to invent new ideas altogether & to offer no sentiment which had ever been expressed before'.[84] Jefferson, with his forceful and elegant prose, had expressed the principles of the *Second Treatise* in a way that would see them remembered through the ages.

The American Constitution itself, with its separation of powers, separation of church and state and bill of rights, is a practical application of the ideas in the *Second Treatise*, and those of other Enlightenment political philosophers such as Baron Montesquieu: 'We the People of the United States, in Order to form a more perfect Union, establish Justice, insure domestic Tranquility, provide for the common defence, promote the general Welfare, and secure the Blessings of Liberty to ourselves and our Posterity, do ordain and establish this Constitution for the United States of America'. Aside from the great moral failing of human slavery, which took a bloody civil war to erase, it has served the American people reasonably well for nearly two hundred and fifty years. The United States of America is not a bad legacy to leave.

Of course, John Locke did not live to see the founding of the United States. He died in 1704. And in his will, he asked that his funeral be modest, and the money saved should go towards buying a new suit of clothes and pair of shoes for four honest labouring men in his home village in Somerset.

William and Mary ruled together until 1694, when Mary died. This was a hard blow for her widower, as she was popular in a way he never would be and he had come to depend on her to rule while he was away on campaign. The War of the Grand Alliance (also called the War of the League of Augsburg or the Nine Years' War) ended in 1697, with Louis XIV contained within his borders and the Netherlands safe. So William had achieved his goal. He never loved England or Scotland and their people never warmed to him, and he had been motivated to overthrow James in order to save his own country. He was a Dutchman first and foremost who preferred to spend his time in the Netherlands and looked on Britain as a foreign country up until the end of his life. But the loveless partnership between the Prince of Orange and the British people was an extremely effective one and brought benefits which were well-appreciated by both sides.

CHAPTER VI

THINKING SCIENTIFICALLY

The Enlightenment is closely bound with the scientific method. The Scientific Revolution was a forerunner to the Enlightenment, and in turn, Enlightenment thinking allowed science to grow and spread. In particular, empiricism, where we begin the process of gathering knowledge through observation of the world rather than principles of philosophy. This is not to say that pre-Enlightenment thinkers did not use science, or the scientific method did not exist before the seventeenth century, but it was only with the Enlightenment that the scientific method became applied rigorously and consistently. And the results have been remarkable—electricity, the internal combustion engine, antibiotics, anaesthetic, computers and hundreds of other innovations which have made our lives better than those of our forebears have come from it.

As with many Enlightenment concepts, there's not a single agreed definition of the scientific method. 'Physicists speak familiarly of scientific method, but they could not readily describe what they mean by that expression' wrote Professor Stanley Jevons in 1874.[85] School science textbooks might explain it in five, six, seven or eight steps.

Put simply, the scientific method goes like this. You make a series of observations, you come up with a hypothesis which could explain those observations, you make predictions based on your hypothesis, you test those predictions with further observation or experiment, change or refine your hypothesis based on what you discover, and when there are no further discrepancies between your observations and the hypothesis you can accept it as a theory. A good scientific theory explains a number of different observations without leaving too much unexplained. The scientific method works because it is based in one of the principles of the Enlightenment—recognising the limits of human reason. Observation and deduction, blind trials, and the peer review of published papers are all designed to counter this frailty.

Today we associate the word 'science' with the scientific method and inductive reasoning. But this is a recent development, dating back only to the nineteenth century. When the word 'science' entered the English language from French in the Middle Ages it was originally used to mean any field of precise and systemic knowledge. The Scholastic philosophers recognised the sciences of grammar, logic, rhetoric, arithmetic, music, geometry and astronomy.[86] Laymen came to use it to mean any knowledge acquired through learning and developed through practice. 'I doubt not that you are an adept in the science yourself, Mr Darcy' Sir William Lucas says of dancing in *Pride and Prejudice*. It is still occasionally used in casual conversation in this way, when someone says something is 'not an exact science'.

The areas of knowledge we refer to today as the physical sciences, like physics, chemistry and biology, were covered by the terms 'natural philosophy' and 'natural history'. But over the 19th century, 'science' became reserved for those areas of knowledge developed and expanded through observation and experimentation, and the word 'scientist' (as opposed to 'natural philosopher') was first proposed in 1834.[87]

At first glance, the distinction between 'science' and 'natural philosophy' seems to be one of semantics. But it makes a difference. Before the Enlightenment, science was seen as an off-shoot of philosophy, like a branch stemming from the trunk of a tree. Descartes used this exact analogy in the introduction to his 1644 *The Principles of Philosophy*, where he described knowledge as being like a tree with metaphysics as its roots, physics as its trunk, and the other sciences as its branches. If this were the case, then you could just as readily reach conclusions about the physical world through philosophy as through observation and deduction. More specifically, the belief that the universe operated according to some pre-arranged purpose which could be deduced through reason hobbled the science of the ancients and the medieval Scholastics.

This can be seen clearly with Aristotle, who pioneered empirical study, but with patchy results. In *On the Heavens* he makes the claim that heavy objects fall faster than lighter ones. Such was the regard in which Aristotle was held for centuries that claims like this were not challenged. Galileo Galilei gets the credit for disproving Aristotle, according to legend, by dropping two cannonballs of different sizes off the Leaning Tower of Pisa.

The Enlightenment thinkers and their successors have been hard on Aristotle for these types of errors. But we should probably cut him some slack—he was doing his best to figure out the world in which he lived with the tools available to him. He might have fared better had his works not been taken up and given a sort of quasi-religious authority in the medieval Christian and Islamic worlds. Rather than allowing his ideas to be individually assessed, challenged and built on, they were made to crystallise into a single fixed edifice, which was finally knocked over and shattered.

***

There have been two basic types of reasoning in philosophy—deduction and induction. Deduction is 'top-down' reasoning, where we draw a conclusion from a number of premises. Induction is 'bottom-up' reasoning, where we develop a general principle from a number of observations. In very simplified terms, Continental rationalist thinkers, like Descartes and Spinoza, preferred deduction. British empiricists, like Hobbes and Locke, preferred induction. In his *An Essay on Human Understanding*, Locke argued that we don't have innate ideas, each person is a *tabula rasa* or blank slate, and we learn about the world through our senses. These ideas permeate Locke's other writings. 'Nobody is born a member of any church' he wrote in his *Letter Concerning Toleration*.

If your premises are true, deduction will give you conclusions which are *certainly* true. Pure maths relies on induction. You calculate that 2+2=4 because you know in advance what '2' is, and what '4' is, and you know by definition that two '2's make a '4'. You could, in theory, solve the sum by doing a series of experiments, putting two groups of two different objects together and counting how many you're left with, but this would be absurd. Induction, by contrast, gives premises which are *probably* true. But you can develop ideas in induction without needing to know anything in advance. The modern scientific method is based in induction—a hypothesis is tested against evidence from observations. Induction is also called empirical thinking, as it involves drawing conclusions based on evidence and experimentation.

The Ancients and Scholastics, however, preferred deduction over induction. Plato believed the physical world to be an imperfect reflection of an ideal abstract one, and hence reason rather than observation was the only sure way to arrive at the truth. In *Timaeus*, his dialogue on the nature of the universe, the titular character says 'that which is apprehended by intelligence and reason is always in the same state; but that which is conceived by opinion with the help of sensation and without reason, is always in a process of becoming and perishing and never really is'. His student Aristotle took a more hands-on approach, wading into the sea off the island of Lesbos to study the marine life there and make observations about it. Aristotle is therefore considered an early empiricist, and one of the founders of scientific thinking. Even so, Aristotle was not a true scientist in the modern sense, combining his observations with supposition and speculation. In *Prior Analytics* and *Posterior Analytics*, his works on formal logic, he recognised induction as a means of gaining knowledge, but devoted most of the book to deduction.

Aristotle's main contribution to logic is the concept of the syllogism, or a valid logical statement which delivers a true conclusion. To cite the most common example (which doesn't actually appear in the book):

All men are mortal
Socrates is a man
Therefore, Socrates is mortal

This is obviously true, and deduction is an important and useful means of reasoning. But as a system of reasoning deduction has an important limitation—if the premises are false then the conclusion will be false. In this case, we have to know for certain that all men are mortal and that Socrates is a man before we can be sure that Socrates is mortal. As it turns out, the premises are true and the conclusion is valid. Where the premises are not true, even a valid syllogism will produce a faulty conclusion. I will show an example of this in the next chapter.

The Scholastics preferred deduction for the same reasons as Plato and Aristotle. To them, the physical world was merely a stage where the conflict between God and Satan for the souls of men would be played out. The only absolute truths could be found in the eternal law, parts of which were revealed in the scriptures.

Of course, induction has limitations as well. The sad tale of Bertrand Russell's inductivist turkey (originally a chicken, but the story is usually recounted today with a turkey) is one such example. One day in the spring a turkey hatches on a farm, and the farmer comes along and feeds him some grain. The next day, at the same time, the farmer again comes along and again feeds him some grain. Many turkeys might assume, at this point, that they would be guaranteed food at the same time every day. But our turkey is a good inductivist, so he holds off on his conclusion until he has made more observations. He observes that he is fed grain at the same time on every day of the week, from Monday through to Sunday. He observes that he is fed when it's hot, or cold, or raining, or sunny. He observes that he is fed at the same time in the spring, and the summer and the autumn. Finally, after making over a hundred observations, he concludes that it is a law of nature that the farmer will feed him some grain at the same time every morning. Then one day, the farmer comes out, takes him from his pen, and cuts his head off. In this case, the turkey would have been better off applying some deductive reasoning to his situation. Even so, Russell still acknowledged that induction is necessary to give us new knowledge.

Here is a more practical example. After observing that swans in all parts of Europe, North America, and western Asia were white, Europeans were comfortable assuming that all swans worldwide were white. Then Dutch explorers found black swans in Western Australia in 1697. The term 'black swan' is used today to mean an unexpected event which defies all previous experience. To learn about the world, we would need to learn how to use induction and empiricism to its fullest potential.

***

Various thinkers between Aristotle and the Enlightenment applied something like the scientific method. These include Archimedes and Epicurus in Ancient Greece, Ibn al-Haytham in the Arab Caliphate, Al-Biruni and Ibn Sina in Persia (the latter known in the west as Avicenna), and the medieval English monk William of Ockham. None, however, seriously challenged the dominance of Scholasticism or its equivalents in the Islamic world.

By the Renaissance, however, cracks were appearing in the foundations. The works of Plato, formerly lost in Europe, were rediscovered in the fifteenth century. Plato was far from an empiricist, but on many issues his books presented an alternative view to Aristotle's. A few Renaissance thinkers like Bernardino Telesio (1509–1588) and Francesco Patrizi (1529–1597) challenged Aristotle, although not to lasting effect.[88] The European discovery of the Americas caused another fracture. Once it became clear the lands Columbus had happened upon in his four voyages between 1492 and 1504 were not the East Indies but were entirely new, questions were asked in royal courts and universities throughout Europe. This was a monumental discovery—two large inhabited continents unknown to the Ancient Greeks and without mention in the Bible. It led to the obvious question—what else was unknown out in the world?

Over the next century and a half, more discoveries raised even more questions. Not only did exploration of the world's seas and oceans reveal more lands and peoples previously unknown in the old world, but the invention and adoption of the telescope and microscope in the first two decades of the seventeenth century showed new things which had been hiding in plain sight. It now took only novel thinkers without preconceived ideas to identify a system where these observations could be turned into new and solid knowledge. They include Galileo with his possibly-apocryphal cannonballs, Francis Bacon, Robert Boyle and Isaac Newton.

Francis Bacon (1561–1626) was a lawyer and politician by profession. In these pursuits he had mixed success. He became Lord Chancellor of England, but found himself cast out of office in disgrace in 1621, in debt and facing charges of corruption. He admitted that he accepted gifts from those whose cases he had judged, but insisted he had not allowed them to influence his judgement. This was not considered as shocking then as it would be today, but it was still not enough to save his reputation.

Bacon has enjoyed more long-term fame from his contributions to science. When the frontiers of human knowledge were still narrow, it was not unusual for one person to pursue study in wildly different fields, and Bacon was one such person. His most significant scientific work was the 1620 *Novum Organum Scientiarum* ('New instrument of science', usually abbreviated to *Novum Organum*). Unlike the works of Copernicus and Galileo it does not contain any new discoveries or revolutionary theories. Rather, Bacon lays down a new way of thinking about science.

In Bacon's view, existing natural philosophy placed too much weight on established authority and overly-broad generalisations, and needed to go back to investigation and induction. In particular, he identified four barriers to clear thinking, which he memorably named the four idols of the human mind. Today, we might call them cognitive biases.

The first, idols of the tribe, are errors of thinking which come from human nature itself. In particular, our habit of assuming the world around us is more orderly and purposeful than it actually is. To use a modern analogy, the gambler who keeps throwing money into the game because he thinks he is 'due' for a win is enthralled by idols of the tribe. The second, idols of the cave (or den), are errors of thinking we fall into through our own background or experience, or quirks of our particular personalities. In Bacon's view, we all have a cave in our mind where the light of reason is filtered and dimmed, and this cave is peculiar to us alone. We can all probably think of the parent who fondly describes their son as a high-spirited lad while everyone else views him as a dangerous menace to society. The third, idols of the market, are errors which come from communication and dealing with others. Someone might write something which is correct, but someone else might misread it and spread the erroneous interpretation to others. If I got Bacon's ideas wrong and described them incorrectly in this book, and others took up my explanation and spread it around, that would be an example of an idol of the market. And finally, there are idols of the theatre, or false ideas established through dogma and existing systems of philosophy.

As an antidote to the four idols, Bacon proposes a system which he describes as 'true induction'. As an example, he demonstrates how he might come to terms with the nature of heat. Putting aside pre-conceived ideas about heat (including, notably, Aristotle's) he makes a list of hot objects, a list of cold objects and a list of objects which might be either hot or cold depending on the situation. Through a series of comparisons, he eliminates certain possibilities. Because the Sun's rays are hot, heat cannot come from the Earth. And because the lava which comes from volcanoes is also hot, heat cannot come from the sky. Heated iron is no heavier than cold iron, so heat is not a corporeal substance of any sort. Nor is it the same as light or fire, as some substances, like water, never light up and catch fire no matter how hot they get. In the end, he concludes that heat must be somehow related to motion. Fire, boiling water, living animals and other things which give off heat are all in motion. Curiously, Bacon was actually fairly close to being right—how hot an object is depends on how rapidly its molecules are moving. Nonetheless Bacon is careful not to draw any more expansive conclusions than he can back up with his observations. He does not claim to have all the answers; only to be asking the right questions.

In the *Novum Organum*, Bacon therefore neatly demonstrates the

Enlightenment principle of recognising the limits of human reason. The system of discovery through induction does not require Aristotelian wisdom; it just requires good observations and a process of elimination. It also does not require the universe to operate according to any purpose, although Bacon himself was a devout Anglican who believed his method could better allow him to understand God's creation. He was also fundamental in developing another key Enlightenment concept—empirical thinking.

Ironically given his interest in heat, Bacon died of a cold he caught while stuffing a chicken full of snow in an early experiment in preserving food through refrigeration. Or at least, he caught the cold after the incident with the chicken. In true Baconian style, we shouldn't assume that the two incidents were related without some sort of evidence lest we fall into the thrall of the idols of the tribe. But the story is too good not to tell.

***

Robert Boyle (1627–1691) was an Anglo-Irish Chemist. High school science students might recognise his name from Boyle's Law, which states that the pressure of a gas increases as the volume of its container decreases. He is best known for the 1661 book *The Sceptical Chymist*, where he broke down many existing ideas about chemistry and matter through rigorous and consistent experimentation. Boyle's work marked a critical development in reproducibility, one of the fundamental principles of modern science. If one person does an experiment and gets a particular result, then someone else should be able to do the same experiment and get the same result. Boyle described his experiments in enough detail so that others could repeat them.

Boyle was also a founding member of the Royal Society, formed in 1600 and granted a royal charter by Charles II in 1662. Established by a group of like-minded physicists and natural philosophers, it was intended to promote science and allow scientific ideas to be shared more easily. A French equivalent, the Académie Royale des Sciences, was founded in Paris in 1666. Both emphasised the importance of conducting experiments.[89]

In 1665, the Royal Society began publishing a monthly journal, the

Philosophical Transactions of the Royal Society, with Henry Oldenburg appointed as publisher and editor. The first edition, published on 30 May, included an article on observations of Jupiter's Great Red Spot by Robert Hooke, Newton's sometime-rival, and a review of a book by Boyle on the experimental history of cold. Other articles covered lead ore, whaling and predictions of the return of a comet.[90] Sufficient material permitting, the Society directed that the journal be published on the first Monday of every month from then on. Oldenburg continued to publish as directed, although it was interrupted by the plague (July–November 1666) and Oldenburg's imprisonment in the Tower of London for treason (June and August 1667)—some of the perils of seventeenth-century life. And it is still published today, 350 years on, although it is now divided into two separate editions covering the physical and life sciences respectively.

Oldenburg was a German who spoke five languages, and he used his connections on the European continent and his polyglot skills to write to learned men throughout Europe to gather articles, many of which he translated himself. Each article was registered and date-stamped, like the submissions to a modern scientific journal. While he reviewed the articles, there wasn't too much originally to guarantee quality.[91] But over time, this practice would evolve into peer review, where a submission to a journal is read by one or more other experts in the field to which it relates before it is accepted for publication. Peer review is obviously imperfect, as it depends on the limitations of the people doing the reviewing. There are very good peer reviewed journals and weaker ones. And over time, a significant number of published scientific findings—perhaps a majority—are discredited by later studies. But peer review does help deal with Bacon's idols, and it has been invaluable in separating science from pseudoscience.

***

The most famous early member of the Royal Society was Isaac Newton, who became a Fellow of the Society in 1672 and served as its president from 1703 to 1727. Newton was born on Christmas Day in the first year of the English Civil War. His father was a well-off Lincolnshire farmer who died before Newton was born, and his mother re-married when he was young. His relationship with both his mother and step-father was troubled, not least of all because his mother tried to make him follow his father's profession without any success. Fortunately for him, his strong academic performance allowed him to go to the King's School, then Trinity College, Cambridge.

Newton was very guarded about his personal life, and he has not left us too much to go on regarding his inner thoughts and feelings. One curious exception is a list of sins he confessed to in his diary in 1662, addressed to God.[92] In contrast to the far more lurid confessions of Newton's friend, Samuel Pepys, in his famous diary, these sins are quite mundane. Sabbath-breaking seemed to be young Newton's most common offence, including 'Squirting water on Thy day', 'Making pies on Sunday night', 'Making a feather while on Thy day' and then 'Denying that I made it'. Others suggested the vindictiveness or outbreaks of temper which troubled him in later life, such as 'punching my sister', 'Putting a pin in John Keys hat on Thy day to pick him' and 'Calling Dorothy Rose a jade'. These also included 'Threatning my father and mother Smith to burne them and the house over them', a definite hint of his stormy relationship with his mother and step-father.

Newton is best-known for gravity. Or more accurately, the theory of universal gravitation—matter attracts matter in proportion to its mass. He also made significant discoveries in optics, physics (his laws of motion), and pure mathematics. There is a long-running controversy over whether he or his German contemporary Gottfried Wilhelm Leibniz discovered calculus—it is likely both men hit on the idea independently of each other.

Newton developed a reputation for eccentricity, both in his academic research and personal life. He scoured the Bible for codes, and concluded the world would not end before the year 2060. He chose to divide the spectrum of visible light into seven colours (Red Orange Yellow Green Blue Indigo Violet, known through the acronym ROYGBIV) because seven was a mystical number. He searched for the philosopher's stone, the magical object which would turn base metals into gold, and developed his own idiosyncratic interpretation of Christianity.

He was friends with John Locke on the latter's return to England, a friendship which was disrupted around the time Newton had a nervous breakdown in 1693. He later wrote to apologise, saying 'being of opinion that you endeavoured to embroil me with women, and by other means, I was so much affected with it, as that when one told me you were sickly and would not live, I answered, "twere better if you were dead". I desire you to forgive me this uncharitableness.'[93] Locke wrote back graciously, asking him to think nothing further of it.

In 1687 Newton published *Philosophiæ Naturalis Principia Mathematica* (the Mathematical Principles of Natural Philosophy, commonly abbreviated as the *Principia*), his most important work. In the second and third editions of his *Principia*, Isaac Newton developed what he referred to as the four rules of reasoning in philosophy. In the third edition in 1726, he states them as follows:

> Rule 1: We are to admit no more causes of natural things than such as are both true and sufficient to explain their appearances.

In his explanation of this rule, Newton wrote that 'Nature is pleased with simplicity, and affects not the pomp of superfluous causes'. Nature, of course, cannot be pleased or displeased, but the rule is still valid. We look for the simplest explanation of something we observe, and consider it more likely than a complex one. It is much simpler to attribute the motion of the planets to impersonal, universal forces than the personal direction of angels, for example, as the forces can be easily explained based on observation and experiment while the presence of angels moving the planets would raise more questions than it would answer.

> Rule 2: Therefore to the same natural effects we must, as far as possible, assign the same causes.

Here Newton gives the examples of breathing in both humans and animals, the descent of stones in Europe and in America, the light of a cooking fire and the light of the Sun, and the reflection of light from the

Earth and from other planets. We now know that a cooking fire and the Sun don't generate light and heat through the same process, but Newton's reasoning is generally sound. Once we know why an object falls towards the Earth, we can assume all objects fall for the same reason unless we have some reason to think otherwise.

> Rule 3: The qualities of bodies, which admit neither intensification nor remission of degrees, and which are found to belong to all bodies within the reach of our experiments, are to be esteemed the universal qualities of all bodies whatsoever.

This is the principle that the laws of nature are universal, one of the basic assumptions of science. There may be some part of the Universe where gravity doesn't exist or works differently to how we understand it, but unless we have some observation suggesting this is the case, we assume Newton's Law of Universal Gravitation applies everywhere.

> Rule 4: In experimental philosophy we are to look upon propositions inferred by general induction from phenomena as accurately or very nearly true, not withstanding any contrary hypothesis that may be imagined, till such time as other phenomena occur, by which they may either be made more accurate, or liable to exceptions.

In short, we cannot reason out of induction. If a theory explains all the observations, we treat it as being true until one which better fits the evidence comes along. We only change our theories as a result of new evidence.

With the approach of the Royal Society, and its equivalents in France and the German states, we can see something like the modern scientific method. We recognise the limits of our reason, rely on induction to gain new knowledge through reproducible studies, generalise from specifics but limit how far we allow our generalisation to go, and submit the results of our research to peer-review before it can be published. It has developed far since then, but the basics were in place. Newton would recognise the methods of a modern science, whereas Aristotle and Aquinas would not.

The scientific method was one of the most important legacies of the Enlightenment. Perhaps even *the* most important. The Scientific Revolution itself happened piecemeal. By 1750 we had a vastly superior understanding of physics, chemistry and astronomy than we did in 1600, but not much more of an understanding of medicine. But the later discoveries in medicine which have played such a crucial role in improving our standard of living have been made, tested and spread using the principles of scientists such as Galileo, Bacon, Boyle and Newton. By recognising the limits to human reason and developing rigorous induction as a remedy, they gave us the lives we enjoy today.

In the next chapter, I will look at a single example of the success of the Scientific Revolution—the rise and triumph of the idea that the Earth orbits the Sun, not visa-versa.

CHAPTER VII

A HERETICAL IDEA

The Sand Reckoner is a book by the ancient mathematician Archimedes, who is remembered for posterity by allegedly discovering the principle of buoyancy bearing his name while taking a bath. It contains, amidst a description of the contemporary account of the structure of the universe, a curious aside. 'Now you are aware that "universe" is the name given by most astronomers to the sphere whose centre is the centre of the earth and whose radius is equal to the straight line between the centre of the sun and the centre of the earth' he wrote.[94] 'But Aristarchus of Samos brought out a book consisting of some hypotheses, in which the premises lead to the result that the universe is many times greater than that now so called. His hypotheses are that the fixed stars and the sun remain unmoved, that the earth revolves about the sun in the circumference of a circle, the sun lying in the middle of the orbit …'

Aristarchus was born sometime around 310 BC and died around 230 BC. No copy of the book Archimedes refers to survives. But from what we know of it, Aristarchus had come up with a fairly-accurate model of the solar system almost two millennia before Galileo and Copernicus. He suggested the Sun was a star, the Earth revolved around it and the other stars were much like the Sun but much further away.

At the time, most astronomers accepted that the sun orbited the earth, a model known as Geocentrism. The alternative as proposed by Aristarchus, Heliocentrism, did not take off until the scientific revolution of the seventeenth century. And the story of how Heliocentrism came to knock Geocentrism off its perch after two millennia of dominance neatly illustrates many of the building blocks of the Enlightenment—the fracturing of central authority following the Reformation, the open challenging of the works of Aristotle and his followers, the rise of empirical and scientific thinking over traditional philosophy and the use of the printing press to spread its new ideas.

The Ancient Greeks already knew the Earth was round, although we do not know exactly when and how they came to this conclusion. The discovery is sometimes attributed to the Pythagorean School, the eccentric half-university half-cult founded by the mathematician of right-angled triangle fame whose members abstained from eating beans for religious reasons and swore oaths on a triangular figure called the tetractys. Aristotle cited the change in constellations as travellers moved north or south and the round shadow the Earth cast on the moon during a lunar eclipse as evidence of a spherical Earth.

On matters of astronomy, the Pythagoreans claimed the Earth and the Sun both orbited a 'central fire' along with an invisible counter-earth, and all the heavenly bodies moved together in a harmonious musical symphony. Most astronomers of the time, however, believed the sun, moon, planets and stars all orbited the Earth. Intuitively, this makes sense. The Earth beneath our feet does not seem to be moving, while all the celestial bodies travel through the sky. The Ancients classified the bodies by type, and assigned to each its own fixed sphere. First, the stars, which did not appear to move except for their nightly rotation through the sky. Referred to as the 'fixed stars' for this reason, they were assumed to be fixed on the inside of a sphere which rotated around the Earth once per day. The stars do move slightly from their positions over the course of the year as the Earth rotates around the Sun, a phenomenon called stellar parallax. As they are so distant from the Earth, however, it is very hard to detect and was not measured until the eighteenth century.

The Sun, Moon and classical planets were then each assumed to move within their own sphere. The Greeks, like the other ancients, knew of Mercury, Venus, Mars, Jupiter and Saturn, and knew they were not stars as they moved independently of them (hence the word *planḗtai*, meaning 'wandering'). Each sphere must be composed of some transparent material which held the object in place and prevented it from falling to Earth. Aristotle called this the *aether*. But there were some unexplained complexities, at least as far as the planets were concerned. The sun, moon and stars all crossed the sky in neat arcs, as would be expected if they were set in heavenly spheres in constant revolution around the Earth. But over time, the planets appeared to move in flat spirals, slowing, turning and reversing at regular intervals. This was exceedingly puzzling.

The apparent motion of the planets made sense if they, and the Earth, were all orbiting the Sun. We do not know if this swayed Aristarchus but it probably swayed another ancient Heliocentrist, Seleucus of Seleucia (*c.*190–150 BC).

On the whole, however, the Ancient Greeks accepted the Geocentric model. The two most significant Greek philosophers, Plato and Aristotle, were Geocentrists. Greco-Roman astronomer Ptolemy of Alexandra (*c.*100–170 AD) built a comprehensive and internally-consistent Geocentric model which accounted for the unusual motion of the planets. He had the planets orbiting the Earth while orbiting in their own little fixed spheres—a system of deferents and epicycles. Both Medieval Christian and Islamic civilisation embraced the philosophy of Aristotle and the Ptolemaic system. Dante's *Divine Comedy*, where a traveller is taken through the three supernatural realms of Hell, Purgatory and Paradise, is based on this model of the cosmos.

Contrary to popular imagination, the Ptolemaic model did not go completely unchallenged throughout the Middle Ages. For example, a medieval French bishop, Nicole Oresme (*c.*1320–1382), wrote of the possibility that the sun was at the centre of the universe. But the first widely-known alternative was proposed by Polish astronomer Nicolaus

Copernicus (1473–1543). Mindful that his ideas were controversial, he initially kept them to himself, finally publishing them in *On the Revolution of the Celestial Spheres* shortly before his death, knowing he would soon be beyond the reach of any worldly censure. Mindful of the potential backlash, Copernicus' publisher Andreas Osiander added a preface encouraging readers to treat the book as a thought experiment.

Some writers date the beginning of the scientific revolution to the publication of *On the Revolution of the Celestial Spheres*. I think this overstates its importance. It was a significant book, but it did not persuade any large part of Europe's intellectual community to abandon Geocentrism any more than any previous Heliocentric book. If the Earth was orbiting the Sun, they reasoned, then the Earth must be moving. Yet it felt motionless. Furthermore, not only must the Earth be moving if Copernicus is correct, but it must also be rotating from east to west. Yet when an object is dropped, it falls straight downwards, rather than a little to the west, as would be expected on a rotating Earth. And, of course, there was the lack of stellar parallax. And aside from Heliocentrism, many of Copernicus' ideas were quite conventional. For example, Copernicus still believed the planets were all in fixed spheres of ether. The Church paid the book little attention.

Danish astronomer Tycho Brahe (1546–1601) was the next person to seriously grapple with the problem. A nobleman who lost his nose in a sword fight and so needed to wear a prosthetic one for the rest of his life, he is well-known today for his rigorous observations of the night sky. By observing that comets passed between the orbits of the planets, he confirmed the celestial spheres could not be solid. Like many scientists of his day, he combined what we would consider proper science with alchemy and astrology—the distinctions between science and pseudo-science were less-clear then. Brahe had to admit that the motions of the planets through the sky made more sense if they orbited the Sun, not the Earth. But he remained troubled by the idea of a moving Earth and the absence of stellar parallax. Copernicus' system, he wrote, 'ascribes to the Earth, that hulking, lazy body, unfit for motion, a motion as quick as that of the aethereal torches, and a triple motion at that'.[95] Nor could he completely disregard the teachings of the Church. He proposed a compromise in 1588, now called the Tychonic System, where the planets orbited the Sun and the Sun orbited the Earth.

Brahe's work was continued by his student, Johannes Kepler (1571–1630). Brahe recruited Kepler for his excellent command of mathematics, and put him to work calculating the orbit of Mars. Kepler spent years on the project, but could not reconcile Mars' position in the night sky with any circular orbit around the Sun. Finally, a solution hit him which was so simple he initially disregarded it on the basis that other astronomers could not have missed it—Mars' orbit is not a perfect circle but rather an ellipse. Not only that, irregularities in Mars' speed could be explained by its position—it moved faster when closer to the Sun and slower when further away. Kepler had discovered his first and second laws of planetary motion.

Kepler's first law states that every planet orbits the Sun in an ellipse, or a flattened circle, with the Sun at one of the foci of the ellipse. In some cases the orbits of planets are very nearly circular, but they are never perfect circles. It is hard to understand just how difficult this had been for the scientific community of the time to accept. The heavens were the realm of the divine, and so it made sense that everything in the heavens would be perfectly even. This is an example of a failure of deductive reasoning—the conclusion was false because the premise was.

Kepler's second law states the time between two positions is directly proportional to the area swept out by a line between the planet and the Sun—this is easier to demonstrate in a diagram.

The details are not that important for our purposes, however. The key principle which Kepler had discovered is that a planet moves faster to the Sun when it is closer, and slower when it is further away. Kepler turned his attention from Mars to the Earth, and found that his discoveries fit far more easily with Heliocentrism than Geocentrism. The observed position of the Sun in the sky throughout the year made sense if the Earth was orbiting the Sun in a way consistent with Kepler's first and second laws.

In 1609, Kepler published *Astronomia Nova* ('New Astronomy') where he went into his findings in great depth. He began with a discussion on theology and scripture, explaining how Heliocentrism was consistent with the Bible. He then followed it up with pages of calculations. 'If thou art bored with this wearisome method of calculation, take pity on me, who had to go through with at least seventy repetitions of it, at a very great loss of time' he informed his readers in Chapter Sixteen.[96] Kepler could not explain why the planets moved, but concluded each planet must create some force holding it in place around the Sun, and the Sun must generate some force causing the planets to move. This was consistent with his second law, where the planets moved faster when closer to the Sun. Later, in 1619, Kepler developed his third law, which states that the square of the orbital period of a planet is proportional to the cube of the semi-major axis of its orbit. This defines the relationship between how close a planet is to the Sun and how quickly it moves.

Kepler's Second Law addressed an oddity in the solar year known to the Ancients but never explained. In the Northern Hemisphere, the summer is slightly longer than the winter. The spring and autumn equinoxes, when there are equal amounts of day and night, fall closer to the December solstice than the June one. For example, in 2017, the March equinox fell on March 20 and the September equinox on September 23, 187 days later. Half a year is actually a little under 183 days. We now know this is because the Earth's orbit is slightly elliptical, and it is closest to the Sun in January and furthest in July. As a result, it is moving through space faster in January than it is in July, and takes less time to move from its September to its March Equinox than it does to move from its March to its September one. Kepler's model of the solar system could explain this oddity in the calendar where no others previously could.

The same year *Astronomia Nova* was published, Galileo Galilei first looked at the night sky with a telescope. The next year, with a more powerful model, he looked at the planet Jupiter and saw three small, bright objects clustered around it. Every night from 7 to 13 January, he looked at the objects. They moved between each observation, so they could not have been stars. And furthermore, one disappeared behind Jupiter and another emerged. Galileo concluded the mysterious objects were orbiting Jupiter. Another astronomer, Simon Marius, named them after Jupiter's lovers in classical mythology—Io, Europa, Ganymede and Callisto. These four moons, Jupiter's largest, are now called the Galilean Satellites. This was a momentous discovery which completely challenged the discipline of astronomy from the ground up. Or, more accurately, from the stars down. Never before in any part of the world at any time had it been shown that one celestial body was orbiting another. In 1610 Galileo published *Sidereus Nuncius* ('Starry Messenger'), where he used the motion of Jupiter's moons and his observations of the phases of Venus to also make the case for a Heliocentric solar system. We did not feel the Earth's rotation, he argued, because we were all rotating with it. We experience this same feeling of motionlessness today when we are on a plane or a train travelling at constant speed. Likewise, Galileo concluded that a dropped object was already moving eastwards with the earth's rotation, and so appears to fall straight downwards to someone standing on the Earth and rotating with it. Galileo could not find any stellar parallax, but if the stars were very distant from the Earth, then this would not be fatal for the Heliocentric theory. Just as trees or buildings far away on the horizon do not appear to change position when you take a few steps to the left or right, so too would very distant stars not appear to change position as the Earth orbited the Sun. Heliocentrism was now looking solid, but it began, for the first time, to attract serious criticism on religious grounds.

***

At no point does the Bible explicitly state that the Sun orbits the Earth. However, a number of verses have been used to support Geocentrism. For example, in the Battle of Gibeon, God commands the Sun to stand still (Joshua 10:12–13). Additionally, he has 'set the Earth on its foundations, so that it should never be moved' (Psalm 104:5) and 'the sun also ariseth, and the sun goeth down, and hasteth to his place where he arose' (Ecclesiastes 1:5). Copernicus' ideas had been discussed in both Protestant and Catholic circles, and had met with some hostility and much ambivalence. Martin Luther was recorded saying in 1539:

> There is talk of a new astrologer who wants to prove that the earth moves and goes around instead of the sky, the sun, the moon, just as if somebody were moving in a carriage or ship might hold that he was sitting still and at rest while the earth and the trees walked and moved. But that is how things are nowadays: when a man wishes to be clever he must needs invent something special, and the way he does it must be the best! The fool wants to turn the whole art of astronomy upside-down. However, as Holy Scripture tells us, so did Joshua bid the sun to stand still and not the earth.[97]

Luther apparently missed the irony of the founder of Protestantism criticising those who sought to 'invent something special', but then again, he only claimed to have taken Christianity back to its fundamentals. The Catholic Church, for its part, was initially not hostile to Heliocentrism. Copernicus himself was a Catholic and a canon in the Church, and he had his book approved by the Church and dedicated it to the Pope. After 1610, however, with Kepler's and Galileo's works published and Heliocentrism rapidly gaining ground, a number of Catholic theologians began to criticise the idea. At stake was not only the Bible, but the centuries of Scholastic philosophy based on the works of Aristotle. The objections to the Copernican Model were not entirely religious. The absence of observed stellar parallax, for example, remained a problem for the Heliocentrists. But the Catholic Church's persecution of Heliocentrism was largely a persecution of heresy.

The Church assembled a group of consultants to consider whether Heliocentrism was heretical. On 24 February 1616, they produced a report describing the idea of the Earth orbiting a fixed sun as 'foolish and absurd in philosophy, and formally heretical since it explicitly contradicts in many places the sense of Holy Scripture, according to the literal meaning of the words and according to the common interpretation and understanding of the Holy Fathers and the doctors of theology'.[98] The Papal Inquisition ordered Galileo to stop writing or speaking in defence of Heliocentrism. Copernican books, including Kepler's *Astronomia Nova*, were banned by the Church. The ban would not be lifted until 1758.

In 1623, Pope Urban VIII asked Galileo to publish a comparative guide to the two systems. In the resulting *Dialogue Concerning the Two World Systems*, Galileo notionally met the Pope's request but in reality took a sledgehammer to Geocentrism. The arguments for Heliocentrism are presented by a scientist named Salviati and those for Geocentrism by a dull Aristotelian philosopher named Simplico. Sagredo, the allegedly-impartial adjudicator, joins Salviati in witty criticism of Simplico. The book was written in Italian rather than Latin, and its engaging style made it a bestseller. The Church was unimpressed, and Galileo was put on trial for heresy in 1633. Facing death by burning, he recanted his Heliocentrism, and would spend the rest of his life under house arrest in his villa. The *Dialogue* was banned. According to legend, Galileo muttered 'and yet it moves' (*Eppur si muove*) as he was led from the courtroom. It's unlikely he took such a risk, but the phrase has become a catch-cry of those who feel they've been barred from telling the truth.

Had the Galileo Affair taken place a century earlier, the Church might have been able to regain the upper hand. But following the Protestant Reformation, it had lost its power throughout much of northern Europe. It could do nothing to stop the re-publishing of the works of Copernicus, Kepler, Galileo and the other Heliocentrists in the German states, the Netherlands, Demark, Scandinavia and Britain. As the seventeenth century progressed, Heliocentrism gradually took hold.

Newton's *Principia* in 1687 finally and convincingly overturned the Aristotelian view of motion, explained how the Geocentric solar system actually worked, and removed once and for all the need for celestial spheres and supernatural forces. Like Archimedes with his overflowing bath, Newton is remembered for being hit on the head with a falling apple. The real story, as far as we know it, is less dramatic. Chronicler William Stukeley wrote of the following conversation with Newton in 1726:

On 15 April 1726 I paid a visit to Sir Isaac, at his lodgings in Orbels buildings, Kensington: din'd with him … after dinner, the weather being warm, we went into the garden, & drank thea under the shade of some appletrees, only he, & myself. amidst other discourse, he told me, he was just in the same situation, as when formerly, the notion of gravitation came into his mind. 'why should that apple always descend perpendicularly to the ground', thought he to him self: occasion'd by the fall of an apple, as he sat in a contemplative mood: 'why should it not go sideways, or upwards? but constantly to the Earths centre? assuredly, the reason is, that the Earth draws it. there must be a drawing power in matter. & the sum of the drawing power in the matter of the Earth must be in the Earths center, not in any side of the Earth. therefore dos this apple fall perpendicularly, or toward the center. if matter thus draws matter; it must be in proportion of its quantity. therefore the apple draws the Earth, as well as the Earth draws the apple'.[99]

So the falling apple story is apparently true, but the apple didn't actually hit Newton on the head. And, of course, Newton was not the first human being in history to observe that dropped objects fall to the Earth. But he was the first to establish the principle that matter draws matter in proportion to its quantity, and so the apple exerts a tiny force on the Earth just as the Earth exerts a much larger force on the apple. This is Newton's law of universal gravitation.

If gravity exerted itself between an apple and the Earth, Newton reasoned, then it must also exert itself in some way between the Earth and the Moon. This was the force which held the celestial bodies in orbit. But why, then, did they move in ellipses and not simply fall into each other? Newton had an answer to this in the *Principia* in his three laws of motion. The first law states that every object will remain at rest or in uniform motion in a straight line unless an external force acts on it. The second states that an object moves in accordance with the sum of the forces acting on it. The third states that, if one object exerts a force on another, the second object exerts a force on the first. Or, as it is commonly put, to every action there is an equal and opposite reaction.

Aristotle had argued the natural state of an object was at rest, and anything set in motion would return to rest unless acted upon by a constant force. This makes sense intuitively—when you throw a rock it doesn't continue indefinitely but steadily loses speed and height until it falls to the ground. But the rock still obeys Newton's laws—it falls to the ground because it is under the influence of the forces of gravity and friction with the air. Likewise, Newton's laws vindicated Galileo's idea of inertia, explaining how we don't feel the Earth's rotation.

The law of universal gravitation and Newton's three laws of motion explain how the solar system works. The planets orbit the Sun because two forces are acting on them—gravity towards the sun and their existing forward motion. Saying the planets orbit the Sun is putting it simply. In reality, one object orbits another around a point between their respective centres of mass called a barycentre. Where one object is much larger than the other, the barycentre of their orbit is very close to the centre of mass of the larger object. The barycentre of the Earth's orbit around the Sun is close to the centre of the Sun, for example. However, in line with Newton's third law, the sun does move slightly under the influence of the Earth's gravity. Gravity explained oddities in the position of the Sun and planets. It also explained the operation of Kepler's Second Law. The Earth moves faster in January than July because it is closer to the Sun, and hence acted on more strongly by its gravity. In the last chapter I wrote that a good scientific theory should explain multiple observations while leaving as little as possible unexplained—Newton's theory of gravity is probably the gold standard.

There was some controversy over whether Newton or another physicist, Robert Hooke, discovered gravity first. 'If I have seen further it is by standing on the shoulders of giants' Newton wrote to Hooke, acknowledging the importance of those who came before him.

It also illustrates an important reason for the success of the Scientific Revolution—the availability of scientific works allowed one scientist to build on the works of another. Nonetheless it was Newton's Principia which essentially explained how the cosmos worked. It is not perfect—we now know the Sun is not the centre of the Universe, as Newton believed, general relativity explains some observations which gravity and motion cannot, and there are likely to be further developments in physics. However, Newton's and Kepler's model is basically correct. The *Principia* is sometimes considered to be the most important single publication in science, and many lists of the world's greatest-ever scientists put Newton at the top.

It was a staggering progression of science. In the course of a single human lifetime, our model of the Solar System had gone from Geocentrism and fixed spheres of aether to Heliocentrism, gravity, and Newtonian motion. As Bertrand Russell put it in his *History of Western Philosophy*, 'In 1700 the mental outlook of educated men was completely modern; in 1600, except among a very few, it was largely medieval'.[100]

Heliocentrism was a triumph of ideas rather than technology. The telescope was an important development, but the technology to build one had existed for centuries. The Ancient Greeks could probably have done it and, with their advances in optics, the Medieval Arabs certainly could. And outside the telescope, everything needed to build a Heliocentric model of the solar system was available through naked eye observation and deduction.

Neither Kepler nor Newton were completely modern in their scientific thinking. Carl Sagan described Kepler as 'the first astrophysicist and the last scientific astrologer'[101] while Newton devoted a significant part of his career to eclectic writings on theology, astrology, alchemy and the quest for the philosopher's stone. But they, and their contemporaries, had moved science for the first time decisively forward from the Ancient Greeks. Putting aside relativity, which has only a small impact on the scale of the planets, Kepler's and Newton's model of the Solar System basically matches our understanding of how it works today. It was a massive scientific achievement, well beyond anything from the best minds of medieval Europe, the Arab world, or China. But just as the triumph of Heliocentrism was not a triumph of technology, so too was it not a triumph of individual people. It was a decisive shift in ideas.

CHAPTER VIII

THE SCIENCE OF MAN AND THE ENLIGHTENMENT IN SCOTLAND

Newton had revolutionised natural science—his *Principia* explained everything from the fall of an apple to the rotation of the Earth, and his principles for reasoning promised an ongoing scientific revolution. But could human behaviour be explained in a similar way? Answering this question occupied the minds of the leading figures of the Scottish Enlightenment. In this chapter, I will look at how a small and previously unimportant country on Europe's northern fringe became a world intellectual and academic leader. And in particular, how this idea of the science of man eventually led Scotsman Adam Smith to write *The Wealth of Nations* and develop the modern science of economics.

We left Scotland on a grim note with the execution of Thomas Aikenhead for blasphemy in 1697. The country had started to modernise, but this modernisation had not been consistent. From the late Middle Ages into the eighteenth century, there were two Scotlands—the Lowlands and the Highlands. They may have been two separate countries.

The first and most obvious division between them was a linguistic one. Lowlanders spoke Scots, and Highlanders spoke Gaelic. The Scots language originated from Medieval English, and spread north from Northumberland. By the seventeenth century, it was spoken widely through the south and east of the country. Centuries of separation from English had made it very distinctive, and even today, there is a lively debate as to whether Scots is a dialect of English or a language in its own right. This is obviously not just a linguistic question. Throughout churches (or *kirks*) in the Scottish Lowlands every Sunday, worshippers would recite the Lord's Prayer and ask God to:

> Gíe us our breid for this incomin day;
> forgíe us the wrangs we hae wrocht,
> as we hae foríen the wrangs we hae dree'd

This is perfectly correct Scots, as is saying *teacht* over *taught*, *leid* over *language* and *bairn* over *child*. It was the language of the royal court of the Stuarts, the courts of law, and the common language of the universities (although the lectures were all given in Latin). Just as the Lowland Scots had their own language descended from English, so too did they have their own legal system, similar in some ways to English common law but different in others. And Edinburgh and Glasgow were recognisable European towns, even if small, dark and poky ones.

The Highlands were another world entirely. The Celtic Gaelic language had held on north of the Firth of Forth, and with it a social system just as distinctive. The Highlands were still the domain of the clans, and the King in Edinburgh had little power compared to the clan chief and his *tacksmen* who collected his rents, mustered his followers for the August hunt, and enforced his decrees. It's easy today to have a romantic idea of the Highland clans, thinking of them of extended families all wearing the same tartan and sticking to each other against an oppressive central authority with bonds of blood. But this is a nineteenth-century image, created after the traditional way of life had faded. For a start, the idea of clan tartans dates from the Victorian era. Highland society was feudal, not tribal. Dirt-poor tenants scraped a living from the rocky soil under the constant threat of violence. Clan law was arbitrary and brutal. When a woman was brought before chief MacDonald of Clanranald, accused of stealing from him, he had her tied by her hair to seaweed out on the rocks at low tide. The rising tide came in and drowned her.

To use the analogy of historian Arthur Herman, if the average Scottish clan was a family, it was a family in the mafia sense of the word. With famine a constant threat and most of the wealth of the Highlands tied up in cattle, cattle-raiding was a fact of life. A cattle-raid, known as a *reive* in Scots or a *creach* in Gaelic, could be directed against other clans or Lowlanders living near the Highlands. Other clans would accept money from Lowlanders in exchange for not raiding them—the word *blackmail* is of Scottish origin.

Needless to say, this state of affairs was of little liking to the royal court in Edinburgh. And with the union of the crowns in 1603, the Scottish Kings for the first time gained the power to exert some more control over the Highlands. This was a long and difficult process. The Highlands remained violent, and in some cases, the central government was the cause of the violence rather than the solution to it. The most infamous example was the 1692 Glencoe Massacre of thirty of the Glencoe MacDonalds by the Argylls when their chief was too slow to swear allegiance to William and Mary.

Scotland was, in other words, an unusual centre of Enlightenment thinking. But it had a few advantages. One was the exceptionally high rate of literacy, driven by the Kirk and its desire to have all people read the Bible and the works of John Knox. By the turn of the eighteenth century this was becoming a reality in the Lowlands. The other was its unusual concentration of universities. Of the seven 'ancient' universities of Britain and Ireland, founded before 1600, four were Scottish—St Andrews, Glasgow, Aberdeen and Edinburgh. However, they were built to train clergy. Like universal literacy, their purpose was to make the Scots more pious. Aikenhead's execution shows the power the Kirk wielded and its intolerance of dissent.

***

Ironically, it was an episode of catastrophic financial speculation which kicked off the Enlightenment in Scotland. In 1698, the Scottish Parliament decided to buy into the high-stakes colonisation game by founding a trading settlement in Central America. This project, called the Darien Scheme, failed disastrously and left half of Scotland's nobles near bankruptcy. Scotland's Parliament looked to extreme measures—a full union with England. England had a growing and increasingly-lucrative colonial empire, but Scotland's merchants were shut out of it. The English Parliament, for its part, was naturally open to the idea of a union. Given that England was so much more populous and powerful than Scotland, England would naturally dominate the new country, and at the same time, the English could remove the threat of the two parliaments disagreeing over succession and creating a dynastic war. It was such an attractive idea the English were willing to shell out some gold to make good the Scottish nobles' losses in the Darien scheme as a goodwill gesture on securing their vote.

This was, needless to say, not particularly popular in Scotland, and the commissioners who signed the treaty spent the rest of the day being chased around Edinburgh by an angry mob. The independence fought for by Robert the Bruce and William Wallace had been given up for trade deals and what seemed an awful lot like straight-up bribery. As the Scottish patriot Robert Burns would later write:

> We're bought and sold for English Gold,
> Such a Parcel of Rogues in a Nation.

On 1 May 1707, the kingdoms were united and Great Britain was born. The crosses of Saint Andrew and Saint George were melded into the Union Jack. The new country would turn out to be one of the most successful which has ever existed.

But some of the worst fears of the anti-Union crowd soon seemed to be realised. The Parliament of Great Britain abolished the Scottish privy council and enforced toleration of Anglicanism in Scotland, ending the Kirk's religious monopoly. Even in England there were second thoughts about the Union, at least among the Tories, who realised that the strong support for the Whigs in the Scottish Lowlands seemed likely to keep them out of power in Westminster indefinitely.

But the issue of succession still hung over Britain, as it had hung over England and Scotland. Mary had been childless when she died in 1694, and the Jacobites were quick to point out that her barren womb was a fitting punishment for breaking the fifth commandment to 'honour thy father'. In 1702, William's horse stumbled on a molehill and he fell, breaking his collarbone and subsequently dying of pneumonia. The Jacobites raised their glasses to the little gentleman in the black velvet waistcoat who had brought undone their most dangerous foe. The crown passed to Mary's sister Anne, who bore five living children amidst numerous stillbirths and miscarriages, but all died in childhood. On her death in 1714, the crown skipped over dozens of Catholic Stuart descendants to pass to a German Prince, George of Hanover, who was a great-grandson of James I through his mother. Great Britain was to get a foreign king who spoke no English, but at least he was Protestant.

There was, of course, an alternative king. James II had died in 1701, but his son, James Francis Edward Stuart, still kept his court in Rome. The Old Pretender, as he was known, was recognised as King James III by both the Pope and the Jacobites. Young noblemen would stop by to visit him on their grand tour of the continent, while Jacobite sympathisers in England would surreptitiously pass their wine glasses over their finger bowls during the royal toast, symbolically toasting the 'King over the Water'.

The Glorious Revolution was still only a generation old, and while it had been popular its support was far from universal. There were a lot of people who remembered the old ways and liked the idea of going back to them. But since the last Jacobite uprising in the Scottish Highlands had been crushed in 1690, they had kept quiet. And they might have stayed quiet, if not for the Earl of Mar.

Mar was a Scottish Tory nobleman who supported the Union, even though it cost him his lucrative post as Secretary of State for Scotland. But following a crushing Whig electoral victory in the election of 1715 he was left sidelined. Shortly afterwards, he was snubbed by the new King, who turned his back on him. It might have been a political gesture, but it could have equally been a display of the notoriously cold and wooden George I's lack of social skills—this was a man who kept his wife a prisoner for twenty years. At any rate, Mar decided to get rid of him. At Braemar during the annual stag hunt on 6 September 1715, he gathered his followers around a bowl of hot punch and declared he would dissolve the 'cursed union', restore Scotland's ancient liberties and put the Old Pretender on his rightful thrones as King James III of England and Ireland and James VIII of Scotland.

Mar had joined two causes—Catholic and Tory opposition to the Glorious Revolution and Scottish opposition to the Union. Neither was strong enough to challenge the House of Hanover alone but together they presented a serious threat. The Highlands largely went over to Mar, as did more than a few Lowlanders. In England, downtrodden Catholics and Tories who had given up on being restored to power by democratic means joined his banner. Within a month Mar had twenty thousand men. The revolt came as a surprise to the Old Pretender, but he optimistically set out for Scotland to claim his throne.

Had Mar been a more decisive commander, things might have gone ill for the House of Hanover. But despite having a two-to-one advantage in numbers, he failed to secure a victory over the government forces commanded by the Duke of Argyll in an indecisive battle at Sherrifmuir on 13 November 1715. France and Spain, which might have been tempted to throw their support behind him had he won, now held back. Mar dithered, and the morale of his army fell. In England, authorities moved quickly to arrest known Jacobites, and a secondary uprising in the north-west of England was quickly crushed. Over the winter, Argyll grew stronger and Mar weaker. The Old Pretender landed in Scotland on 22 December, finding the Jacobite army disintegrating and Argyll advancing. In February 1716, he returned to exile, taking Mar with him. Another much smaller Jacobite uprising broke out in the western Highlands in 1719, backed by Spain, but it too was defeated. Many of the Jacobites were pardoned, and Scotland returned to normal.

***

George I adapted to his new role surprisingly well. Despite being an absolute monarch in Hanover, he proved able to govern as a constitutional one in Great Britain. Already middle-aged when he took the crown and very set in his ways, he preferred Hanover to Britain and seemed content to let his Parliament and his ministers govern. He learned some English, but otherwise spoke to his ministers in French, the Europe-wide language of aristocracy and diplomacy. And so constitutional government became more established. In particular, the principle of cabinet government and the office of prime minister dates from George I's reign, although the title itself only became official in the twentieth century. Indeed, having a foreign king uninterested in micro-managing the kingdom was probably to Britain's advantage.

And contrary to Mar's predictions, Scotland did not suffer in the long run from the Act of Union. The Act did quash Scotland's independence and abolish its parliament and give it the much higher taxes England was used to, but Scotland kept its legal system, its universities and its church. In some ways, Scotland had the best possible situation—a distant government with less interest in meddling in its affairs and, at the same time, sound institutions of its own. Benign neglect, in other words. And critically, Scottish merchants now had access to English markets, and the Scottish economy began to grow. By 1755, Scottish imports had doubled.[102]

Against this background of precarious peace and improving material conditions and increasing introspection, Adam Smith was born in June 1723. His home town was Kirkcaldy, on the east coast of Scotland about twelve miles from Edinburgh. Kirkcaldy was then a trading port of around 1,500 people. Meaningfully for anyone who has ever read *The Wealth of Nations*, it had a nail factory, which may have given the young Smith his first sight of the effects of the division of labour. His father, also named Adam Smith, was a Writer to the Signet, a type of senior solicitor within the Scottish legal system, although he does not seem to have actually practised law. He served as judge-advocate, a lawyer within the military responsible for advising courts-martial, but courts-martial were few and so this job was not demanding. Ironically, given his son's later views, his main occupation and main source of income was as the controller of customs for Kirkcaldy. This made him responsible for calculating the import duties on the twelve hundred or so items then subject to tariffs. He was paid a modest but respectable salary of £40 per year, but the fringe benefits of the position were worth much more. As the younger Adam Smith wrote in *The Wealth of Nations*, '… the perquisites [fringe benefits] of custom-house officers are everywhere much greater than their salaries; at some ports more than double or triple those salaries'.[103] The elder Smith's wife, and younger Smith's mother, Margaret Douglas, came from a landed and military family.

Smith's prospects at life therefore seemed very solid, but he faced an immediate setback when his father died around the same time he was born. His mother did come from a wealthy family, but children left without a father's support faced challenges nonetheless. Fortunately for the young Smith, Kirkcaldy boasted an excellent school, one of the network of schools the Kirk had compelled local landowners to fund throughout the Scottish Lowlands. At school from 1729 to 1737, Smith studied writing, mathematics, history and Latin. He also saw, and probably participated in, plays. The Kirk had long maintained an absolute prohibition on the performing arts, but they were starting to catch on, and while the Kirk had required the schools be built, the town councils funded them. After a brief tug-of-war, the councils won out and Scottish school students were able to watch and play roles in *Hamlet* or *Macbeth*. It was an early sign of social change.

Smith was, for his entire life, notoriously absent-minded, prone to daydreaming and talking to himself. He was solitary, but made firm and lasting friendships. And perhaps from being the only child of a widow, he remained extremely close to his mother for his entire life. However, it quickly became apparent that reaching his potential would involve leaving Kirkcaldy. In 1737, at the age of fourteen, he commenced an arts degree at the University of Glasgow. Today we would consider this very young, but at the time it was common for boys to start at university when still in their mid-teens. And in Glasgow, Smith would be thrown headfirst into the developing Scottish Enlightenment.

Glasgow was where Scotland's growing prosperity was most readily-apparent. Following the Union, tobacco from Carolina and Virginia began passing through the hands of Glasgow merchants. Eight million pounds a year in the 1740s, up to 47 million pounds a year in the 1770s.[104] Glasgow went from 15,000 residents in 1700 to 77,000 in 1800. Daniel Defoe described it in 1706 as a city of 'rabble and riots', twenty years later it was 'one of the cleanest, most beautiful and best-built cities in Great Britain'.[105] In 1733 its residents built a statue of William III on horseback in the centre of their city, a symbol of the powerful effect of the 1688 settlement. Much of Glasgow's trade was tied to slavery, a fact which was not lost on some of its clearer-thinking residents, but this would not start to become a large political issue until the late eighteenth century.

At Glasgow, Smith studied Latin, Greek, mathematics and moral philosophy. This put him in the lectures of one of the leading figures of the early Scottish Enlightenment, Francis Hutcheson (1694–1746). The 'never-to-be-forgotten Hutcheson', as Smith called him later in life, would be his biggest intellectual influence.[106]

Hutcheson was born in the north of Ireland, the son of a non-conformist minister of Scots-Irish background. He studied at Glasgow but then returned to Ireland, where he was licensed to preach by the Synod of Ulster. He returned to his alma mater to take Glasgow's prestigious chair of moral philosophy in 1729.

Moral philosophy was a very broad subject back then, and included what we today would call politics and economics. Hutcheson was heavily-influenced by Locke, writing:

> ... each one has a natural right to exert his powers, according to his own judgment and inclination, for those purposes, in all such industry, labour or amusements as are not harmful to others in their persons or goods, while no more public

interest necessarily require his labours ... This right we call *natural liberty*.[107]

Hutcheson was also a utilitarian who believed the natural liberty of individuals could be limited if the welfare of society as a whole demanded it. In his words, the best possible outcome for society was 'greatest happiness of the greatest number'. There was then an expectation that university professors would be in holy orders and give sermons as well as lectures, but Hutcheson adhered to an optimistic and humanistic theology often at odds with the dour and solemn Calvinism of the Kirk. On philosophy, he is best-known for writing about the 'moral sense' and exploring how human beings might naturally know right from wrong.

Hutcheson is not widely-remembered for his writings, but he was a magnetic lecturer who left a lasting impression on those who listened to him. He abandoned Latin in favour of speaking to his students in their own language, and would walk around in front of his audience, lecturing with energy and charisma.

But his popularity was far from universal. In Smith's first year, the local Presbytery tried to have him removed for teaching two false and dangerous ideas—firstly, that the standard of moral goodness was the promotion of the happiness of others rather than obedience to God's law, and secondly, it was possible to have a knowledge of good and evil without prior knowledge of God. Hutcheson survived, thanks in a large part to the advocacy of his students, and kept up his teaching.

Scotland's universities were then in a state of rapid change, and Hutcheson was one of the major drivers of that change. Newton's *Principia* had first appeared in 1685, and over the next few decades his principles of scientific reasoning had become firmly established in Scottish institutions of learning. They expanded their fields of researching and teaching into practical subjects such as medicine, chemistry and agriculture, all based on empirical study.

***

Smith did well enough at Glasgow to be selected for one of the Snell exhibitions, a prestigious scholarship which allowed Glasgow students to study at Balliol College at Oxford University. Established by the will of a Scots Anglican, their purpose was to send bright young Scotsmen south to study at Oxford and then bring them home to preach Anglicanism to the Presbyterians. By the mid-eighteenth century the original arrangement had broken down and the Snell alumnus were no longer exclusively going into the Church, but Glasgow kept sending them to Balliol regardless.

In June 1740, Smith rode down from Scotland to Oxford on horseback. Once he crossed the border, he could not help but notice how much richer England was than his own country. The agricultural revolution was more advanced, the climate milder, the fields more productive and the cattle fatter. On his first night at Balliol, when he sat daydreaming at the dinner table, the undergraduate who was waiting on him told him he better set to the food as he wouldn't get as good back in Scotland. It was a stark reminder to him that he was now in a country which viewed his homeland as poor and backwards. And it would not be the last.

Oxford University was then in something of an intellectual slump, and Smith was shocked by the poor standards of teaching and learning. According to historian Edward Gibbon, who studied at Oxford around the same time, the dons were completely ignorant of new developments in their fields, the lectures either dull or non-existent, the tutors not actually tutoring and the students occupied with inane conversations about college business, Tory politics, personal anecdotes and private scandal.[108] Balliol, Smith's college, was known for being a hothouse of Jacobite opinion. One story, perhaps more than any other, is illustrative of Smith's time at Oxford. Back in Glasgow Hutcheson had introduced him to David Hume's newly-published *Treatise on Human Nature*, a major work of Scottish Enlightenment philosophy. The Balliol authorities confiscated the book, believing it to be dangerous.

As a quiet and eccentric young man, Smith would have probably faced difficulties in Oxford in any case. Then there was his limited income, and above all, the fact that he was one of only eight Scots at Balliol out of a hundred students. He was an outsider in every sense of the word. He made no lasting friendships at Balliol, never returned to Oxford after he left, and the university did not confer on him an honorary degree even when he became its most famous living alumnus later in life.

Still, Smith did not consider his time at Oxford wasted. Balliol had an excellent library, and he was able to keep up with his studies of Latin and Greek and teach himself French. He learned to speak English perfectly (his native language being Scots). He completed his B.A. in 1744 but opted to stay on while the money for his scholarship lasted. He left and returned to Scotland in 1746, to find the country convulsed by the momentous events of the previous year.

***

The Whig politicians who controlled Scotland, like the Duke of Argyll, remained concerned about the Highlands. Little of the benefits of the trade flowing through Glasgow or the research and scholarship of the universities reached the Highlands. True, the chieftains had started buying houses in Edinburgh and sending their sons to university, but back home they still lived in hovels and their tenants remained as poor and bullied as ever. The government started building roads up the Lowlands in order to improve commerce and speed the passage of troops to crush any uprising, but they were progressing slowly. The Highlands proved very resistant to change. The chieftains may have appreciated Carolina tobacco, Jamaican rum and fine shirts of Virginia cotton, but some looked with increasing scepticism on the developments in the towns.

In 1739, Britain became embroiled in a war with Spain. The next year, when Smith left Glasgow for Oxford, this turned into a general European war, the War of the Austrian Succession. Great Britain, allied with Austria, was pitched against its traditional enemies, France and Spain, as well as Austria's enemy, Prussia. Britain was now fighting on the continent to protect Hanover, and after some initial successes at sea and in the colonies the war in Europe itself began to go badly. In May 1745, the British army in the Low Countries was trounced by the French under Marshal Saxe at Foutenoy. The Government was forced to strip the country of troops to reinforce its army on the continent. Two months later, Bonnie Prince Charlie landed at the Firth of Ariseag and raised the banner of rebellion at Glenfinnan. The 1745 Jacobite uprising had begun.

Charles Edward Stuart was the Old Pretender's son. At the age of twenty-three, he decided to take advantage of the War of the Austrian Succession to win back his grandfather's throne for his father, who still lived in Rome. He tried to get French support for a full-scale invasion of England, but the French were reluctant to pull their successful army out of the Low Countries and risk losing it in a major entanglement with the Royal Navy, so in the end he needed to satisfy himself with having a French warship land him and a small band of loyal followers on the rugged west coast of Scotland.

It was a mad scheme. The Earl of Mar had tried and failed thirty years before, and since then, the House of Hanover and the 1688 settlement had become even more established. Now a youth who had never set foot in Scotland and spoke French as his native language stood before 700 Highlanders and shouted over the cold winds blowing off the Atlantic that he would march on London and overthrow King George II and his government.

Fortunately for Charlie, he found Britain poorly-prepared to deal with him. Most of its soldiers were across the Channel, and Scotland was held by a couple of thousand inexperienced men under Sir John Cope. The government had tried to disarm the clans, but had only succeeded in disarming the loyal ones. And the roads which had been built with so much labour to allow redcoats to march quickly through the highlands to suppress revolt now allowed the Jacobites to travel just as swiftly in the other direction. Not all the clans joined him, but there were enough chiefs with either a sense of loyalty to the House of Stuart or a romanticised image of a fading past to take up musket and broadsword in support of his cause. By the second week of September, he was marching on Edinburgh with 2,500 men.

There were no government troops in Edinburgh, but moderate

Presbyterian clergyman and university professor William Robertson (1721–1793) promised to lead the defence. The students mustered for battle. But as they marched to the gates, the townspeople urged them to stand down. They were too few, and would only be massacred by the Highlanders. In small groups, they melted away. Their time would come, but not yet. On 17 September, the Jacobites took the city unopposed. Four days later, they routed Cope's weak government army with a dawn attack at Prestonpans. The redcoats crumbled before a charge of the broadsword-wielding Highlanders in a battle commemorated by the Scots folk song 'Hey, Johnnie Cope, are Ye Wauking Yet?' On 8 November, Bonnie Prince Charlie invaded England, marching south.

He got as far as Derby. By then, his commanders were compelled to sit him down and force-feed him a dose of reality. The Duke of Cumberland, King George II's younger son, had been raced back across the Channel with 12,000 experienced troops and was then marching north. France had provided some money and some troops, but nowhere near enough. Some Englishmen had gone over to Charles, particularly from Manchester, but far fewer than he needed. Many highland and lowland Scots had remained loyal to the king. And Charlie's Scottish troops had joined him to put a Stuart back on the throne in Edinburgh—it didn't matter to them who was on the throne in London. The Jacobite army began an ignominious retreat to the north through the oncoming winter weather. Order broke down, as the soldiers began looting towns they passed through. Charlie arrived in Glasgow to find a reception as frosty as the weather. The statue of King William loomed over his army as it marched past it, a stern reminder of which side the booming commercial port with its university was on.

It's a mistake to think of the Forty-Five, as the rebellion is now called, as being a contest between England and Scotland, or between the Scottish Highlands and Lowlands. Cumberland's army was mostly English and Charlie's mostly Scottish, but there were Englishmen and Highland and Lowland Scots in both. Four of Cumberland's twelve battalions were Scottish and over a third of the Jacobites were lowlanders. Twenty-two Highland clans joined the revolt, while ten remained loyal to the House of

Hanover. Overwhelmingly, the loyal were the most commercially-active. Nostalgia, romanticism and old loyalties pushed Scots to join Charlie's doomed rebellion, while peace, prosperity and progress pushed others to risk everything to keep their German king on his London throne.

The last serious attempt to overthrow the Government of Great Britain by force came to a predictable end on a wet spring day in 1746. Against the advice of his generals, Charlie decided to give battle to Cumberland's vastly-superior army on 17 April on a soggy stretch of highland moor near Inverness, overlooked by Culloden House. The charging highlanders were cut down by musket fire and canister shot, and the army of the grandson of King George I completely crushed the army of the grandson of King James II.

Maybe it was anger over the humiliation at Prestonpans. Maybe it was the false rumours of Jacobite atrocities. Or it could have simply been Cumberland's youthful hot-headedness—he was ten days away from his twenty-fifth birthday. But whatever the reason, the British Army behaved atrociously in the aftermath of Culloden. The eighteenth-century rules of combat did not apply to rebels or savages, and as far as Cumberland was concerned, the Scottish highlanders were both. Wounded Jacobites were left to lie on the field for days, with guards placed around it so none could come to their aid. Houses in which wounded Jacobites had sought refuge were set alight. Eyewitnesses wrote of finding destroyed villages and naked bodies of women raped and hacked apart by dragoons. The Earl of Culloden, who had perhaps done more than anyone in the Highlands to limit the spread of the rebellion, even spending his own money in bribes, had to stand by helpless as his tenants were beaten up by redcoats. Over the summer, the reign of terror spread over the Highlands. The wearing of tartan was banned, villages were burned and actual or suspected Jacobite sympathisers were executed without trial or loaded onto penal transports bound for the Americas. The 'Highland Clearances' or the 'Harrying of the Glens' finally smashed the old clan system, but at a high cost in blood and bitter resentment. When the stories reached London, the Tories damned the king's son as 'Butcher Cumberland'. And so Bonnie Prince

Charlie became something of a romantic figure, a fighter for Scots freedom against oppression rather than a foolish and idealistic young man. He escaped and returned to the continent. But when his father died, the Pope refused to recognise him as rightful king of Great Britain. He died in 1788, embittered and still refusing to accept any responsibility for the failure of the Forty-Five Rebellion.

***

In the summer of 1746, as the redcoats still ranged through the Highlands, Adam Smith returned to his mother's house in Kirkcaldy. Shortly before he left Balliol, a group of pro-Jacobite students had staged a raucous celebration on the birthday of Henry Stuart, Bonnie Prince Charlie's younger brother. The party turned into a riot and they were arrested for damaging property and assault. They were given short gaol sentences, even though the college authorities were in favour of letting them off. At the same time, men were being summarily hanged in the Highlands for even a hint of sympathy with the House of Stuart. It was a sharp reminder of the double standards which cut across the British Isles.

Smith lived fairly quietly and looked for a job. He didn't correspond much, and as biographers depend so heavily on letters much of his inner life remains a mystery. At this time, though, he came under the patronage of another major figure of the early Scottish Enlightenment, Henry Home (1696–1782). Or, as he is known from 1752, Lord Kames.

Kames was both a leading jurist and a pioneer in anthropology and sociology. He is best-known today for his theory of the four stages of human development—hunter-gatherer, pastoralist, farmer and finally, city-dweller. He could see all four in his native Scotland, from the fisher-folk on the windswept rocky coasts of the Hebrides to Edinburgh's burgeoning New Town. It was a model typical of the Enlightenment concept of progress, as it viewed human societies not as fixed but as in development. The downside of Kames' model was that it justified Europeans giving indigenous peoples a helping hand to push them along the four stages, usually with disastrous adverse consequences. But Kames did turn Scotland's courts into a new field of Enlightenment thinking. Under Kames' guidance, Smith began delivering public lectures in Edinburgh on English literature. 'We must every one of us acknowledge Kames as our master' Smith would later write, showing his intellectual debt to the jurist.[109]

In 1750, Smith finally met David Hume (1711–1776), whose work he had first encountered as an undergraduate at Glasgow University. The two men would become not only the leading figures of the Scottish Enlightenment, but also close and lifelong friends.

Hume was born in Edinburgh to a middle-class family. His father was an advocate (the equivalent of a barrister in the Scottish legal system), and Hume's elder brother followed in the same profession. The law, however, had little appeal to the young David, who professed 'an insurmountable aversion to everything but the pursuits of Philosophy and general Learning'.[110] These pursuits took him to Edinburgh University, although he tired of the professors and did not graduate. Needing an income he became a merchant's assistant, then a tutor to an insane nobleman, then a secretary to a general.

Hume's great project was pulling together a rational and complete science of man, a *Principia* of understanding and ethics. In 1738, aged twenty-eight, he published *A Treatise on Human Nature*, today considered to be his most important work. He eagerly awaited praise, or failing that, criticism, but got nothing. 'Never literary attempt was more unfortunate than my Treatise of Human Nature. It fell dead-born from the press, without reaching such distinction as even to excite a murmur among the zealots. But being naturally of a cheerful and sanguine temper, I very soon recovered from the blow, and prosecuted with great ardor my studies in the country' he reflected later.[111]

Hume was in England during the Jacobite rising, and his various jobs meant he spent most of his twenties and thirties out of Scotland. He finally settled in Edinburgh in 1751, mostly remaining there except for time spent in France in the company of the *philosophes* of Paris. He considered settling in southern France permanently to enjoy the mild climate, but as Adam Smith pointed out, he would miss Edinburgh and his friends.

His various attempts to get academic tenure were thwarted due to his alleged atheism, so he turned to writing history. Between 1754 and 1761 he produced a mammoth six-volume *History of England*, which became a best-seller and guaranteed him an income. He had learned to improve his prose and make himself accessible to a general audience. Hume's thinking and writing covered almost every field of philosophy, so I will only describe a few of his ideas most-relevant to this chapter.

Hume was an empiricist who had deep doubts about the power of human reason. Perhaps more than anyone else, his philosophy explores this critical Enlightenment concept. He wrote extensively about the problem of induction. Just because the sun rose in the east today, and yesterday, and every day of my life up until now, can I assume it will rise in the east tomorrow? Or if every swan I've ever seen is white, can I assume every swan I ever will see will also be white? If I see one event always follow another, can I assume the first causes the second? Hume offers no solution to this problem, but points out that we can learn from experience and develop an instinct for when our inductive reasoning is valid. This touches on another key aspect of Hume's philosophy—his belief in what we might call practical common sense.

Western philosophy had traditionally taken the view that we should use our reason to override our passions and train ourselves to be more rational. Hume rejected this, because only our passions can drive us to action. I know through reason I will be fitter and healthier if I eat fewer cakes and exercise more, but only my passions will compel me to actually put that knowledge to use—fear of death, for example. Our preferences may be irrational, but that's OK. Someone vandalising my car will probably make me feel more anger than the massacre of a hundred people I've never met in a distant country I've never been to, even though the latter is self-evidently much worse. I like dark chocolate, but you might find it bitter—there's no rational basis for my like and your dislike. Following Bacon and his idols of the mind, Hume observed that we often use reason to justify holding a conviction we like rather than using reason to find the truth. Our reason can easily be conscripted to serve our preferences—in modern terms, we're susceptible to cognitive bias. As Hume famously summarised, 'Reason is, and ought only to be the slave of the passions, and can never pretend to any other office than to serve and obey them'.[112] But, he added, we can train our passions. We just need to accept them and respect their central role in our thinking. Hume rejected Hutcheson's 'moral sense', preferring our feeling of sympathy towards others as a basis for morality.

Hume's religious writings were, and have remained, controversial. In *The Natural History of Religion* (1757), he argued that the three Abrahamic religions descended from earlier beliefs and speculated that God was unnecessary and the world could have a natural order. Like Spinoza, he disputed the existence of miracles, and like Locke, favoured religious toleration on the basis people couldn't be compelled to believe or disbelieve. Although in his case, he went further, pointing out that reason could not persuade any more than force. If we are attached to an idea, we might stick with it even in the face of sound evidence contradicting it.

His own beliefs remain unclear, and may have fallen somewhere between deism and atheism. In a famous story he liked to relate, he was walking one night beside the marshes to the north of Edinburgh when he fell in. A fishwife came past, and he asked her for help getting out. Recognising the 'infamous atheist' David Hume, she refused to help him unless he recited the Lord's Prayer. This he did, and true to her word, she pulled him out. Hume's religious writings certainly denied him academic tenure, but he was still able to live and write openly—such had been the changes from the days of Servetus, or even Spinoza in the previous century.

On politics, Hume was more sceptical of the Whigs and more favourable to the Tories than many of his contemporaries, and his *History of England* earned criticism from the Whigs for its somewhat sympathetic portrayal of the Stuarts. 'My views of *things* are more conformable to Whig principles; my representations of *persons* to Tory prejudices' he wrote.[113] He remained a Scottish patriot but was hostile to the Jacobites. He wasn't sure if there was a right to private property, but said it made sense to have it because resources were limited—a point relevant to Smith's work.

Hume was a third significant influence on Smith, after Hutcheson and Kames. In 1751, Smith returned to Glasgow as a professor, but he kept up his correspondence with Hume and visited Edinburgh regularly. Otherwise he remained in Glasgow for thirteen years, and the city would shape him just as much as it had a decade earlier. Amidst burgeoning commerce and the Scottish Enlightenment, he would apply the science of man to a new field—economics.

CHAPTER IX

FREE TRADE OVER MERCANTILISM

I have a complaint to make against my local supermarket. In the years in which I have lived in my neighbourhood, I have spent thousands of dollars buying groceries there. Yet in that time, the supermarket hasn't bought so much as a dollar's worth of anything from me. Clearly, I'm being ripped off, and should endeavour to find ways to produce my weekly groceries myself. Most people will intuitively understand that this argument is nonsense, even if they have trouble explaining exactly why. But it illustrates a type of thinking which was common in Europe into the nineteenth century—an ideology called mercantilism.

Mercantilism was the dominant system of economic thinking in Europe from the collapse of feudalism to the rise of modern classical economics in the late eighteenth century. In mercantilist thinking, trade was a zero-sum game. Imports were seen as bad and exports as good. Accumulating gold was good, but giving gold to others in exchange for goods was bad. Countries should acquire colonies, prohibit their colonies from trading with anyone else, and discourage their people from buying goods from other nations by means of tariffs, import restrictions and managing trade through state-backed monopolies. As a 1549 English economic text stated, 'We must always take heed that we buy no more from strangers than we sell them, for so should we impoverish ourselves and enrich them'.[114]

Mercantilism arose alongside the post-feudal centralised state and the massive growth of international trade which accompanied the expansion of European colonial empires. It was a natural accompaniment to the absolute monarchism of rulers like the Stuarts in Britain and Louis XIV in France. And like many pre-Enlightenment ideas, it made intuitive sense.

Joyce Appleby begins her history of capitalism, *The Relentless Revolution*, with this puzzle: why did it take capitalism so long to materialise? Today, the nations of the West have economies where the means of production are privately owned, people invest collectively by buying shares in companies, and international trade is generally free. Governments tax private enterprise and use the revenue to build infrastructure and provide services like healthcare, education and old age pensions. This seems natural to us, but it is fairly recent. The mercantilist system which preceded modern capitalism, like many pre-Enlightenment ways of thinking, proved unusually resilient.

Just as mercantilism was a natural partner to the divine right of kings, so too did *laissez-faire* capitalism become the natural partner to a liberal and secular state where the powers of the government are limited by a constitution. As with constitutional government and secularism, modern capitalism had precedents before the Enlightenment, and we can find examples of pre-capitalist or nearly-capitalist societies before modern Britain and the Netherlands. Merchants in Renaissance Italy made use of *Comeda* contracts to share risk and reward (a bit like a modern limited-liability company) and developed shipping insurance contracts, double-entry book-keeping and the use of bills of exchange rather than cash. Limited agricultural options in the dry and hilly countryside of Northern Italy and the importance of Mediterranean trade both drove urbanisation and economic development, and the merchants of Venice and Genoa had exposure to Jewish and Islamic financial practices which they could adopt. On the other side of the continent, the commercial cities of northern Germany formed a free trade bloc called the Hanseatic League. However, the German and Italian city-states still had economies tied up by guilds and restricted with mercantilist trade practices, and the discovery of a sea route to India in 1498 and the rise of the Dutch and English trading empires left them lagging behind.[115] And outside of very urbanised regions of the world, the economy often remained in a post-feudal state. It was kept there by a series of barriers—religious, cultural and institutional.

The world's major religions have historically tended to have an ambivalent (at best) attitude towards the accumulation and exchange of material wealth. In times when most people could expect to live their lives at a level little better than subsistence luxury could only be hoped for in the afterlife. In Matthew 19:21 and Luke 18:22, Jesus tells a rich young man to give away his money to the poor on the promise of attaining spiritual treasure. Attachment to the material world was looked down upon, and people were encouraged to be satisfied with their lot in life. As the Tenth Commandment (by the Catholic reckoning) reads: 'You shall not covet anything that is your neighbour's. You shall not desire your neighbour's house, his field, or his manservant, or his maidservant, or his ox, or his ass, or anything that is your neighbour's.'[116] And unsurprisingly, most religions viewed priests as being more important than tradesmen. The Hindu caste system placed *Vaishyas* (merchants, tradesmen and farmers) below *Kshatriyas* or *Rajanyas* (warriors and administrators), with *Brahmins* (priests) at the top. Aquinas wrote in *Summa Theologica* that monks and priests should not engage in commerce 'both because it is directed to worldly gain, which clerics should despise, and because trading is open to so many vices [and] because trading engages the mind too much with worldly cares, and consequently withdraws it from spiritual cares; wherefore the Apostle says (2 Timothy 2:4): "No man being a soldier to God entangleth himself with secular businesses"'.[117]

For a specific example of a religious impediment to economic growth, consider the traditional prohibition against usury, or lending money for interest, in Christianity and Islam. Today, almost everyone in the western world deposits income they don't require to meet their immediate needs in a bank account, expecting to be paid a little bit of interest for it. Most of us save some money long-term by investing in retirement savings accounts or managed funds. The banks, in turn, lend the money to people for interest so they can buy homes or start and expand businesses. Without this arrangement, our economy and society couldn't function. Without some means of collectively investing money, it wouldn't be possible for anyone except for the government to undertake any project too large to be funded by a few business partners.

But the idea of making money without producing anything yourself has been shunned by thinkers throughout history. In *Politics*, Aristotle wrote that making wealth purely through exchange 'is justly censured; for it is unnatural, and a mode by which men gain from one another. The most hated sort, and with the greatest reason, is usury, which makes a gain out of money itself, and not from the natural object of it. For money was intended to be used in exchange, but not to increase at interest.'[118] The Scholastic philosophers followed Aristotle closely. Thomas Aquinas discusses economics in the second part of the second part of *Summa Theologica*. Question seventy-seven deals with cheating in buying and selling, and question seventy-eight deals with usury. Interestingly, he puts both questions in the section where he deals with vices contrary to the virtue of justice. To Aquinas, to make money without producing anything new was unjust.

> To take usury for money lent is unjust in itself, because this is to sell what does not exist, and this evidently leads to inequality which is contrary to justice [...] Now money, according to the Philosopher (Ethic. v, 5; Polit. i, 3) was invented chiefly for the purpose of exchange: and consequently the proper and principal use of money is its consumption or alienation whereby it is sunk in exchange. Hence it is by its very nature unlawful to take payment for the use of money lent, which payment is known as usury.[119]

To Aquinas and the Scholastics, usury was therefore a crime 'against nature'. In his description of the Medieval Catholic version of hell in *Inferno*, Dante put usurers and sodomites in the same circle of hell. Usury was gaining wealth divorced from production, just as sodomy was sexual pleasure divorced from procreation. In 1311, Pope Clement V declared that the belief that usury was not sinful was heresy.[120]

In practice, the prohibition on usury could be circumvented. Christians could still borrow money from non-Christians, particularly Jews. And the pioneers of the banking industry in northern Italy created a series of legal fictions which effectively allowed money to be lent on interest, such as disguising the loan as a joint venture or profit-sharing arrangement. Sophisticated banking arrangements in cities such as Florence and Genoa were critical to the Italian Renaissance. But commerce was still constrained by the need to ensure finance arrangements were compliant with religious law.

Many of these religious restrictions were loosened by the Protestant Reformation, as described earlier. Perhaps because of the importance of trade and commerce to the Netherlands, England, and the north German states and the power of their merchant classes as a result, Protestant theologians were willing to be more flexible on the question than their Catholic counterparts. Luther upheld the Scholastic prohibition against usury, but John Calvin challenged it. 'I do not consider that usury is wholly forbidden among us, except it be repugnant to justice and charity' he wrote in a 1545 letter to his friend Claude de Sachins.[121] Calvin was a hardliner on theology, but on economics his views could be quite modern. He rejected Aristotle's and Aquinas' claim that money was sterile. It was sterile, he said, if left locked in a box, but out in the real world it could be put to use. And if both the lender and the borrower in a transaction ended up benefitting, what was the harm done? He outlined his views in *Commentaries on Jeremiah* and *De Usuris*, where he held that there was no Biblical prohibition against lending money for interest, only excessive interest, as this violated the principle of reciprocity (he thought 5% a reasonable figure). He also held that charging interest on loans to the poor would violate the Christian concept of charity. But in a commercial arrangement, lending money for interest was acceptable. In England, the *Act Against Usury* of 1545 permitted lending money on interest but set a maximum interest rate at 10%. Even so, while Protestant countries continued to grow steadily richer, they didn't see an immediate take-off in their GDP per capita. England and the Netherlands were certainly richer than Spain and Italy in 1700, but not markedly so. The Protestant Reformation was a start, but it wasn't enough on its own.

Aside from the Church, there were arbitrary monarchs who could take property on a whim, plundering mercenary armies, and the labyrinthine restrictions of the pre-capitalist economy. Feudalism had been a very economically rigid system, tying peasants to land, and while it had broken down across most of the continent many of these restrictions remained. Various national and local government authorities imposed a network of tolls, tariffs, and other barriers on the production, consumption and transport of goods. The Rhine is lined with *Zollburgen*, or 'toll castles', from which a myriad of feudal lords would take their share of the traffic on the river.

Trade and commerce were controlled by craft guilds in the same way knowledge was controlled by the scholastic universities. While we might have a romantic view of medieval guilds today, in practice they worked something like a combination between a government-enforced monopoly and closed-shop trade union. Certain goods could only be manufactured by guilds, and anything which would make their manufacture more efficient, and hence less-labour intensive, was a threat to the guild members. As Renée Lettow Lerner wrote:

> The guilds formed an elaborate regulatory apparatus. To have a dress made in France, for example, one had to buy cloth from a draper, get accessories or ornaments from the mercer, and bring it all to a tailor, who then set to work according to the rules established by his guild for cutting cloth. The tailor was forbidden to stock or sell cloth.[122]

The patent system was another barrier. Patents date back to the fifteenth century, with a 1474 law in Venice creating the first recognisable patent system, and the concept spread to the rest of Europe from there.

Early patents, though, were often completely arbitrary. Today, if you invent something new (or a significant improvement to something which already exists) you can apply for a patent to have an exclusive licence to produce it for a set period of time. If someone else produces it without your permission, you can sue them for infringing your patent. In other words, a patent protects your intellectual property, like a trademark or copyright. If you print and sell copies of this copyrighted book without my approval then the law views your conduct as being similar to driving my car without my permission. The purpose of a patent is to provide an incentive for people to create new things by giving the creator a certain time to exclusively make money from it, while making it open to wide competition at some point in the future. In the sixteenth century, though, English kings would award patents to anyone they liked for any reason, giving them exclusive rights to produce or import something. Patents had no real connection with invention, and were often just a way for the king to reward someone. For example, by giving them an exclusive licence to import salt. Patents were the subject of one of the early clashes between the Stuarts and Parliament, when Parliament passed a 1624 *Statute of Monopolies*, limiting royal power to grant patents and reserving this power for itself. But the system took time to develop.

***

Adam Smith arrived in Glasgow in 1749 to find the city and the port both growing steadily. Glasgow had gained a tannery and linen print factory in 1742. During Smith's time there, he would see the opening of a pottery in 1758, a carpet factory in 1759 and a bank in 1760. And with the deepening of the River Clyde in 1768, tall ships would sail straight up to the wharves to take on their produce. In 1773, after Smith had left, Samuel Johnson wrote of Scotland as 'a nation of which the commerce is hourly extending, and the wealth increasing'.[123] Culturally, the city was in transition. It got its first theatre in 1764, but the building was burned down on opening night by an angry mob spurred on by a Calvinist preacher—a sign the old moral code remained strong. Still, things were changing.

Smith described his thirteen years in Glasgow as the most useful, happiest and most honourable of his life.[124] In April 1752, he took over the Chair of Moral Philosophy formerly held by his mentor Hutcheson. He earned a respectable income of £170, more than the highest stipend in the Presbyterian Church, allowing him to take a house and support himself, his mother and his aunt in some comfort. He worked hard and became popular with his students, most of whom were studying for the Presbyterian Ministry. 'During one session a certain student with a plain but expressive countenance was of great use to me in judging of my success' he wrote later of his method of lecturing.

> He sat conspicuously in front of a pillar: I had him constantly under my eye. If he leant forward to listen all was right, and I knew that I had the ear of my class; but if he leant back in an attitude of listlessness I felt at once that all was wrong, and that I must change either the subject or the style of my address.[125]

Around Scotland's dining-rooms and drawing-rooms, people began to suggest that promising young men of means should be sent to Glasgow to study under Mr Smith.

Like his predecessor, Smith was not free from controversy. He was known for his friendship with the 'notorious atheist' David Hume, said prayers which hinted at deism and was sometimes seen smiling during divine service (although given he was a lifelong daydreamer this was probably not any sort of act of rebellion). From the start he lectured on liberal ideas and free trade, and at times had occasion to put his ideas into practice.

Traditionally, students would bring sacks of oatmeal with them to the University so they would have a supply of porridge for breakfast for the whole term. In 1757, the town council began charging import duties on the oatmeal, even though it had traditionally been exempt as it was for the personal use of the students, not for sale. Smith was among those who forced the council to back down and repay the students.

And, of course, he kept up with his connections in Edinburgh, particularly with the founding of the Select Society in 1754. Its members included Kames and Hume, and also Presbyterian Minister William Robertson (1721–1793). Robertson had volunteered to defend Edinburgh against the Jacobites in 1745, although his services were not required on that occasion. But in 1762 he became the moderator of the General Assembly of the Kirk, from where he could exert far more influence. He was the leader of the faction called the moderates, who may have been very devout in their own lives, and emphasised Christian conduct in public affairs, but also supported religious pluralism. They were friendly to Enlightenment ideas, and so within a lifetime the Kirk went from pushing for the execution of blasphemers to co-operation with Enlightenment thinkers.

***

In 1759, Smith published his first book, the *Theory of Moral Sentiments*. The title shows the influence of Hutcheson and Hume, although it contained the ideas he had been lecturing on for nearly a decade. Adam Smith is often overlooked as a philosopher—for example, he doesn't appear in the index of my edition of Bertrand Russell's *History of Western Philosophy*. But the *Theory of Moral Sentiments* is a significant stepping-stone towards *The Wealth of Nations* and an interesting work of Enlightenment thinking in its own right.

Like Hume and Hutcheson, Smith didn't believe morality could be reasoned. Instead, he saw it as being based in sympathy—our ability to conceive of the feelings of others. Sympathy gave us a natural inclination to morality, which could be trained. And by living in society, we become socialised to consider the needs of our fellow men and women. Smith rejected attempts to build intricate systems of philosophy in favour of deferring to the judgements of ordinary people, and made no effort to develop rules which were universally applicable. He also disagreed with Hume and Hutcheson, on the basis that Hume relied too much on utility (what is useful) and Hutcheson on benevolence (the 'moral sense').

The *Theory of Moral Sentiments* leads to a political conclusion—because it's not possible to develop universal systems of moral behaviour, the government should not promote religion or virtue. Here is the link to *The Wealth of Nations*, in which Smith outlines a role for the government which doesn't include trying to control the economy and dictate the exchanges of citizens. Rather, these exchanges are based on our understanding of each other's needs and wants. *Theory of Moral Sentiments* was not hugely-influential, but earned Smith additional honours over the next two decades, including a Doctor of Laws and membership of the Royal Society.

Then, in 1764, Smith left Glasgow to become a tutor to the young Duke of Buccleuch. Leaving the university was difficult, but Smith's new job gave him the opportunity to accompany the duke on his traditional grand tour of Europe.

Smith spent two years overseas with Buccleuch. But while the tour on the whole was important for Smith's development as a writer and thinker, it was probably the summer of 1766 in Paris which was the most important. He was thrown into the world of the French *philosophes*, with their dinners and coffee-house meet-ups. The shy and eccentric Scottish academic was pulled out of his shell, and some of the ladies of Paris found him charming company. He met the physiocrats, French economists who challenged the mercantilist policies of their government with the slogan '*Laissez faire et laissez passer, le monde va de lui même!*' (Let it do and let it pass, and the world will go along by itself!).

He was also able to observe conditions in different countries firsthand. While the poorest people in England had leather shoes, Smith noticed the poorest French people wore wooden clogs or went barefoot. Why? He concluded France suffered from an inefficient and oppressive tax system which raised less money but imposed more of a tax burden on common people. By his calculation, tax raised 25s per head per year in Great Britain, but only 12s 6d in France, yet the French peasants seemed to be paying more. It was an astute observation—a tax system which lightly-taxed the nobility and clergy yet burdened the peasants would be a driver of the French Revolution. Smith returned to Scotland in 1766 and began to write in earnest about economics.

***

In the concluding paragraph of *The Theory of Moral Sentiments* Smith had promised his readers a book about political economy, but they would need to be patient. *The Wealth of Nations* had a long gestation. Its ideas date back to 1749 when Smith first began lecturing at Glasgow, and its writing occupied him for a decade. The book was finally published on 9 March 1776 in two volumes, available for £1 16s.

What makes a country rich? Smith proposed three causes—the division of labour, the free market and capital accumulation.

The Wealth of Nations begins with the division of labour, and Smith's well-known example of the pin factory. A single untrained worker, Smith claims, could not make a single pin in a day. A trained one would make more, but no more than twenty. However, once the process of making the pin is broken down into separate operations performed by separate men—drawing out the wire, straightening it, cutting it, pointing it and the like—then ten men in a factory could make 48,000 pins in a day. In other words, 4,800 pins each.

The gains of the division of labour are possible through exchange. Through education and training we can become specialised in a field and far more productive than others. And in turn, we can rely on exchanging some of what we make with someone else who is specialised in a different field. This exchange is based on mutual self-interest, which Smith establishes is the basis of the economy. As he wrote in a widely-quoted sentence, 'it is not from the benevolence of the butcher, the brewer, or the baker that we expect our dinner, but from their regard to their own interest'.[126]

Between the *Theory of Moral Sentiments* and *The Wealth of Nations*, Smith establishes self-interest and sympathy as the two great drivers of human behaviour. When we offer to sell (or buy) something we consider our own self-interest but also exercise our ability to put ourselves in someone else's position to consider what they might want. Smith observes that the division of labour will yield the most benefits when the market is bigger. More buyers lead to more opportunities for specialisation and more efficiency. If there is a small economy where all metal goods are produced by one man, he will need to make everything from spoons to spades and so will not be able to specialise between them. But in a larger economy, there can be separate spoon- and spade-makers, and workers doing one task in the production of spoons and spades.

Of course, there is a downside to specialisation. A worker who produces a pin from start to finish and then sells it to a customer gets to admire his or her handiwork and see the customer's satisfaction. Doing nothing but stretching wire leads to a worker becoming a cog in a machine. Smith recognised this was a problem, and proposed educating workers as a solution. But it remains a challenge, and is a downside to the division of labour. This separation of the worker from the final product of his or her work is part of what Marxists refer to as alienation.

Smith then goes onto exchange in detail, and specifically, how we know how much something is worth. This problem had occupied philosophers for millennia. Thomas Aquinas, for example, held that goods had a just price and buying below or selling above it would be giving in to the sin of greed. But calculating just price was difficult. Smith observed that things have different value to us in use and exchange. 'The things which have the greatest value in use have frequently little or no value in exchange; and, on the contrary, those which have the greatest value in exchange have frequently little or no value in use' he wrote. 'Nothing is more useful than water: but it will purchase scarce anything; scarce anything can be had in exchange for it. A diamond, on the contrary, has scarce any value in use; but a very great quantity of other goods may frequently be had in exchange for it.'[127] The diamond-water paradox illustrates the principle that the price of a good will not always relate to its utility.

Smith's view was that the market price of a good was the amount of labour the good allowed the seller to purchase or command—not, as some had previously argued, the labour which had gone into the production of the good. This could not be established on objective grounds, though, so the only way to determine the price of a good was to have it put on the market. Smith observed that people will pay more for scarce goods and less for abundant ones, so market prices were not fixed but could change. Smith's work, along with the writings of other economists at the same time, gave rise to modern classical economics with the laws of supply and demand.

In Book IV, Smith writes a devastatingly-effective critique of the mercantilist system which flows neatly from the economic principles he establishes in Book I. It was thirty times as expensive to produce wine in Scotland than in the Mediterranean countries, so it was absurd for the Scots to put labour and capital into viticulture. International trade was no different to any other sort of trade, and just as the pin-maker is better off producing pins for sale and using the proceeds to buy his other needs and wants, so too are the merchants of any country better off being left to produce whatever they can make most profitably. Gold and silver were useful in exchange, but there was no point hoarding them, any more than there was a point in buying up wine and hoarding it:

> A country that has no mines of its own must undoubtedly draw its gold and silver from foreign countries in the same manner as one that has no vineyards of its own must draw its wines. It does not seem necessary, however, that the attention of government should be more turned towards the one than towards the other object. A country that has wherewithal to buy wine will always get the wine which it has occasion for; and a country that has wherewithal to buy gold and silver will never be in want of those metals. They are to be bought for a certain price like all other commodities, and as they are the price of all other commodities, so all other commodities are the price of those metals. We trust with perfect security that the freedom of trade, without any attention of government, will always supply us with the wine which we have occasion for: and we may trust with equal security that it will always supply us with all the gold and silver which we can afford to purchase or to employ, either in circulating our commodities, or in other uses.[128]

In one of Smith's most famous passages, he writes that an investor in pursuit of his self-interest may be '... led by an invisible hand to promote an end which was no part of his intention'.[129] Smith used the term 'invisible hand' three times in his work, but never quite in the sense modern economists use it to refer to the laws of supply and demand setting market prices.

Smith concludes that the Mercantilist system was set up to benefit producers by protecting them from competition, not the consumers who are denied cheaper goods (or other producers, who are denied cheaper raw materials or tools). The Mercantilist system was ultimately based on flawed thinking. I shouldn't care that the local supermarket doesn't buy anything from me, or that I can't produce the goods it sells myself, provided I can produce something else which I can sell for money to buy them. Likewise, a country has no reason to care if its people buy foreign goods, as they presumably have made the money to buy those goods by producing something else. Mercantilism had led to hardship for the poor, restrictions on innovation and destructive trade wars like the three Anglo-Dutch Wars between 1652 and 1674.

If it wasn't the role of the government to direct the economy, hoard gold and silver, and keep out foreign goods, what was its role? Contrary to popular opinion, Smith was not a radical libertarian who viewed government as an impediment to a free market. According to Smith, every tax '... is to the person who pays it a badge, not of slavery, but of liberty. It denotes that he is subject to government, indeed, but that, as he has some property, he cannot himself be the property of a master.'[130] Smith's principal concern was with the poor, and just as he favoured free trade to make cheap goods available to them, he also advocated for a utilitarian rather than a strict rights-based system.

In Book V of the *Wealth of Nations*, Smith outlined the proper functions of government. First came defence and the judicial system (there was no professional police force in Britain in the eighteenth century). Next:

> [T]hose public institutions and those public works, which, though they may be in the highest degree advantageous to

a great society, are, however, of such a nature that the profit could never repay the expense to any individual or small number of individuals, and which it therefore cannot be expected that any individual or small number of individuals should erect or maintain.[131]

Firstly, institutions of trade and commerce, including ports, bridges, canals and military forces to defend trading colonies. Then the public education system, of which Smith himself was a beneficiary. Smith saw public education as a way of counteracting the ill-effects to a worker's mind of becoming increasingly specialised.

***

The *Wealth of Nations* became immediately popular and influential. The first edition sold out in six months, and it was praised by David Hume (unsurprisingly) and Edward Gibbon, author of seminal *The Decline and Fall of the Roman Empire*. Smith's publisher William Strahan wrote that the book's success was '… more than I could have expected from a work that requires much thought and reflection (qualities that do not abound among modern readers) to peruse to any purpose'.[132] It began to be quoted in Parliament. In 1791, Prime Minister William Pitt said the book would 'furnish the best solution of every question connected with the history of commerce and with the system of political economy' when presenting his budget to the House of Commons.[133]

Some critics thought it odd that a work on commerce should be written by a man without practical experience of business. But Smith was simply applying empirical thinking to trade and production—he had created economics as a field of discipline. Along with his contemporaries like Jean-Baptiste Say and David Ricardo, he had established the principles of classical economics. Over time, the institutions of mercantilism fell away. Finally, in 1846, Britain abolished the corn laws, which restricted importing of grain. The corn laws protected British grain growers, but made bread more expensive. With the repeal of the corn laws, free trade finally and completely won over mercantilism.

The Scottish Enlightenment thinkers had set out to find the equivalent of the *Principia Mathematica* which would apply to the science of man. They didn't find the single theory which bound all of human behaviour together in one set of rules, and we may have never such a work. But the *Wealth of Nations* still did for economics what the *Principia* did for physics. It was a triumph of Enlightenment thought and one of the most important books of the modern world.

CHAPTER X

ENCYCLOPÉDIE AND THE ENLIGHTENMENT IN FRANCE

When I was a child, our family had an old, brown, leather-bound edition of the *Encyclopædia Britannica*. After I graduated from picture-books, I got into the habit of consulting it if I wanted to know something. As a source, it was obviously imperfect. There's only so much information which can be fit into two feet of bookshelf space, and as it dated from the 1950s, if I wanted to know anything about the Apollo Program or the Vietnam War, I would be out of luck. For anything more, I'd need to arrange a trip to the local council library.

When I was in high school, we got our first computer, and with it, a copy of Microsoft's Encarta encyclopedia on CD-ROM. Encarta was an improvement on the *Britannica*. It was much more up-to-date, contained a lot more information in a much smaller space, was easier to search, and was much cheaper than a new edition of the *Britannica*. It also had what we today call multimedia. Some of the biographical articles had voice recordings of their subjects, the article on France let you play an extract of *La Marseillaise*, and the article on the Battle of Waterloo had a little animation with red and blue dots on a map showing the movement of the British, French and Prussian armies across the field.

By then the internet was emerging, and in the last two decades it has changed the way we access information more than any invention since the printing press in the fifteenth century. I have access to information from the significant (I was able to do much of the research for this book from academic articles and primary sources available online), to the useful (the next train from my local station leaves for Melbourne Central in eight minutes), to the trivial (Josef Stalin was a fan of westerns and liked to watch them in his home cinema). I can get a lesson in how to conjugate Spanish verbs, do a bench press with proper form, bake pumpkin scones, or understand the philosophy of Immanuel Kant quickly and for nothing.

This collection and dissemination of knowledge is critical to the success of modern society, and was an important legacy of the Enlightenment. No medieval king cared if his subjects knew Aristotelean physics. It wasn't expected, or even desirable, for ordinary people to know much more than their own trade and the basic tenets of their religion. Women, in particular, were expected to be ignorant. By the eighteenth century, with the rise in literacy brought about by the Protestant Reformation, the growing wealth of the urban merchant classes, and new ideas about the importance of knowledge, this was beginning to change in Enlightenment Europe. The *Encyclopædia Britannica* itself came out of the Scottish Enlightenment, with the first edition published in Edinburgh between 1768 and 1771. In his 1784 essay *Answering the Question: What is Enlightenment*, Immanuel Kant coined the phrase *Sapere aude* (dare to know) as the slogan of those who advocated Enlightenment against its enemies. In particular, he wrote, 'those guardians who have kindly taken supervision upon themselves see to it that the overwhelming majority of mankind—among them the entire fair sex—should consider the step to maturity, not only as hard, but as extremely dangerous'.[134]

There is probably no more potent symbol of the spread of knowledge through the Enlightenment than *Encyclopédie, ou dictionnaire raisonné des sciences, des arts et des métiers* (*Encyclopedia, or a Systematic Dictionary of the Sciences, Arts, and Crafts*), the mammoth encyclopedia written and published as a joint effort by over a hundred writers in France between 1751 and 1772. From a simple commercial enterprise, *Encyclopédie* became the central project of the French Enlightenment and, in the words of historian Philipp Blom, a 'triumph of free thought, secular principle, and private enterprise'.[135]

The advocates of Enlightenment thinking in France had long faced a solid barrier in the form of King Louis XIV (1638–1715). He became King when still a young child in 1643, and the years of minority were marred by the Fronde, a destructive civil war between the nobles and the central government. Taking the helm of the ship of state himself in 1661, he became determined to centralise power and create a strong, unified France. In this he had great success, and by the 1680s his country was the most powerful in Europe and he became known for his brilliance as *Le Roi Soleil*, the Sun King. Louis expanded its borders through bargaining and conquest, dismantled the feudal system, and promoted the idea of the divine right of kings. The phrase *L'etat, c'est moi*, 'I am the state', is attributed to him. The last three decades of his long reign were not as successful. In 1685, perhaps influenced by his very pious Catholic second wife Madame de Maintenon, he revoked the Edict of Nantes and made Protestantism illegal. Hundreds of thousands of Huguenots, including many of the most skilled craftsmen in France, were forced to flee to the Netherlands, Germany and Britain. This naturally enriched and strengthened Louis' enemies at his expense. Then France was embroiled in almost-continuous war from 1688 to 1714, leaving the country bankrupt.

The Sun King died in 1715 to be succeeded by his five-year-old great-grandson, Louis XV (1710–1774). The country was initially led by a regency of Philippe II, Duke of Orléans, who restored the right of the *Parlement* of Paris, one of the assemblies of nobles suppressed after the Fronde, to petition the King. Then, when Louis XV did reach adulthood, he showed much less inclination towards politics than his great-grandfather. He occupied himself with the pursuit of stags and young women, and allowed his principal mistress, Madame de Pompadour, to appoint and dismiss his ministers and military commanders. His shy, quiet and very pious Polish wife bore him ten children but then lived in secluded retirement. Unlike Britain and the Netherlands, France was still an absolute monarchy. But from 1715, it no longer had a monarch with the inclination or energy to stamp out dissent. France therefore entered its own Enlightenment, the *Siècle des Lumières* (century of light), which French historians conventionally date from 1715 to the beginning of the Revolution in 1789.

The French Enlightenment is notable for coming later than its equivalents in England, Scotland and the Netherlands. France was also the only Catholic country to become a significant centre of Enlightenment thought. Perhaps because it faced an absolute monarchy and a powerful established Catholic Church, the French Enlightenment was more radical and more anti-clerical than its earlier and more northern counterparts. 'God, in order to exercise the patience of the faithful, also allowed the Greek and Latin churches to separate in the ninth century. He likewise permitted in the east no less than twenty-nine horrible schisms with the See of Rome' wrote Voltaire sarcastically in the article on Christianity in his *Philosophical Dictionary*.[136] It is difficult to imagine Baruch Spinoza or even the openly atheistical David Hume being so irreverent.

The French Enlightenment was centred around the *philosophes*, as its thinkers and writers were known. They were, it should be said, frequently disreputable men who sought alternatives to making a regular living and kept many mistresses. Dozens became involved in *Encyclopédie*.

Encyclopédie was not a particularly original project. Other encyclopedias had been published before, the most famous at the time being the *Historical and Critical Dictionary* (*Dictionnaire Historique et Critique*) by Pierre Bayle (1647–1706). Bayle was a Huguenot who had been forced to flee to the Netherlands, and his encyclopedia, aside from containing a great deal of information, pushed a line in favour of scepticism, religious tolerance and empirical thinking. Bayle also invented the idea of arranging the articles in alphabetical order, an innovation future dictionaries and encyclopedias would follow. Even the Jesuits found Bayle's encyclopedia useful, once they had first purged it of heretical content.

Encyclopédie, however, began as a proposal to translate a different encyclopedia. In the early 1740s a German scholar of some repute,

Gottfried Sell, commonly known as Sellius, ended up in Paris, having fled his creditors in Germany. He approached a publisher, André-Francois le Breton, with a proposal to produce a French translation of a 1728 English encyclopedia, the *Cyclopædia* by Ephraim Chambers. He had hired a young Englishman, John Mills, to undertake the translation, and had produced a prospectus of a few specimen articles. Le Breton took on the project, gaining the necessary royal *privilege* (right to publish) in February 1745 and advertising for subscribers in April. It all seemed simple enough—translating *Cyclopædia*'s two volumes and two and a half thousand words into French.

Within a few months, however, Le Breton ran into two significant problems. Firstly, he learned that Mills didn't even have a copy of *Cyclopædia* to work off. And secondly, he couldn't speak French well enough to translate it even if he did. Nonetheless, Mills kept asking for money. On 7 August, Le Breton visited Mills at his lodgings and expressed his displeasure at the direction the project was taking by punching him in the stomach and hitting him twice in the head with his cane. Unsurprisingly, Mills left Paris shortly afterwards.

Having advertised for subscribers and invested money in the project, Le Breton needed to push on. He engaged a new editor, Abbé Jean-Paul Gua de Malves. However, he found the abbé difficult to work with, and his editorship lasted only thirteen months. Le Breton then engaged two co-editors, young men who had already done some work on the developing encyclopedia. He had no idea how large the project would turn out to be, but the two men he chose turned out to be the right choice, and their names are forever associated with *Encyclopédie*—Denis Diderot and Jean-Baptiste Le Rond D'Alembert.

Diderot was born in the provincial city of Langres, Champagne, in 1713. His father was a successful craftsman, a cutler who specialised in medical and surgical instruments. His upbringing was conservative. He attended the local Jesuit College, earning a Master of Arts. He considered making the Church his profession, although he later dismissed this urge as youthful idealism. As he subsequently wrote:

> There comes a moment during which almost every girl or boy falls into melancholy; they are tormented by a vague inquietude which rests on everything and finds nothing to calm it. They seek solitude; they weep; the silence found in cloisters attracts them; the image of peace that seems to reign in religious houses seduces them. They mistake the first manifestations of a developing sexual nature for the voice of God calling them to himself; and it is precisely when nature is inciting them that they embrace a fashion of life contrary to nature's wish.[137]

He then intended to make a career in the law, enrolling in the Paris Law Faculty. But he dropped out, finding the law no more satisfying than the Church. His father refused to keep supporting him, and so he lived a poor Bohemian lifestyle in Paris. In 1742 he met Jean-Jacques Rousseau in a café, and the two men became good friends, although their relationship would later sour. In October 1743, much to his family's disapproval, he married Antionette Champion, a poor and devout woman who lived with her mother in the same rooming house as him. In August 1744 they had a daughter, Angelique. With a family to support, Diderot made something of a living writing translations from English into French, having taught himself the language from an English-Latin dictionary. This is how he first became involved with Le Breton and *Encyclopédie*. He brought tremendous energy to the project, not only in finding contributors and editing their articles but, particularly in the early years, writing many himself—7,000 in total.

D'Alembert was, like Diderot, a *philosophe*, but was otherwise a very different man. He was born illegitimate in 1717, the son of writer and socialite Claudine Guérin de Tencin and her lover, Army officer Chevalier Louis-Camus Destouches. His mother abandoned him to the care of the Church, but his father found him and paid for his education. Even at thirty he was already distinguished as a mathematician and scientist, and had been elected into the Académie des Sciences in 1741. D'Alembert provided the project with much-needed credibility. He was also a significant contributor in his own right, writing over a thousand articles. He also wrote the Preliminary Discourse which led the first volume and remains one of the major pieces of Enlightenment writing.

Aside from writing articles themselves, Diderot and D'Alembert needed to recruit others who had expertise in their respective fields. Early on, the group of *encyclopédists* remained small, but as the volumes rolled out, the list of authors became longer and longer. Chevalier Louis de Jaucourt (1704–1779), a wealthy aristocrat and scientist, wrote over 18,000 articles on science, particularly biology, and political history—a quarter of the entire encyclopedia in total. He was a hard worker but prone to plagiarism. Paul-Henri Thiry, Baron d'Holbach (1723–1789), a French-German aristocrat, translated significant German works into French, wrote a number of articles of his own, and perhaps most importantly, made his Paris *salon* the central hangout of the *encyclopédists* and their friends. His guests included David Hume and Adam Smith. D'Holbach's later writings were openly atheistical and defended political and economic freedom, but his privileged position in society accorded him some protection. Not all the *encyclopédists* were deists or atheists, however, and quite a number were churchmen. In particular, *Abbés*, clergymen who were not members of any monastic order and generally worked as tutors or scholars. The most famous was Abbé Morellet, to whom Voltaire gave the nickname *Abbé Mords-Les* (Father Bite-Them) for his pugnacity in debate. Formally, all of the *encyclopédists* were men. At least three women, however, are believed to have contributed to *Encyclopédie*—Jaucourt's sister-in-law the Marquise du Jaucourt, Suzanne Verdier and Madame D'Epinay.

Louise D'Epinay was the daughter of an army officer, who received a conventional genteel upbringing and married another officer at eighteen. Her husband turned out to be shiftless, licentious and drunk, and she ended up leaving him, but not before he infected her with syphilis. She became the long-term partner of an idealistic German aristocrat Friedrich Melchior, Baron von Grimm (1723–1807), said to be the only German who mastered the French language. Grimm wrote for *Encyclopédie* on music and operas, while Diderot's friend Rousseau wrote about music theory and political economy.

As its name suggested, *Encyclopédie* had a focus on science, geography, craft and philosophy. History played only a minor role, and there were no long and hagiographic articles on past kings of France, epic battles, or major conquests. There were, however, many long and beautifully-illustrated articles on trades and professions. *Encyclopédists* visited the workshops of glass-blowers, blacksmiths, printers and other craftsmen. Never before had men of letters paid so much attention to such humble yet so important subjects.

Encyclopédie had a definite editorial slant. It was imbued with thinking of John Locke on politics, it favoured empiricism and scientific inquiry, and (unsurprisingly given the commercial interests of its backers) promoted modern economic ideas and free trade. Of course, it was of its time in many respects. The article on *Humaine Espece* (Human Species) by Diderot makes uncomfortable reading today. The great *philosophe* writes confidently, but without any authority, that ugly people are fat, superstitious and stupid. He runs through the world's nations making broad and sometimes bizarre generalisations about their residents. The Swedes, according to Diderot, live underground, have never heard of God or religion and offer their wives or daughters to strangers. It doesn't seem likely that the article was peer-reviewed by a Swede, or, for that matter, anyone who had ever been to Sweden.

Encyclopédie had a complex relationship with race. On one hand, it showcases the theories of scientific racism which were beginning to take hold and which run through so much of Enlightenment thought. But on the other, it ridicules the idea of mistreating people even if they were members of an 'inferior' race. As Diderot wrote: 'Although Negroes generally have little wit, they do not lack feeling. They are sensible to good and bad dealings. We have reduced them, I do not say to the condition of slaves, but to those of beasts of burden. And we are reasonable! And we are Christians!'

In other words, black people were less intelligent than white people, but they were still humans and entitled to human rights. As eighteenth-century views go, it could be better, but it could be worse.

When it came to religion, the *encyclopédists* knew they were on perilous ground. Non-Christian religions, of course, could be cheerfully ridiculed and condemned as superstition and absurdity. Diderot's writings on Judaism and Islam are fiercely critical. It's easy to get the impression they were on the receiving end of Diderot's pent-up frustration at the Catholic Church, which he was forced to direct towards a more socially-acceptable target. And many of his criticisms of non-Christian religions would apply equally to Christianity, something Diderot must have been aware of but, for obvious reasons, couldn't make explicit. *Encyclopédie's* challenge to conventional religious doctrine is often based in these sorts of subterfuges, where it doesn't plainly say anything heretical but leaves the reader to join the dots.

This can be seen, most clearly (or unclearly) in Abbé Mallet's writings on theology. Diderot and D'Alembert knew they would need to exercise utmost caution when writing on Christianity, lest a single hole in the theological hull sank the whole project. To this end, they found what seemed to be the perfect contributor, Abbé Mallet, an extremely learned theologian who came recommended by a bishop. Mallet, obligingly, wrote thousands upon thousands of meticulously-researched words on topics related to religion, as well as history more broadly. His style was dull, but nobody could doubt his erudition.

Mallet's articles, however, often analysed the episodes described in the Bible in such detail that they couldn't possibly stand up to scrutiny. His article on Noah's Ark (appearing in the first volume under *Arch*) is a case in point. Mallet wrote page after page exploring the theories of leading scholars from Saint Augustine onwards on how a man and his three sons, using bronze-age technology, could possibly build a seaworthy boat capable of carrying a pair of every kind of animal, plus all their food and water, for forty days. Quoting the calculations of John Wilkins (1614–1672), an eccentric English bishop whose writings explored topics from invented languages to the practicality of space travel, he concluded the animals on the Ark would have eaten the equivalent amount of food of

27 wolves (for the carnivores) and 208 oxen (for the herbivores), meaning the Ark would have needed to carry 1,825 sheep and 109,500 cubits of hay in order to feed all the other animals. These could fit comfortably on the second floor, leaving the lower floor for the beasts and the third floor for Noah, his family, and the birds. Not one word of the mammoth article contradicted established Church doctrine, but by the end Mallet had made it abundantly clear that the entire episode could never have happened. To this day, nobody knows whether Mallet simply was a profoundly unimaginative man used by Diderot as a blunt instrument to attack Christianity, or whether he was some sort of sceptic Manchurian candidate working inside the ranks of Catholic scholars. The latter theory is very entertaining but very far-fetched.

Diderot went to a lot of effort to find information on subjects not well known in Europe, but in a few cases, he gave up completely. Finding out nothing on the South American plant aguaxima aside from its name, he wrote despairingly in the article

> [F]or what do we care that there is a tree in Brazil named aguaxima, if all we know about it is its name? What is the point of giving the name? It leaves the ignorant just as they were and teaches the rest of us nothing. If all the same I mention this plant here, along with several others that are described just as poorly, then it is out of consideration for certain readers who prefer to find nothing in a dictionary article or even to find something stupid than to find no article at all.

These sorts of asides make *Encyclopédie* more interesting to read than most encyclopedias, although they wouldn't pass academic standards today.

Encyclopédie was not Diderot's only project, for reasons both practical (he needed more money) and personal (he craved recognition for his writing, recognition which was unlikely to come from being the editor of an encyclopedia). In addition to his wife and daughter he now had a mistress, the writer and women's rights advocate Madeleine de Puisieux, which meant he had further calls on his purse. His first foray into philosophy came in 1746 with *Philosophical Thoughts* (*Pensées Philosophiques*) where he discussed the reconciliation of reason and passion and defended deism. Trying to cash in by titillating the reading public he also wrote an erotic novel, *The Indiscreet Jewels* (*Les bijoux indiscrets*) in 1748. As his reputation grew, he would come to regret the book.

Needless to say, he was sailing close to the wind with projects like this. One manuscript he wrote in 1747, *Skeptics' Walk* (*Promenade du sceptique*) was too dangerous to publish and only appeared after his death. In 1749, however, he did publish a highly controversial book. In *Letter on the Blind* (*Lettre sur les aveugles à l'usage de ceux qui voient*) he described the first successful cataract surgery ever, carried out on a Prussian girl. What must it be like, he wondered, to see the world for the first time having been blind your whole life? This, on its own, was unremarkable. The deist and anti-clerical sub-text which ran through the whole book was not, and Diderot opted to publish anonymously. In a bold move showing how confident he was in the work, Diderot decided to send a copy of *Letter on the Blind* to the most famous *philosophe* in Europe.

***

To speak of the French Enlightenment is to speak of Voltaire. The name, today a by-word for freedom of speech and thought, was the *nom de plume* of François-Marie Arouet (1694–1778). He was born in Paris, his father was a lawyer and public servant, his mother the daughter of a minor noble family. Alleged father, for Voltaire liked to claim he was the illegitimate son of an aristocrat. His father intended for him to follow in the same profession and apprenticed him to a notary, but he spent his time writing poetry. Thinking a change of scenery might knock some sense into the wayward boy, his father then sent him to the Hague. He began a scandalous relationship with a Protestant woman, forcing his father to return him to Paris. His wit and daring won him admirers and enemies. Writing a satirical verse accusing the *Régent* of incest with his daughter landed him in the Bastille for nearly a year. Released from prison, he decided to adopt a new name. His current surname, Arouet, sounded a bit too much like *à rouer*—to be beaten up. This was a fate which did befall him at times when his enemies found themselves unable to respond to his wit with anything other than brute force, but wasn't something he wanted to draw attention to. Instead, he decided to suggest agility and motion. *Vol* means to fly, and *voltage* is acrobatics (the English word 'vault' as in 'pole vaulting' is a cognate). So in 1718, François-Marie Arouet became Voltaire. Today, the name makes us think of electricity, but this is a happy coincidence. Volt, the unit of electricity, is named for Italian scientist Alessandro Volta (1745–1827), the inventor of the battery.

Voltaire spent long periods of the 1720s outside France. First in the Netherlands (where he was seeking a publisher who would publish his controversial writings) then in England (where he was forced into temporary exile following a dispute with a nobleman which ended with a beating at the hands of the nobleman's hired thugs). He might have been present at the funeral of Isaac Newton in 1726. In England he was won over to the thinking of John Locke, and became an advocate for secularism, constitutional monarchy, freedom of speech, and the removal of the privileges of the aristocracy and the church.

Returning to France, Voltaire settled in Cirey-sur-Blaise in rural northeastern France with his mistress, Madame du Châtelet. She was a formidable scholar in her own right who had translated Newton's *Principia Mathematica* from Latin into French and added a helpful commentary for readers unfamiliar with mathematics. She also became the first woman to have a scientific paper published by the Paris Academy. Voltaire called her the 'Minerva of France' (in reference to the Roman goddess of wisdom and strategy) and 'a great man whose only fault was being a woman'. Voltaire wrote plays, novels and works of popular history. He corresponded with Frederick the Great of Prussia, who admired him.

Voltaire and Châtelet decided to read the Bible together. At the time, Catholics generally did not read scriptures, which remained inaccessible to the majority of the people who could not read their own language, let alone the Latin in which Catholic Bibles were published. Even those who benefitted from a Jesuit education, like Voltaire and Châtelet, would still have only seen the scripture in bits and pieces, wrapped up in the commentaries of Scholastic philosophers.

Voltaire and Châtelet could read Latin, and so they opened the Bible to Genesis 1:1 and set off from there. They were not impressed. Voltaire found 'historical monstrosities which are repellent to nature and good sense' and a God who violated every principle of 'purity, chastity, justice, good faith, and universal reason'.[138] He found himself decidedly uninspired by Jesus, 'one of a large number of prophets without a mission who, not being a priest made a living by being inspired'. He expressed scepticism at the account of miracles. Coming across a Gerasene man possessed by demons, Jesus exorcises them and sends them into a herd of pigs, who then go mad and throw themselves off a cliff. Voltaire simply observes that the owners of the pigs probably weren't impressed by the trick. He also wonders why no contemporaneous sources from any society speak of the global darkness at noon accompanying the crucifixion. Some of these criticisms worked their way into Voltaire's *Philosophical Dictionary*, the first edition of which came out in 1764. He rejected atheism, but nonetheless refused to accept that the Bible could possibly contain God's word. 'Believe a hundred things either visibly abominable or mathematically impossible; otherwise the God of Mercy will burn you in hell-fire, not only for millions of millions of ages, but for all eternity, whether you have a body or have not a body' he wrote in the article on Christianity.[139]

They also appeared in Châtelet's extensive commentary on the Bible. It was while he was living with Châtelet at Cirey-sur-Blaise that Voltaire received a copy of Diderot's *Letter on the Blind*. He was impressed with it, and wrote a warm letter back to Diderot, who was overjoyed. The great Voltaire himself had praised him.

***

As it turned out, Diderot was to get more recognition than he bargained for. Unfortunately for him, he had brought out the *Letter on the Blind* just when the French Government was looking for enemies. From 1740 to 1748, Europe (including France) had been embroiled in the War of the Austrian Succession, one of several pointless dynastic conflicts to consume Europe's blood and treasure over the eighteenth century. France was partnered with Prussia against Britain and Austria. The War had not gone too badly for France, and a brilliant campaign by Marshal Saxe had left France in control of the Austrian Netherlands. Then, with the Treaty of Aix-la-Chapelle in 1748, the French Government agreed to hand them back. The public was enraged—eight years of fighting and sacrifice had left them with nothing. Indeed, Europe was returned to more or less the state it had been in at the outbreak of the War in 1740, with the questions left unresolved and war certain to resume again as soon as the combatants had refilled their treasuries and refreshed their alliances (the outbreak of the Seven Years' War in 1756 would prove them right). Faced with this seething discontent, Louis XV's ministers ordered a crackdown on troublemakers.

While Diderot had published *Letter on the Blind* anonymously, he was soon outed as the author. And to make matters worse, his parish priest, Hardy de Levaré, had denounced him to the government in a lengthy letter as 'a young man who has passed his early years in debauchery ... the remarks that Diderot sometimes makes in his household clearly proves that he is a deist, if not worse. He utters blasphemies against Jesus Christ and the Holy Virgin that I would not dare put into writing.'[140]

At half-past seven in the morning of 24 July 1749, Diderot answered a knock at his door to find two constables standing on his front step. They searched his house, seized all the manuscripts they could find (including, no doubt, the extremely transgressive *Sceptic's Walk*), then bundled Diderot into a waiting carriage. After a short and bumpy ride, he was cast into a cell in the Château de Vincennes, a grim prison on the outskirts of Paris.

The Minister for War had received Levaré's letter, and despite having read none of Diderot's books, nor even being familiar enough with the author to spell his name correctly, ordered the Lieutenant-General of Police to arrest and detain Diderot under a *Lettre de Cachet*. This was a convenient instrument of the French Government, allowing any of Louis XV's ministers to throw into prison indefinitely without charge or trial anyone believed to be an enemy of the state. Diderot was in a cell in the keep at Vincennes, and he had no idea when, or if, he would get out.

His father was not particularly sympathetic to his plight. If he would have simply prayed to God and obeyed the King like a good subject, he wrote sternly to his son, he wouldn't have gotten himself into this mess. Fortunately for Diderot, though, he was not simply a renegade author—he was also the director of a major commercial project on which investors had placed large sums of money. Le Breton and the Paris booksellers who were depending on the success of *Encyclopédie* wrote to the Government, pushing for Diderot's release. For his part, Rousseau wrote to the King's mistress, Madame de Pompadour, on his friend's behalf, and regularly came to visit him in prison.

Diderot knew what he needed to do if he had any chance of getting back to his family, the *Encyclopédie* and his mistress. He wrote to the Lieutenant-General of Police, confessing that his books had come from a moment of intemperance and promising not to write anything challenging the authority of King or Church again. As an author, I can say the idea of writing a book in a moment of intemperance is pretty far-fetched, but Diderot's letter had some effect and, while he was not released, he was given freedom of the prison and allowed to work and receive visits from Antionette. It might have helped that the prison governor François-Bernard du Châtelet was a relation of Madame du Châtelet, Voltaire's mistress, and she might have advocated on his behalf. On 3 November 1749, he was released. He had been in Vincennes only six months—many others who were imprisoned under a *Lettre du Cachet* were not so lucky. But his release was effectively a parole. The Minister for War had his letter promising to write nothing more criticising the King and the Church. If he broke his promise, he would be back in gaol for life. Or worse. But he kept this promise, at least on the surface, and returned to *Encyclopédie*.

Work progressed well, and in November 1750, Le Breton was able to announce to his customers that the finished work would be available in ten volumes, one published every six months, for a total subscription of 280 *livres* over five years. True to the promise, the first volume, covering A-Azymites, appeared in June 1751 (if you're curious, an azymite is a priest who delivers the Eucharist with unleavened bread, as opposed to a prozymite, who administers it with leavened bread—both terms are now used pejoratively by those who believe the bread in the Eucharist should be leavened or unleavened respectively).

Before it could be delivered to its waiting subscribers, though, the book needed to receive a pass from the official censor, the lawyer and nobleman Guillaume-Chrétien de Lamoignon de Malesherbes (1721–1794). Fortunately for the *encyclopédists*, the customers who paid subscriptions, and the progress of the Enlightenment generally, Malesherbes had liberal sympathies. After looking through the volume, he admitted it was a bit unorthodox at times but said it contained so much useful knowledge it should be allowed. The book was shipped off to the subscribers. Malesherbes' role proved critical—without him, *Encyclopédie* might never have existed.

The volume received mostly favourable reviews, but was not met with universal acclaim. The Jesuits recognised it for what it was. Their scholars were far from stupid, and the order had some of the sharpest minds and sharpest pens in Europe. If there was one page in the volume which epitomised their concerns, it was the diagram of the Tree of Knowledge appearing at the start. It divided all of learning into three branches: memory, which included subjects such as history and geography, reason, including maths and science, and imagination, including literature and the creative arts. Reason was broken down into branches such as the science of nature and the science of man, and on a very small sub-branch, the science of God. To the Jesuits, this was deeply problematic. Theology had gone from the base of the tree, where the Scholastic philosophers had rightfully put it, to a little branch alongside such things as superstition and the worship of idols.

But the Jesuits opted to attack *Encyclopédie* with a chisel rather than a sledgehammer. They began to undermine its credibility, making accusations of, among other things, plagiarism. Being a summary of existing knowledge, *Encyclopédie* naturally drew on a large number of existing sources. But some of its contributors, such as the overenthusiastic Jaucourt, had lifted a lot of content from others. 'One may harvest the way bees do ... but the thievery of the ant, which walks off with the whole thing, ought never to be imitated' wrote the first volume's Jesuit reviewer.[141]

All problems aside, the second volume, B-Cezimba, was published on schedule in January 1752. Then the entire thing nearly came tumbling down thanks to the particularly unwise decision of a theologian, Abbé Martin de Prades. Prades wrote a doctoral thesis at the Sorbonne, the theological faculty of the University of Paris. Apparently without bothering to read it, his examiners awarded him a doctor of theology in November 1751. At some point—perhaps to pass time on a long winter evening—someone at the Sorbonne did actually read the thesis and realised it was full of a litany of heresies. Prades pointed out inconsistencies between the books of the Old Testament, and then questioned the historicity of Jesus' miracles in the New. There was an uproar. The Government immediately issued a *Lettre de Cachet* for Prades' arrest, which he escaped by fleeing overseas.

Unfortunately for Diderot and D'Alembert, Prades had contributed an article for the second volume of *Encyclopédie*. Ironically, on *Certitude* (Certainty). The Jesuits, who had been quietly questioning the accuracy of the projects, now proudly rode the wave of indignation over the Prades affair. Whatever its merits as a source of information, *Encyclopédie* was also a public platform for heretics.

It was Malershebes who came to the project's rescue, brokering a deal between the *encyclopédists* and their enemies where the publication could continue provided the Jesuits could censor future volumes. The first two volumes were now notionally illegal, but still circulated. Madame de Pompadour was also a defender of *Encyclopédie*, and she may have used her influence at court in its favour. In a 1755 portrait, a copy of the fourth volume appears on the shelf behind her.

This new arrangement was less than ideal, but it allowed the publication to continue and Le Breton to continue shipping the product to his customers. The six-monthly intervals proved impossible to keep up, and volume 3 (Cha–Consécration) did not come out until October 1753, volume 4 (Conseil–Saint-Dizier) until October 1754, and Volume 5 (Do–Esymnete) until November 1755. Voltaire now joined the ranks of the *encyclopédists* himself, contributing articles in the fifth and sixth volumes on *Elégance* (elegance), *Espirit* (wit), *Fantasie* (fantasy) and *Fausseté* (falsehood). These were not weighty topics, and showed that, as much as Diderot admired Voltaire, he didn't entirely trust him.

The two men had not met. After Madame du Châtelet died in childbirth in 1749, bearing the child of her other lover, Voltaire briefly returned to Paris. He then left for Prussia, where he enjoyed for a while the hospitality of Frederick the Great, until they fell out. Louis XV banned him entirely from Paris in 1754, so in 1758, he settled on a country estate at Ferney a few miles from the Swiss border. He was still in France, but while he remained in a distant corner of the Kingdom the authorities seemed content to leave him alone. In 1764, he published the first edition of his witty but scandalous *Philosophical Dictionary*.

In May 1756, while the preparation of the sixth volume of *Encyclopédie* was approaching completion, the much-awaited war broke out again. The great powers had switched partners, and France was now allied with Austria against Britain and Prussia. While the drums of war beat across Europe and armies mustered for battle, the sixth volume (Et-Fne) was dispatched to *Encyclopédie's* subscribers in October. There was a lot of grumbling about the slow pace of the project, but they were getting a lot more content than they had been promised. Given the sixth volume finished still only halfway through 'F', it was clear there would be a lot more than ten.

The next year, 1757, saw events once again move against the project. On a frigid night in January 1757, a mentally ill domestic servant named Robert-François Damiens stabbed Louis XV with a penknife as he boarded his carriage outside the Palace at Versailles. The King called for a priest and began to confess his multiple liaisons, until his doctor examined the wound and bluntly told the King it was so slight it would not stop another man from attending a ball. Damiens was arrested, and even though the King had only a minor wound and Damiens was clearly delusional, he was still sentenced by a court to a truly gruesome public execution. Over several hours in front of a large crowd, he was torn with red-hot pincers, tortured with boiling oil, lead and wax, dismembered by horses, and then burned to death. The assassination attempt made the Government more suspicious, even though Damiens was a lone fanatic.

Then there was the War, which, in contrast to the successful campaigns of the previous decade, was going badly. France suffered defeats from the British at sea and the Prussians on land. In November 1757, the same month volume 7 of *Encyclopédie* was released (covering Foang–Gythium), Frederick the Great inflicted a crushing defeat on a French Army which outnumbered his forces two-to-one at Rossbach. Louis XV, long since fully recovered from Damiens' wound, was thrown into depression.

Volume 7 of *Encyclopédie* contained a great triumph for Diderot, an article by Baron de Montesquieu himself. Surprisingly, though, it did not cover any of the great liberal jurist's usual subjects of constitutional law and the basis for government power, instead simply dealing with *Goût* (taste). But the volume also contained yet another troublesome article. D'Alembert had written a lengthy piece on Geneva which, while it contained both praise and criticism for the city-state, was not well received by its residents. This would be D'Alembert's last contribution—he left the project after Volume 7, leaving Diderot as sole editor.

With *Encyclopédie* under renewed attack from both at home and abroad and the Government again on the hunt for scapegoats, the project was in jeopardy. And this time, neither Meleshebes nor Pompadour could save it. In March 1759, it was condemned by the Royal Council, its *privilège* was revoked, and it was banned by the *Parlement* of Paris. Work continued, but in secret. Diderot was under enormous pressure, but he kept up his writing and editing.

Then, for once, events moved in his favour. In 1759, a scandal erupted within the Jesuit order. Antoine Lavalette, a Jesuit missionary who had been carrying out commercial activities throughout the Caribbean, went bankrupt. And when it turned out he had tried to defraud his creditors, the courts found the Jesuit Order itself liable for them. It was sued, then suppressed, then finally abolished by royal decree in 1764. The previous year, the War (the Seven Years' War, as it became known) ended in a disadvantageous but tolerable peace for France.

With his most dangerous enemies gone and the Government less-concerned with suppressing suspected internal threats, Diderot was able to finish the final ten volumes of text. In December 1765, volumes 8 to 17, covering H to Zzuéné, were shipped to the subscribers, who at this point had probably despaired of ever seeing them. They were printed outside Paris carrying the mark of a foreign printer. Le Breton took it on himself to edit them to remove material he thought was controversial, much to Diderot's outrage, but they were done nonetheless. In March and April 1766, another ten volumes of illustrations followed. By the time it was finished, *Encyclopédie* comprised 28 volumes of 71,818 articles, totalling twenty million words and 3,129 illustrations, representing the work of over a hundred contributors. Nothing like it had been seen before.

CHAPTER XI

HUMAN RIGHTS

In 1765, a wooden crucifix in Abbeville in north-eastern France was vandalised by a person or persons unknown. To the councillors of the conservative and very Catholic town, the episode was proof of the declining morals of French society and the baleful influence of the *philosophes* in their Paris cafés. Then, the next year in the same town, a young and not particularly bright minor nobleman, Chevalier François-Jean de la Barre, refused to take off his hat in the presence of a passing procession of Capuchin Friars. Worse, he sang an obscene and impious song at them. Worse again, after he was arrested authorities searched his room and found pornographic books and, more dangerously in their view, a copy of Voltaire's *Philosophical Dictionary*. He was convicted of blasphemy, and sentenced to have his right hand cut off, his tongue torn out, and to be burned to death. The Paris *Parlement* slightly amended his sentence. Burning him alive did seem a little excessive, so after his tongue was torn out he would be beheaded and his body burned. However, they also ordered that he be tortured by having his legs crushed, or, as they called it, 'putting the question'. On 1 July 1766, the sentence was carried out in public in central Abbeville. For good measure, the executioner threw Barre's copy of the *Philosophical Dictionary* into the flames after his body, sending a clear message to the *philosophes*. Voltaire used the episode to condemn both religious intolerance and torture in later editions of the dictionary. His disgust that such an episode could happen in France in the late eighteenth century shows clearly as he wrote:

> ... the judges of Abbeville, men comparable to Roman senators, ordered not only that his tongue should be torn out, that his hands should be torn off, and his body burned at a slow fire, but they further applied the torture, to know precisely how many songs he had sung, and how many processions he had seen with his hat on his head. It was not in the thirteenth or fourteenth century that this affair happened; it was in the eighteenth.[142]

Today, the story of Chevalier de la Barre horrifies us much as it horrified Voltaire and the *philosophes*. We would argue that Barre should be able to own a copy of Voltaire's book if he wanted, and while it is wrong to disrupt a procession of capuchin friars, this would be, at most, worthy of a fine for causing a public nuisance. He should not be prosecuted for damaging the crucifix without evidence, and even if he did damage it, he could be punished with an order to make restitution or undertake community service. And above all, no matter what he did, he should not have been put to death in such a cruel fashion. In short, Barre's human rights were violated.

Our modern concept of right and wrong is grounded in human rights. If you hit me, or steal my car, or lock me up in gaol without giving me a fair trial, I will complain that you have violated my rights (to person, property and liberty respectively). This is why we treat such acts as wrong and make them illegal—not because they are offensive to God, nor because they are disruptive to social harmony, nor because they go against the arbitrary will of an all-powerful ruler.

Consider the second line of the American Declaration of Independence of 1776: 'We hold these truths to be self-evident, that all men are created equal, that they are endowed by their Creator with certain unalienable Rights, that among these are Life, Liberty and the pursuit of Happiness'.

This neatly summarises four key elements of the modern understanding of human rights. Firstly, they are self-evident and require no justification. I don't need to prove to a court that I have a right to property before someone can be convicted of stealing from me, for example. Secondly, the rights are innate to us as humans and are not granted by the government. People living under a dictatorship still have rights; rights that are presumably being violated. Thirdly, the rights are unalienable, we can never lose them no matter what we do. And finally, they are universal, and attach equally to all people. You, me, the King and a refugee fleeing Myanmar all have the same human rights (here's the Enlightenment idea of universality again).

We have already seen the influence of Enlightenment thinking on the American Founding Fathers. The Declaration of Independence obviously draws on older ideas, such as the Christian notion of man being created in God's image, but it, and every other modern charter of human rights, is an Enlightenment document. As Micheline Ishay wrote in her history of human rights, 'the legacy of the European Enlightenment, for our current understanding of human rights, supersedes all other influences'.[143]

Prior to the Enlightenment, many societies had a concept of human rights with either a religious or secular basis. The Abrahamic religions—Judaism, Christianity and Islam—are all based in the premise that every human being is created by God in his image and so is entitled to justice: 'Whoso sheddeth man's blood, by man shall his blood be shed: for in the image of God made he man' (Genesis 9:6), and 'slay not the life which Allah hath made sacred, save in the course of justice' (Surah 6:151).[144] The Common Law of England recognised certain legal rights, such as *habeas corpus*, the right not to be arrested and detained without facing a court.

In practice, though, these systems were all mixed. Hinduism, for example, emphasised non-violence but upheld a restrictive caste system. And none were particularly effective at mitigating the brutality of everyday life in the Ancient, Medieval and Early Modern world. The widespread use of punishments such as mutilation and burning to death, the acceptance of slavery, and the sack of cities and massacre of civilians and prisoners in warfare were all common and frequently supported by religious edicts, such as the Old Testament's endorsement of punishments such as stoning to death, or God's instructions regarding captured cities in Deuteronomy 20:13–14:

> And when the Lord thy God hath delivered [the city] into thine hands, thou shalt smite every male thereof with the edge of the sword. But the women, and the little ones, and the cattle, and all that is in the city, even all the spoil thereof, shalt thou take unto thyself; and thou shalt eat the spoil of thine enemies, which the Lord thy God hath given thee.

Secular systems were likewise limited. *Habeas corpus*, for example, provided little benefit in practice to Englishmen locked up on the King's orders. It took two Acts of Parliament, in 1640 and 1679, to make it a workable remedy for those locked in the King's dungeons.

Earlier we looked at John Locke and his idea of a government founded to protect the natural rights of citizens, and how his ideas were applied by Montesquieu and the American Founding Fathers. Now, let's see how this idea of natural law and the limitations of government authority led to the modern concept of human rights.

The Enlightenment concept of natural law and human rights was different to what came before it for a few key reasons. One is that it recognised that people were formally equal when it came to rights of life and liberty. Another is that it was critical generally of dealing with problems through violence. And finally, by putting a focus on the physical world over the spiritual one it promoted ideas which improved life for people in the here and now. In other words, what we call humanism.

This is quite obvious when you compare a modern legal system with a pre-Enlightenment one. Take a well-known example, the system of Mosaic law established in the Old Testament and summarised in the Ten Commandments. The First Commandment is to worship God and only God, the Second (by Catholic reckoning) is not to take God's name in vain and the Third is to keep the Sabbath. In other words, religious and ritual matters come first. This is true of the broader code, where the entire book of Leviticus and the early part of Deuteronomy handle liturgy, ritual cleanliness and religious orthodoxy. The system prioritises establishing a community and a single system of belief and practice, and the most serious and most often-repeated offences are those which threaten this unity, such as worshipping idols.

The laws surrounding sexual morality in Deuteronomy 22 begin with the penalties for a man who makes a false allegation that his wife was not a virgin when he married her (payment of 100 shekels of silver to her father as compensation for slandering his family) and for a woman who is found not to have been a virgin when she was married (death by stoning). A woman's virginity is treated as a man's property throughout the chapter—a man who rapes a woman can escape any punishment if he pays compensation to her father, for example. The book also deals with slavery, and draws very clear distinctions between Hebrew and non-Hebrew slaves. Hebrew slaves are to be freed after seven years and rewarded, whereas foreign slaves (who might be seized in war) may be kept for life. Here we see a legal system which pre-dates the Enlightenment concept of universal human rights and draws clear distinctions between members of the in-group and out-group. This is not to condemn Mosaic Law for being unusually harsh or brutal—most pre-modern legal systems incorporated elements like these.

We can contrast this with the Enlightenment concept of rights which made it into the French Declaration of the Rights of Man and the Citizen (1789), and the Bill of Rights in the United States Constitution (1791). Critically, the Enlightenment concept of human rights were inalienable and could not be given up. As Thomas Paine wrote in *The Rights of Man* (1791):

> When I contemplate the natural dignity of man, when I feel (for Nature has not been kind enough to me to blunt my feelings) for the honour and happiness of its character, I become irritated at the attempt to govern mankind by force and fraud, as if they were all knaves and fools, and can scarcely avoid disgust at those who are thus imposed upon ...
> The fact therefore must be that the individuals themselves,

each in his own personal and sovereign right, entered into a compact with each other to produce a government: and this is the only mode in which governments have a right to arise, and the only principle on which they have a right to exist.[145]

In this book I have emphasised the importance of judging ideas by how they work in practice. Therefore, I will explore three examples of how the Enlightenment concept of human rights made a real and tangible difference to human wellbeing—the treatment of civilians and prisoners in wartime, torture and slavery.

***

We have already looked at the brutality of the Thirty Years' War of 1618 to 1648 as an example of pre-Enlightenment thinking about warfare. For a more detailed explanation of these attitudes, we can look to Shakespeare's *Henry V*, first performed in 1599. The play is fictional, but is closely based on the real events surrounding the central character's invasion of France during the Hundred Years' War in 1415 and the Battle of Agincourt. It is interesting in that it reflects a view of warfare and the laws around the treatment of prisoners and civilians recognisable to its audiences. This view is, to modern eyes, often wildly inconsistent. For example, during their march through the countryside the King has a man hanged for robbing a church, declaring:

> We would have all such offenders so cut off, and we give express charge that in our marches through the country there be nothing compelled from the villages, nothing taken but paid for, none of the French upbraided or abused in disdainful language; for when lenity and cruelty play for a kingdom, the gentler gamester is the soonest winner.[146]

However, previously, before the walls of the town of Harfleur, he warns the mayor that if he does not surrender he will allow his army to sack the city, describing the results in graphic terms. 'The gates of mercy shall be all shut up', soldiers will act as they will, and he will be powerless to restrain them.¹⁴⁷ This reflects the idea that a King cannot always be accountable for his army, and would bear no moral responsibility if he lost control of it. As it turned out, the city did surrender, and Henry ordered his army to treat the population with mercy.

In both cases, Shakespeare's Henry's basis for treating civilians well was pragmatic. He does not seem to think that he should forbid his soldiers from robbing, raping or killing the French villagers because it would violate their human rights, or even because they were his fellow Christians and Catholics. The historical Henry V did issue ordnances regarding the treatment of women and priests during his march through northern France, but these were likewise simply rules of discipline rather than a recognition of existing rights. And as in Shakespeare's play, they were observed imperfectly. There is an ongoing historical debate on whether Harfleur was sacked, but the English army did massacre a sizeable portion of the citizenry of Caen when it captured the town in 1417. And Henry V himself starved the women and children of Rouen to death by refusing to allow them passage through his lines during the siege of the town that same year.

Perhaps the play's most interesting scene from a legal perspective occurs between two captains in the English army, Gower and Fluellen, during the Battle of Agincourt.¹⁴⁸ The men learn that the retreating French have attacked the English camp and slain the non-combatants minding their supplies. The excitable Welsh soldier Fluellen exclaims 'Kill the boys and the luggage! 'Tis expressly against the law of arms', making it clear that men viewed that the indiscriminate killing of non-combatants was actively illegal. Gower responds by praising the King for ordering his soldiers to kill their prisoners: 'the king, most worthily, hath caused every soldier to cut his prisoner's throat'. In practice, Henry V ordered his prisoners killed out of military necessity, fearing his outnumbered men were facing another French attack. Shakespeare makes it out to be an act of vengeance. Either way, both recognised a doctrine of collective responsibility where killing prisoners in some cases was lawful.

But even amidst the brutality of the seventeenth century, a formal western theory of just warfare based in human rights began to develop through the works of writers like Francisco de Vitoria (1486–1546), Balthasar Ayala (1548–1584), Francisco Suárez (1548–1617) and Alberico Gentili (1552–1608). Probably the most famous of these writers was Hugo de Groot, more commonly known by the Latinized version of his name, Hugo Grotius (1583–1645). A child prodigy who completed a doctorate of law by fifteen, he became a high-profile lawyer and politician and took part in the peace negotiations between the Dutch Republic and Spain.

Grotius was an eminent lawyer and politician who fell from favour when he became embroiled in the Arminian controversy. Jacobus Arminius, a professor of theology at Leiden University, proposed an alternative set of ideas to the teachings of the Dutch Reformed Church. The dispute was extremely complex, but in brief, rather than accepting the Calvinist idea that mankind was absolutely depraved and completely dependent on God's will for salvation, Arminius argued that people could take some action to save themselves.

The argument crossed over from the religious into the political and so became inflamed. Finding himself on the wrong side of the present *Stadtholder* Grotius was imprisoned as a political prisoner in Lovestein Castle—an example of the limitations of tolerance of dissent in the Dutch Republic. While there, he commenced his most influential book, *De Jure Belli ac Pacis* (On the Law of War and Peace). Smuggled out of Lovestein Castle in a chest of books, he finished the work in 1625 while in exile in Paris. In the Prologue, he wrote:

> Fully convinced by the considerations which I have advanced that there is a common law among nations, which is valid alike for war and in war, I have had many and weighty reasons for undertaking to write upon the subject. Throughout the Christian world I observed a lack of restraint in relation to war, such as even barbarous races should be ashamed of; I observed that men rush to arms for slight causes, or no cause at all, and that when arms have once been taken up there is no longer any respect for law, divine or human; it is as if, in

accordance with a general decree, frenzy had openly been let loose for the committing of all crimes.[149]

Grotius based his argument in both the laws of nature and the commandments of God, which he viewed as being different in source but complimentary in application. He wrote at length on the distinction between *jus ad bellum* (starting a war for a just cause) and *jus in bello* (acting justly within a war). Grotius argued that the same logic for the just use of force for citizens within a state should apply to the use of force between states—it was just to start a war for self-defence, to recover property, or punish wrongdoers. This meant that only one side could be just, but Grotius acknowledged that it could be unclear which side that was, and therefore soldiers should not be punished merely for fighting an unjust war.

Grotius also argued that the laws of nature and God placed limits on what was acceptable for soldiers to do in warfare itself. Grotius argued absolutely against the killing of whose who had surrendered, even where some of his predecessors had acknowledged exceptions:

> Against these principles of natural law and equity an objection is sometimes derived from the necessity of retaliation, or striking terror, in cases of obstinate resistance. But such an objection is by no means just. For after a place has surrendered, and there is no danger to be apprehended from the prisoners, there is nothing to justify the further effusion of blood.[150]

He denied that hostages could be put to death, unless they themselves had committed crimes deserving of capital punishment. He also stated absolutely that prisoners of war should not be enslaved, even if they were non-Christian. Grotius also called for moderation in despoiling an enemy country. While he acknowledged that it could be justified to seize property in war, 'driving off some of our cattle, or burning a few of our houses, can never be pleaded as a sufficient and justifiable motive for laying waste the whole of an enemy's kingdom'.[151]

Importantly, Grotius based his argument in natural rather than divine law. Like Thomas Aquinas, Grotius believed that people could find what was right through reason, and people, like other animals, were inclined to seek what was naturally good for them. In this case, the human tendency to live together in societies inclined them to seek out a natural law which would facilitate this. 'What we have been saying would have a degree of validity even if we should concede that which cannot be conceded without the utmost wickedness: that there is no God, or that the affairs of men are of no concern to Him' he concluded.[152]

Grotius' book is still considered to be a foundation work of international law, but at the time his ideas found limited practical application. Nonetheless, from the end of the Thirty Years' War, warfare in Europe became much more regulated. As the nation-state became more centralised and more bureaucratic over the seventeenth and eighteenth centuries, governments were better able to feed and pay their troops, reducing the need for them to live on plunder. A series of bilateral treaties were established between different countries for prisoner exchange, extending the medieval custom of ransom to ordinary soldiers. This is an example of how theory and practice moved together.

Governments recognised there was little point in waging expensive wars in order to capture ruined and depopulated territory, and restrained their own armies under the expectation that their enemies would do the same. These considerations were all pragmatic rather than moral, however. European nations may have shown restraint fighting each other, but still often showed none towards rebels and non-European peoples in their colonial wars. Likewise, the customs of surrender permitted showing no quarter in some cases, such as with garrisons which insisted on holding out for too long. 'I believe that it has always been understood that the defenders of a fortress stormed have no claim to quarter' wrote the Duke of Wellington in a letter to George Canning, although he never acted on this principle.[153]

Europe in the eighteenth century was still beset by wars. But the two biggest conflicts, the War of the Spanish Succession (1701–1714) and

Seven Years' War (1756–1763) killed fewer Europeans than the Thirty Years' War by a factor of ten.[154] The French Revolutionary War and Napoleonic Wars were devastating, killing some two million soldiers and a million civilians.[155] But even with larger armies and deadlier weapons, this was a much smaller proportion of the world's population—some 400 out of 100,000 rather than 1,000 in 100,000 as in the Thirty Years' War. And while it is important not to minimise the atrocities of the irregular war in Spain or the war in the Vendée, they did not bring destruction and cruelty on the scale of the seventeenth century.

***

Prior to the Enlightenment, torture was widely used throughout human societies both as a means of extracting confessions from suspects and a method of punishment. Neither religious nor secular law offered much protection against it. The Old Testament endorses stoning to death as the punishment for a range of offences, including adultery, witchcraft, sabbath-breaking and apostasy. English common law traditionally permitted confessions to be forced out of suspects by crushing them under weights (the *peine forte et dure*) and execution by boiling alive, burning at the stake, and hanging, drawing and quartering.

The latter punishment befell the regicides who signed Charles I's death warrant. One account of Major-General Thomas Harrison's execution on 16 October 1660 described the grisly process in detail:

> [He] was upon a Hurdle drawn from Newgate to the place called Charing-Cross; where within certain Rails lately there made, a Gibbet was erected, and he hanged with his face looking towards the Banqueting-house at Whitehall, (the place where our late Sovereign of eternal memory was sacrificed) being half dead, he was cut down by the common Executioner, his Privy Members cut off before his eyes, his Bowels burned, his Head severed from his Body, and his Body divided into Quarters, which were returned back to Newgate upon the same Hurdle that carried it. His Head

is since set on a Pole on the top of the South-East end of Westminster-Hall, looking towards London. The Quarters of his Body are in like manner exposed upon some of the City Gates.[156]

The dismembered corpses on display were a constant reminder of the brutality of the contemporary criminal justice system. 'I saw the limbs of some of our new traitors set upon Aldersgate, which was a sad sight to see; and a bloody week this and the last have been, there being ten hanged, drawn, and quartered' wrote famed diarist Samuel Pepys in his entry of 20 October 1660.[157]

Enlightenment thinkers challenged both the justice and usefulness of such spectacles. One was Italian criminologist Cesare Beccaria (1738–1794), one of the founders of modern criminology. As he wrote in his *Essay on Crimes and Punishments*, an offender is either guilty or not guilty. 'If guilty, he should only suffer the punishment ordained by the laws, and torture becomes useless, as his confession is unnecessary. If he be not guilty, you torture the innocent; for, in the eye of the law, every man is innocent, whose crime has not been proved.'[158] Furthermore, torturing confessions out of suspects, rather than arriving at the truth, would only lead to the conviction of the feeble and the escape of the robust, regardless of their guilt or innocence. Finally, he argued that putting prisoners to work would be a more effective deterrent and would allow criminals to repair some of their damage to society.

'The death of a criminal is a terrible but momentary spectacle, and therefore a less efficacious method of deterring others, than the continued example of a man deprived of his liberty, condemned as a beast of burden, to repair, by his labour, the injury he has done to society.'[159] He also argued, quite convincingly, that there was no evidence that such extreme punishments made violence any less common. The Enlightenment argument against extreme punishments was therefore based in both empirical thinking and humanist considerations.

Beccaria proved influential with other Enlightenment thinkers, and he was cited with approval by Voltaire in his *Philosophical Dictionary*

(1764). 'Providence sometimes puts us to the torture by employing the stone, gravel, gout, scrofula, leprosy, smallpox; by tearing the entrails, by convulsions of the nerves, and other executors of the vengeance of Providence' he wrote. 'Now, as the first despots were, in the eyes of their courtiers, images of the Divinity, they imitated it as much as they could.' He was fiercely-critical of the continuation of torture in the French legal system. 'Woe to a nation which, being more civilized, is still led by ancient atrocious customs!' 'Why should we change our jurisprudence?' say we. 'Europe is indebted to us for cooks, tailors, and wig-makers; therefore, our laws are good.'[160]

We can use England as an example of how Enlightenment thinking spread through the criminal justice system. The 1689 English Bill of Rights was an initial pushback against the bloody public executions which had characterised the previous three decades. The Bill provided 'that excessive bail ought not to be required, nor excessive fines imposed, nor cruel and unusual punishments inflicted'. Many of the cruellest punishments remained on the books, but over the next century and a half, they gradually fell out of use.

We can start with burning, which had fallen out of use for heresy but was retained as the penalty for treason for women (it was seen as indecent to hang, draw and quarter them). Not only high treason, directed against the King, but petty treason, which included the murder of her husband. In 1726, Catherine Hayes became the last woman to be burned to death in public for this offence. From then on, as a humane consideration, women sentenced to death by burning were strangled first by their executioner. The last woman strangled and then burned was Catherine Murphy, executed for counterfeiting coins in 1789. Her execution caused an outrage in Parliament, which replaced burning with hanging in the *Treason Act 1790*.

Hanging, drawing and quartering also fell from favour. From the late seventeenth century, anyone condemned to this fate was hanged until dead first, and beheaded and cut up after they were dead. The last such execution, and the last beheading in England, was in 1820, when the Cato Street Conspirators were executed for treason. Their heads were cut off with a butcher's knife when they lay in their coffins, and when the executioner held them aloft and gave the traditional cry of 'behold the head of a traitor!' the crowd reacted with disgust. It was a far cry from Harrison's execution of one hundred and sixty years earlier.

From the late eighteenth century, the death penalty itself began to fall from use, replaced by penal transportation and the penitentiary for all but the most serious crimes. Under the 'Bloody Code' of the seventeenth and eighteenth centuries, all thefts of goods worth forty shillings or more were capital. But increasingly, these sentences were commuted to penal transportation. A harsh penalty by today's standards, but one which didn't kill the criminal and gave him or her a chance at a new life in the colonies. There were about two thousand executions annually in the seventeenth century, five hundred in the mid-eighteenth century, and about two hundred by the 1780s.[161] Then they were wound back. The 1823 *Judgement of Death Act* removed the mandatory death penalty for every offence save treason and murder.

One particular beneficiary of the British Government's changing policy was an Irishman named James Fines, who was born in Kildare in 1799. In 1823 he was convicted at the Dublin Assizes of breaking and entering and transported to New South Wales. A century earlier, he would certainly have been hanged. As it turned out, he served his sentence, was granted freedom in 1830 and lived the rest of his life peacefully near Bathurst, west of Sydney. His case is of particular interest to me, because he was my great-great-great grandfather.

Torturing confessions out of suspects fell out of use at the same time. The last known case of someone being pressed under weights by *peine forte et dure* was in 1741; the practice was banned in 1772. Corporal punishments also followed. Public whipping was phased out in the 1830s, although flogging continued in English prisons until 1948. The pillory was abolished in 1837, and the stocks fell from use and were finally banned in 1872. A large modern prison was opened in Pentonville in 1842, symbolising the new commitment to a private, orderly, regular and bloodless criminal justice system.

***

There is perhaps no more potent symbol of the injustice of the pre-Enlightenment world than slavery. Millions of human beings kept as the property of others, merely as a means to an end. Hunter-gatherer societies have no division of labour and therefore no need for slaves, but slavery has been widespread throughout human societies which get their food from farming.

The Ancient Greeks used slaves, and in *Politics*, Aristotle argued that some people were simply slaves by their nature. So did the Hebrews, and the Books of Exodus and Leviticus outlined the rules for taking, keeping and releasing slaves.

An interesting take on pre-Enlightenment views of slavery can be seen in the Valladolid debate of 1550–1551, discussing the treatment of native Americans in the Spanish Empire. In Spanish-controlled territories, each group of Native Americans would be assigned to a Spanish landlord (*Encomendero*) to work land and pay him triubute. He would be obliged to instruct them in Christianity, protect them and pay a tax on them to the government. In exchange, he would get their labour for two generations. It was effectively a form of communal indentured servitude. The *Encomienda* system had come under pressure from a 1537 Papal Bull (decree) declaring that the Native Americans were rational beings and not beasts, and 1542 laws designed to bring the system to an end were proposed. Troubled by the reports he was hearing from his colonial possessions, Charles V of Spain and the Holy Roman Empire called for a debate on the *Encomienda* system and colonial conquest generally at the Spanish city of Valladolid in 1550.

The affirmative case was argued by an Aristotelian philosopher, Juan Gines de Sepúlveda, who was speaking for the *Encomenderos*. Standing before the assembled scholars, Sepúlveda spoke for four hours and made four arguments in favour of further Spanish expansion into the New World. He spoke with reference to the works of Aristotle, Saint Augustine and Aquinas. Firstly, the Native Americans were naturally inferior to the

Spanish and incapable of self-government, and so it was natural that they should be in a subordinate position. Here he cited Aristotle, who argued in *Politics* that some men were by nature masters and some by nature slaves: '... there is in some cases a marked distinction between the two classes, rendering it expedient and right for the one to be slaves and the others to be masters: the one practising obedience, the others exercising the authority and lordship which nature intended them to have'.[162] Secondly, the Native Americans engaged in practices repugnant to both divine and natural law, like human sacrifice and cannibalism, and it would be immoral in the eyes of God to allow such practices to continue. Thirdly, the Spanish had a duty to protect innocent native Americans who might fall victim to such practices as God entrusted to each the care of all his fellow men (whether Sepúlveda was right on this particular point is obviously still debated today in the context of military interventions to protect human rights, although more commonly with secular rather than religious arguments). Finally, waging war against the Native Americans and conquering them would allow them to be converted to Christianity, improving their lives and saving their souls.

Sepúlveda was opposed by Bartolomé de las Casas, a Dominican friar and a Christian humanist from the School of Salamanca. Unlike Sepúlveda, he had spent a significant amount of time in the New World, first as an *Encomendero*, then as the Bishop of Chiapas in Mexico. He has appeared in this book before, in the first chapter, as the eyewitness to the massacre in Cuba. He had written prolifically on the mistreatment of Native Americans, and drew on his personal experience for his arguments, although he also quoted extensively from Aristotle, Augustine and Aquinas.

Speaking over several days, he challenged each of Sepúlveda's four arguments point-by-point. First, he accused Sepúlveda of oversimplifying Aristotle. He argued that the Native Americans were as developed as the Spanish in all ways except spiritually, and so could govern themselves. The Spanish had no natural right over them save evangelisation.

Secondly, while Casas admitted that the Native Americans had committed crimes, he denied that the Spanish had any jurisdiction to punish them. Catholics had a natural right to punish heretics, who had been baptised into the Church but rejected its teachings, but not to punish Infidels who had never been Christian. And furthermore, he argued that accounts of native crimes were exaggerated. Far more damage could be done in war and conquest, which risked making the Native Americans hate the name of Christ and associate it with violence.

Finally (pre-empting Locke by a century and a half) Casas pointed out that warfare would be ineffective at converting the natives—they would need to be called by God like the Europeans had been.

The debate was indecisive. Both sides claimed victory, and a tighter system of regulation around the *Encomienda* system was introduced, but Spanish conquests in the New World continued.

But no continent is more associated with slavery than Africa. The Europeans did not bring slavery to Africa; Africans had been buying and selling each other before the first Portuguese mariners arrived, and the Arabs had established a vast network of slave routes throughout the Sahara and Indian Ocean in the Middle Ages. But the shipping of millions of Africans across the Atlantic in chains, and keeping them in their American colonies in a state of the utmost oppression and degradation for centuries, is probably the blackest indictment that can be made against the nations of Europe. All up, as many as 10% of Africa's people were dragged from the continent in bondage, and a plurality of those to the waiting holds of Atlantic slave ships. As Elikia M'bokolo wrote in 1998 on the hundred and fiftieth anniversary of the abolition of slavery in the French Empire:

> The African continent was bled of its human resources via all possible routes. Across the Sahara, through the Red Sea, from the Indian Ocean ports and across the Atlantic. At least ten centuries of slavery for the benefit of the Muslim countries (from the ninth to the nineteenth). Then more than four centuries (from the end of the fifteenth to the nineteenth) of a regular slave trade to build the Americas and the prosperity of the Christian states of Europe. The figures, even where hotly disputed, make your head spin.

Four million slaves exported via the Red Sea, another four million through the Swahili ports of the Indian Ocean, perhaps as many as nine million along the trans-Saharan caravan route, and eleven to twenty million (depending on the author) across the Atlantic Ocean.[163]

By the eighteenth century British ships had come to dominate the trans-Atlantic slave trade, but Slavery was always viewed with suspicion by English liberals, and Blackstone confirmed a line of eighteenth-century cases which established that the air of Britain was too free to allow anyone to kept in slavery there:

> And this spirit of liberty is so deeply implanted in our constitution, and rooted even in our very soil, that a slave or a negro, the moment he lands in England, falls under the protection of the laws, and with regard to all natural rights becomes eo instanti a freeman.[164]

This did not change the fact that dozens of British ships continued to carry slaves from Africa to the West Indies and North American colonies, and then return to Britain laden with cotton and sugar, before taking on goods with which to buy more slaves in Africa; the extremely lucrative 'triangle trade'. Calls for the abolition of slavery met fierce resistance from merchants in port cities such as Liverpool and Bristol as well as from the legislatures of the West Indian Colonies. Elected by the planters on narrow franchises, they responded to any criticism of slavery by insisting that the brutalised slaves were treated with Christian charity and were content with their lot. It was an example of where the Enlightenment notions of free commerce and scientific racism came into conflict with the concept of inalienable and universal human rights. Indeed, it was a classic example of practices notionally repugnant to English notions of freedom in Britain post-1688 being readily tolerated in the colonies.

From the mid-eighteenth century onwards, though, abolitionist movements rapidly gained strength in Britain, France and America. Slavery was condemned by Baron Montesquieu in *The Spirit of the Laws*

(1748) and in *Encyclopédie*. Adam Smith wrote against it in both moral and economic terms in his books and in his unpublished lectures on jurisprudence. The 1772 case of *Somerset v Stewart* established that slavery was odious to English common law; the 1778 case of *Knight v Wedderburn* came to the same decision in Scotland (Lord Kames was one of the judges on the bench). Slavery was slammed in an influential article called *African Slavery in America* published in Philadelphia in 1775; Thomas Paine is believed to be the author. The Society for Effecting the Abolition of the Slave Trade was formed in London in 1787, centred around leading abolitionist William Wilberforce.

The abolitionist movement was based in religion as much as Enlightenment philosophy, and in England and America, many of its leading advocates were Quakers. Wilberforce, whose name is more closely associated with abolition than anyone else, was an evangelical Christian. And while the Enlightenment provided much of the intellectual justification for abolition, the prospect of God's judgement provided much of its urgency.

Ultimately, though, the abolition of slavery came in the wake of the Enlightenment; the religious objections to the institution had failed to gain traction before then. Britain abolished the slave trade in 1807 and slavery throughout the Empire in 1833. France abolished slavery in 1794, re-established it in 1802, then finally abolished it for good in 1848. America's northern states began passing legislation to abolish it in the wake of the Revolution, although its abolition in the cotton-dependant south only came with the Union victory in the Civil War of 1861–1865.

The 1948 United Nations Convention on Human Rights confirmed that slavery was a violation of international law, and the remaining countries in which the institution was legal have now banned it. The last was Mauritania, which abolished slavery in 1981 and criminalised it in 2007. But in practice, tens of millions of people in the developing world are still held in conditions of forced labour, and many thousands are trafficked every day. The fight against slavery and involuntary servitude is a major Enlightenment project which is continuing.

CHAPTER XII

BRIDGING SCIENCE AND TECHNOLOGY

It seems perfectly natural to us today for science and technology to go together. If you hear one of these two words, you often think of the other. Someone discovers radio waves, someone else invents the radio, and then we can all go buy a radio in a shop (or online from Amazon or eBay). We're used to the image of Steve Jobs in his jeans and black turtleneck presenting the latest model iPhone to eager Apple consumers. There's a clear chain from scientific discovery to invention to the manufacture of consumer goods.

But this chain is a recent development. As physicist Count Rumford wrote in 1799, 'there are no two classes of men in society that are more distinct, or that are more separated from each other by a more marked line, than philosophers and those who are engaged in arts and manufactures [preventing] all connection and intercourse between them'.[165] Most human societies have tended to establish clear distinctions between people who worked with ideas and those who made things. Plato's ideal society in *The Republic* draws a very sharp line between the propertyless guardians trained in philosophy and the artisans who manufacture and sell goods, and places the guardians over the artisans. The Hindu caste system cemented this idea in practice. In China, Mandarins working for the state may have written books on agriculture, such as Wang Chen's 1313 *Nong Shu*, but these were intended to be read by other Mandarins, not the illiterate farmers who actually worked the soil.[166] In Medieval Europe, ideas were for the Church and the Scholastic Universities and making things for the guilds.

From the fourteenth century, the guilds went into decline in Britain and the Netherlands. In the eighteenth century, they were criticised by Baron Montesquieu in *The Spirit of the Laws* and Adam Smith in *The Wealth of Nations*. At the same time, alternatives to the Scholastic universities appeared in the form of technical colleges such as the Ponts et Chauseés in France in 1748 and the Mining Academy of Freiburg in Saxony in 1765. Empirical thinking was applied to agriculture and manufacturing. Over the eighteenth century, Britain underwent an agricultural and industrial revolution.

Plants take nutrients from the soil, so if the same field is used year after year it becomes less and less productive. Since ancient times, farmers have therefore rotated their crops and left fields lying fallow to give them a chance to recover. Since the Middle Ages, most farmers in Europe followed a three-field system, leaving a third of their fields fallow. In the sixteenth and seventeenth century, farmers in Belgium and England began experimenting with a four-field system, using the fallow field to grow turnips, which lie deeper in the soil than wheat, grass or barley and hence don't use the same nutrients as them. This system was spread throughout Britain by agriculturalist Charles Townshend (1674–1738). The Dutch developed a new plough which could be pulled by three or four oxen, not six or eight, drastically reducing the expense of ploughing fields. And Robert Bakewell (1725–1795) pioneered the selective breeding of cattle. The Norfolk four-course system and improved farming technology steadily pushed up crop yields:[167]

Year	Bushels per Acre
1250–1299	8.71
1300–1349	8.24
1350–1399	7.46
1400–1449	5.89
1450–1499	6.48
1550–1599	7.88
1600–1649	10.45
1650–1699	11.36
1700–1749	13.79
1750–1799	17.26
1800–1849	23.16
1850–1899	26.69

Then, around 1760, there was a decisive shift in manufacturing and engineering in Britain. Civil engineering projects, which had been steady at between three and thirteen per decade from 1700 to 1760, jumped to thirty-five in the decade between 1760 and 1769.[168] At the same time, there was a spike in the number of books being printed.[169] Then, in the 1770s, there were decisive changes in the textile industry. Before then, textiles such as cotton and wool were prepared in a cottage industry with thousands of weavers working in families using spinning wheels and hand looms. A series of inventions including the spinning jenny (1764), the spinning mule (1779) and the power loom (1784) vastly increased the potential output of a single worker and so changed everything. Rather than have a family prepare the fabric from start to finish, it became more practical to have one worker working at one machine doing one part of the process. Cotton mills, often powered by water-wheels, began to spring up around Britain, particularly in Lancashire. Workers in these factories could produce dozens of times as much cotton and at a better and more consistent quality than the weaving families in their cottages, and so the cottage industry died out.

It started with textiles, but it did not end there. From the mid-1750s, Britain's iron smelters found they could produce cheaper and better-quality iron using coke, made from coal, rather than charcoal, made from wood. Then, in the 1780s, further advances were made allowing iron to be produced ten times faster than it had been only a generation before.

Ordinary people didn't initially see much, if any, improvement in their lives as a result of these changes. In fact, if they depended on cottage industries to make a living, they would have seen their lives get worse. This was the beginning of the dilemma we still face today, where technological progress leads to labour savings, which in turn, leads to unemployment. Others among the rural poor would have been left destitute by the enclosure acts, which locked up land previously held in common for farming. Many more people would have seen no change at all. Before the spread of railways in the 1830s, the Industrial Revolution was mostly confined to the north of England.

The Industrial Revolution obviously didn't herald a time of plenty. The Dickensian image of stunted factory workers toiling for long shifts in dirty and dangerous conditions, living on a poor diet of bread and dripping, is close to reality. Charles Dickens himself had first-hand knowledge of this—as a twelve-year-old in 1824 he had needed to get a job in a shoe-blacking factory, working twelve hours a day for six days a week to help support his family. But these jobs, as miserable as they were, kept people alive who would previously have starved during lean times. This harsh reality is why many people in third-world countries today choose to abandon subsistence farming for jobs in factories, as difficult as the conditions are.

***

At first glance, it's easy to assume the Agricultural and Industrial Revolutions were inevitable results of scientific progress. A combine harvester can harvest far more wheat than a labourer with a scythe, a sewing machine can assemble clothes faster than a seamstress and a truck can bring far more vegetables to market far more quickly than a farmer in a horse cart. But this isn't the whole story, as previous periods of scientific advance had failed to trigger sustained GDP growth. China during the Song Dynasty (960–1279) developed gunpowder, the first use of the magnetic compass for navigation, moveable type printing, paper money and the pound lock in canals, but the average Chinese peasant still lived a meagre life by modern standards. There was no Chinese Manchester.

The other important point to make about the Agricultural and Industrial Revolutions is that they didn't use much cutting-edge science. Many of their innovations were discovered through trial-and-error by people ignorant of the underlying science. The pioneers of selective cattle breeding had no knowledge of genetics, and Charles Darwin's theory of evolution through natural selection was still a century away. The agriculturalists who developed the Norfolk four-course crop rotation system knew nothing of molecular biology. The improvements in metallurgy were made by people who wouldn't have recognised the periodic table. This shows the critical importance of empiricism—reason alone could not have delivered these outcomes and nobody knew of their causes.

This is not to say science was unimportant. Scientific discoveries did lead to some real and practical benefits. One example is the solution to the longitude problem. To know where in the world you are without reference to landmarks, you need to know how far you are to the north or south (latitude) and now far you are to the east or west (longitude). Finding your latitude is fairly straightforward—the height of the sun at noon or the height of a recognisable star at night will tell you. But measuring longitude is much harder, and having no accurate means of finding it made navigation in the Age of Discovery difficult and dangerous. Particularly in the Pacific Ocean, where there were very few landmarks. For example, Álvaro de Mendaña de Neira became the first European to visit the Solomon Islands in 1568, but another European did not land there until 1767 simply because no one could find them again. It is possible to know your longitude if you know what time it is relative to the time at a known location, but no clocks were accurate enough to determine this within hundreds of miles.

Anyone who solved the longitude problem would gain a huge

advantage to exploration, commerce, and warfare, and so Europe's rulers began offering prizes for a solution. In 1755, a German astronomer, Tobias Mayer of the Observatory of Göttingen, published a means of calculating local time from observations of the moon. In 1767, English astronomer Nevil Maskelyne published tables which removed the need to undertake the difficult and laborious calculations while at sea. Maskelyne's tables used the Royal Observatory at Greenwich as the fixed point from which time would be calculated, hence the adoption of Greenwich Mean Time as the global standard. James Cook used Maskelyne's tables on his first voyage of exploration in the Pacific with great success, accurately mapping New Zealand and the east coast of Australia. But many of the other early advances were made through trial and error in ignorance of the scientific principles behind them.

***

Let's look at the invention symbolic of the Industrial Revolution—the steam engine—and the story of Scotsman James Watt. Watt did not invent the steam engine, as is commonly claimed, but he did improve it to the point it became practical, reliable and economically feasible to use on a large scale. Watt's experience neatly illustrates how science, technology and commerce came together through the Enlightenment.

Anyone who has ever watched the lid bouncing on a boiling pot knows steam can cause motion. But building a machine to put this knowledge to practical effect proved impossible for centuries. There were some models, of course. Simple steam engines were designed by Hero of Alexandria in the first century AD, Turkish polymath Taqi al-Din in 1551, and Giovanni Branca in Italy in 1629. But it was only English military engineer Thomas Savery who made one with a practical application in 1698. Noticing how the mines of his native Devon tended to fill with water, he built a machine which he called the 'Miner's Friend'. He was granted a patent, No. 356.

Savery's engine consisted of a boiler and two chambers called receivers. Steam was forced into one and it was then cooled, which created a vacuum which could suck up water. The pump alternated between the receivers, so one was being filled with steam while the other was filling with water. The machine worked, but it was too big to fit in mines and not powerful enough to reach deep mines—it had a limit of about thirty feet. Existing metalwork techniques were not precise enough to seal it entirely, and it wasted a lot of energy.

A significant improvement was made by ironmonger Thomas Newcomen. With his assistant, a plumber, he built the 'atmospheric engine' in 1712. Newcomen's engine worked on the same principle as Savery's—condensing steam creating a vacuum. But Newcomen's engine used the vacuum to pull a piston in a water-lubricated cylinder—a pivotal development. The piston worked an arm, and the arm drove the pump. It was still slow and inefficient compared to later steam engines, but it worked better than Savery's engine. After a squabble over Savery's patent, Newcomen engines with their recognisable see-sawing bat-wing beam began popping up at English coal mines.

For the next five decades, the Newcomen engine represented the pinnacle of British technology. It wasn't efficient enough to work away from ready supplies of coal, but it could pump out coal mines.

***

Then we come to James Watt. Watt was born in 1739 at Greenock on the west coast of Scotland. His father was a maths teacher and baille (civic officer), his mother was well-educated, and both parents were devout Presbyterians who had been Covenanters.

The young Jamie Watt (as the family called him) was not academic, but showed a remarkable aptitude for anything mechanical. Given a small set of tools as a present, he was soon using them to dismantle and rebuild his toys, often improving them in the process. Then there is the famous anecdote of Watt and the kettle. 'James Watt, I never saw such an idle boy; take a book or employ yourself usefully' his aunt said to him one evening.

> For the last hour you have not spoken one word, but taken
> the lid off that kettle and put it back on, holding now a cup

and now a silver spoon over the steam, watching how it rises from the spout; and catching and connecting the drops of hot water it falls into. Are you not ashamed of spending your time in this way?[170]

I consider this story far too pat to be true. It seems unlikely to me Watt's aunt would have described exactly what he was doing in such detail, and I cannot imagine why the kettle at the Watt household would need to be left boiling for an hour. But as with George Washington and the cherry tree, it conforms to the fad for distilling something essential about someone's character to an episode in their childhood.

As an eighteen-year-old, Watt was apprenticed to an instrument-maker in London. He then moved to Glasgow, intending to set up the first instrument-making shop in the city. According to a popular account, his bid to go into business on his own was blocked by the Glasgow Guild of Hammermen. Having a monopoly on all metal craftsmen, they refused to permit Watt to join them unless he served a seven-year apprenticeship. Watt could not serve such an apprenticeship as there was no instrument-maker in Glasgow to be apprenticed to, so he was stuck. Then the University came to his rescue. Believing it would be beneficial to their scientific program, they furnished him with a small workshop and a shop front from which he could sell his instruments. Adam Smith, who opposed the monopoly of the guilds, may have had a hand in this. Smith and Watt certainly knew each other at Glasgow, but having Smith going in to fight a monopolistic guild on behalf of the pioneer of the steam engine might also be too pat as well.

Regardless of the circumstances of how he came there, Watt worked at Glasgow University, steadily growing his business. And one day, someone from the science faculty brought in a small model of a Newcomen steam engine. Using a practical model to teach scientific principles was itself a radical idea by the standards of the time, but sadly, the little engine had stopped working. Could Watt, with his skilled hands, fix it? Watt took the engine, and his great love affair with steam began.

Watt fixed the engine, but noticed how inefficient it was to heat and cool the cylinder for every stroke. He began working to improve it. In 1762, at the same time Watt was working on the engine, and at the same university, physicist Joseph Black discovered latent heat. Latent heat is 'hidden' heat; the heat absorbed by something without changing its temperature. Converting 1 kg of water at 100°C to 1 kg of steam at 100°C requires 2,260 kJ of energy—that 2,260 kJ is latent heat. Black and Watt were friends, and Watt credited Black's discovery with helping him towards his new steam engine. But it's also possible Watt would have got there on his own, through trial and error.

In 1765, Watt had his major breakthrough—the discovery for which he is best known. If the steam could be condensed in a separate chamber to the cylinder, then the cylinder could be kept hot and the condenser kept cool. There would be no need to expend the energy to heat and cool the cylinder with every stroke, and much more work could be done burning much less coal. Watt soon had a working model.

But creating a full-sized engine proved extremely difficult. With existing tools it was not possible to build a piston which fit exactly into the cylinder, leaving a gap for steam to escape. Watt tried everything, including lining the piston with felt from old hats, but it didn't work. And while the condenser worked on the small model, on the full-sized machine steam also kept escaping from the seals joining the condenser to the cylinder.

Watt needed capital. Fortunately for him, he caught the attention of John Roebuck, the founder of the Carron Iron Works. Roebuck entered into partnership with Watt, backing him in the hope the improved engine would prove commercially viable. Patents were expensive then, and Roebuck put up the funds. Watt's engine was now taking shape thanks to the combined efforts of a scientist, a craftsman and a businessman—Black, Watt and Roebuck. It was a radical arrangement.

Sadly, things didn't work out. Watt couldn't perfect the steam engine. He married in 1764, and while he made a fine partnership with Peggy Miller, who helped him tremendously, he now needed more income. He took various jobs, including as a surveyor and a civil engineer. Then, in 1772, Roebuck went bankrupt. Watt had lost his partner. But all was not lost—Roebuck sold his two-thirds share in the patent for Watt's steam engine for £1,200 to a Birmingham industrialist named Matthew Boulton. Putting Watt and Boulton together in Birmingham proved remarkably fortuitous.

***

Today, Birmingham is the second most populous city in the United Kingdom. For centuries, though, it was a successful but fairly-unimportant market town. Situated in the West Midlands away from the coast or any major rivers, it could never compete as a commercial centre with London, Bristol, Plymouth, or Portsmouth. Over the sixteenth and seventeenth centuries, though, it was able to build a highly-successful metalworking industry. Metal goods were small and high-value, and so the lack of water transport didn't matter as much. Feudalism and the guild structure collapsed early, and the town became a major centre of religious non-Conformism. It strongly supported Parliament in the Civil War, and became the armoury of the Parliamentary Army.

Unsurprisingly, this history made Birmingham naturally receptive to Enlightenment ideas, and Watt arrived to find the town in the midst of a revolution in thinking called the Midlands Enlightenment. Prominent scientists, academics and industrialists (including Boulton) had formed a group called the Lunar Society, similar to the Edinburgh Select Society. Bookshops and booksellers were multiplying, with the city's tradesmen taking up reading on a wide scale. Steady improvements were being made to local industry—Birmingham got the world's first mechanical cotton mill in 1741, and Boulton himself built the Soho Manufactory in 1766 where production lines were used to make consumer goods like buttons and buckles. 'By the many mechanical contrivances and extensive apparatus we are possess'd of, our men are enabled to do from twice to ten times the work that can be done without the help of such contrivances' he wrote in 1770.[171] In 1772 the Birmingham Canal was finished, joining the city to the rest of the English canal network.

In Birmingham, Watt found the skilled artisans and the money he needed to finish the steam engine. He also had, in Boulton, a partner who could make up for his deficiencies. By his own admission he hated business, and 'would rather face a loaded cannon than settle an account or make a bargain'.[172] Boulton, however, was a natural. And while Watt was nervous and prone to stress and episodes of depression, Boulton was naturally steady and unfazed by failure. Boulton lobbied Parliament to have the now-expired patent renewed to 1800, and engaged John 'Iron Mad' Wilkinson, an iron foundry owner, to cast a cylinder made to the best modern standards.

Watt went through several years of ups and downs. His wife died in 1773, and he re-married in 1775. The steam engine struggled, but steadily improved. Finally, it was good enough to be sold. In 1775, Watt and Boulton had their first orders. And in March 1776, the first Boulton and Watt engine went into action at the Bloomfield Colliery at Tipton. As the Birmingham Gazette recorded:

> On Friday last a Steam Engine constructed upon Mr. Watt's new Principles was set to work at Bloomfield Colliery, near Dudley, in the Presence of its Proprietors, Messrs. Bentley, Banner, Wallin, and Westley; and a Number of Scientific Gentlemen whose Curiosity was excited to see the first Movements of so singular and so powerful a Machine; and whose Expectations were fully gratified by the Excellence of its performance. The Workmanship of the Whole did not pass unnoticed, nor unadmired. All the Iron Foundry Parts (which are unparalleled for truth) were executed by Mr. Wilkinson; the Condensor, with the Valves, Pistons and all the small Work at Soho, by Mr. Harrison and others; and the Whole was erected by Mr. Perrins, conformable to the Plans and under the Directions of Mr. Watt. From the first Moment of its setting to Work, it made about fourteen to fifteen Strokes per Minute, and emptied the Engine Pit (which is about ninety Feet deep, and stood fifty-seven Feet high in Water) in less than an hour.[173]

The machine had worked faster than any Newcomen engine and used a third of the coal. It was truly revolutionary. Mines which were flooded could now be re-opened. Orders began to arrive from coal mines in Cornwall, and Watt had an anxious few years amidst patent and payment disputes as they went in. Soon there were Boulton and Watt engines at work up and down England.

Then, in 1783, Watt improved his engine further, so it could run at constant speed. This meant it could drive a mill wheel, freeing factories from water power for the first time. From there, it was only a matter of time before the engine was used to drive a vehicle. The first experimental steam locomotive was built in 1804 and the first steamboat in 1807. By the time Watt died in 1819, steam-driven travel had become a reality. The Liverpool-Manchester Railway opened in 1830, leading to a transformation in the lives of ordinary people. For the first time, they could travel for work or pleasure, and goods could be bought to them to cater for local shortages. Markets widened.

Watt was a very clever man, but he benefitted enormously from the world he was born into. No doubt countless other Watts, men and women alike, have laboured in obscurity in rice paddies and barley fields around the globe, known in the village for their dexterity and problem-solving but unknown to anyone else. But Watt was able to produce his steam engine through empiricism, markets, capital accumulation and, above all, the breakdown of the barriers which separated those who had ideas and those who made things for sale. In the Watt steam engine, the ideas of Isaac Newton were combined with those of Adam Smith.

There was another smaller driver behind the Industrial Revolution—the standardisation of weights and measures. Watt created the concept of horsepower, which was formerly used to measure how powerful engines were. Today, though, we measure power in a standard unit of one joule per second, and apply it to everything from engines to light bulbs. It is, appropriately, called the Watt.

CHAPTER XIII

ENLIGHTENMENT'S END?

When did the Enlightenment end? In one sense, the answer is 'never'. Every mainstream political party in the western world, to some extent, embraces liberal ideas. We still treat the scientific method as the best way to learn about the world around us, and our body of knowledge has kept growing. The United States has kept the constitution it started with, and Britain has not had a revolution since 1688.

Still, if the Enlightenment as a period of history had an end, it is usually placed between the start of the French Revolution in 1789 and the end of the Napoleonic Wars in 1815. These events fractured the Enlightenment coalition and gave rise to the counter-Enlightenment. Enlightenment ideas, by this stage, were too well-entrenched to be torn out by the roots, but they were no longer at the cutting edge of thought in Europe.

How obvious was the Enlightenment in the 1780s? This was, after all the decade in which Immanuel Kant published *What is Enlightenment?* (1784), and the United States created its Bill of Rights. Prussia and Russia were still absolute monarchies, but their monarchs—Frederick the Great and Catherine the Great—were sympathetic to Enlightenment ideas. The Whigs had dominated Britain for a century.

But in many ways, Enlightenment ideas had little effect on the lives of ordinary people. For all the advances in physics and astronomy, European science still had little understanding of disease, and infant mortality was unchanged. The Bubonic Plague was gone, but epidemics of influenza and cholera remained a real threat from which there was no security.

Europe was slowly becoming less violent. From 1500 to 1700, the great powers had been at war almost continuously. But over the eighteenth century, the periods of peace became more common. From the end of the War of the Spanish Succession in 1713 to the outbreak of the War of the Austrian Succession in 1739, Europe had an unprecedented generation without the beating of drums and the marching of armies. And then again, from the end of the Seven Years' War in 1763 to the entry of France into the American Revolutionary War in 1778, a shorter but still significant episode of peace. Civil war, too, was rarer. After Culloden in 1746, there would not be another battle fought in Great Britain. State-sanctioned violence was also becoming rarer. In Britain, the number of executions carried out remained steady from about 1750 onwards, even as the population increased.[174] The brutal execution of Robert-François Damiens in Paris in 1757 was the last of its kind in France.

In Europe and America, there was a growing interest in human rights. True, the interest was mostly in the rights of property-holding white men, but even this was changing. Mary Wollstonecraft (1759–1797) was working on her *Vindication of the Rights of Woman*, a pioneering work of feminist literature published in 1792. Slavery was coming under criticism. In the 1772 case of *Somerset v Stewart*, the Court of King's Bench established that even if slavery were legal in Britain's colonies, it could not be tolerated in Britain itself. As Lord Mansfield wrote in his judgement:

> The state of slavery is of such a nature that it is incapable of being introduced on any reasons, moral or political, but only by positive law, which preserves its force long after the reasons, occasions, and time itself from whence it was created, is erased from memory. It is so odious, that nothing can be suffered to support it, but positive law. Whatever inconveniences, therefore, may follow from a decision, I

cannot say this case is allowed or approved by the law of England; and therefore the black must be discharged.[175]

But in France, things were far from going well. The country was bankrupted by wars and economic crises, and the new and mostly-ineffective king, Louis XVI, found himself unable to ease the concerns of his discontented subjects.

France was an absolute monarchy, but it had a parliament-like body in the form of the Estates-General of three estates—the first of the clergy, the second of the nobility, and the third representing everyone else. The Assembly had little power, and the Third Estate the least power of all. In May 1789, pointing out that it represented the interests of the overwhelming majority of French people, the Third Estate begin agitating for a new constitution. When this agitation was initially unsuccessful, a large group of Parisians decided to take matters into their own hands. On 14 July, a mob stormed the Bastille, the Paris prison which was a hated symbol of the *Ancien Regime*. They freed the prisoners (all seven of them), decapitated prison governor Bernard-René Jourdan de Launay, and paraded his head on a pike. For the rest of the summer, the country seethed with unrest.

In August, the Third Estate finally got its wish when the Assembly passed sweeping reforms.

It abolished special privileges of the aristocracy and the church, enacted the Declaration of the Rights of Man and the Citizen, and set out drafting a new constitution. On 14 July 1790, amidst public celebration in which the King actively participated, France became a constitutional monarchy. Absolutism in France had come to an end speedily and with relatively little bloodshed (poor Launay notwithstanding), and a year exactly after the storming of the Bastille, France had taken steps which would make political violence unnecessary. In September 1791, France adopted a new constitution, and four million men who met a tax threshold cast a vote by secret ballot for a new Legislative Assembly. With the King's blessing, it met for the first time on 1 October.

Enlightened Europe was thrilled, as were the advocates of constitutional government across the Atlantic. Thomas Jefferson, serving as America's ambassador to France, had witnessed the Fall of the Bastille, and had watched the events which followed with optimism. 'The nation has been awaked by our revolution, they feel their strength, they are enlightened, their lights are spreading, and they will not retrograde' he wrote to George Washington. And later, to James Madison, he was cautiously optimistic that the French were 'advancing to a limited, moderate government, in which the people will have a good share'.[176] In Königsberg, the aging Immanuel Kant avidly followed the developments in France in the newspapers and wrote extensively of the Revolution in letters to his students.

But at some point, things began to go wrong. Badly wrong. In public, Louis XVI appeared to endorse the new constitutional monarchy. But privately, he was becoming more and more concerned for his safety. In June 1791, he tried to flee with his family, but was arrested and returned to Paris. He was in an uncomfortable position, half-monarch, half-prisoner, when he was met with applause by the new Legislative Assembly.

The Assembly was dominated by a moderate faction called the Girondins, but on the benches on the far left a new and much more radical party was forming. Called the Montagnards, or Jacobins, they found an able spokesman in the Arras lawyer Maximilien Robespierre. Austria and Prussia, which remained absolute monarchies, understandably looked on events in Paris with alarm. France's Queen was Austrian, and both the King and Queen remained in close contact with her family.

In April 1792, with the Assembly struggling to deliver on its promises and the perceived threat of foreign interference growing, France declared war on Austria and Prussia. Austria and Prussia placed their armies under the command of the Duke of Brunswick, who issued a manifesto on 25 July. He was preparing to invade France, he wrote, with the intention of restoring the king to his rightful position and bringing anarchy in the country to an end. Right-thinking French people would be with him, and he would treat any who fought against him as rebels with no right to the protection of the laws of war. Any towns or villages which resisted him would be burned to the ground.

Far from encouraging the people of France to take his side, the Duke's manifesto merely hardened French resolve. It also drove a further wedge between the French and their king, whose restoration to absolute power was now the stated aim of France's enemies. On 10 August 1792, an angry crowd stormed the Tuileries Palace, forcing the King and his family to seek shelter with the Assembly. Three days later, Louis XVI went from being a refugee to a prisoner, with the Assembly locking him up in the Tour du Temple in Paris. And three days after that, Brunswick's invasion began.

In battle after battle, the Revolutionary French Army crumbled before the onslaught of the disciplined Prussian infantry. The Assembly declared a state of total war, and ordered that all of the resources of France be mobilised for her defence. For the first time, war became not just the business of kings and armies, but the responsibility of each and every citizen.

And then, after a series of defeats, the *levée en masse* of the French population finally brought results. On 22 September, the French defeated Brunswick at Valmy. Overjoyed, the Assembly declared the end of constitutional monarchy, established the first French Republic, and inaugurated a new calendar with 1792 as 'Year One'. Shortly after, the Legislative Assembly replaced itself with a new revolutionary body, the National Convention.

The King remained in prison. The Girondins were partial to keeping him there, potentially to use as a hostage to negotiate the recognition of the legitimacy of the Republic with Vienna and Berlin. But louder and more radical voices prevailed. Over December and January, as the winter weather slowed the fighting along France's eastern frontier, he was tried before a Convention of 721 delegates for high treason and crimes against the state. A chest of incriminating documents suggesting collusion with the Austrians was presented as evidence. 693 members of the convention voted to find him guilty, the others abstained or were absent, and none voted to acquit.

But on the question of sentence, the Convention was more divided. Some wanted the King imprisoned, some wanted him executed, others couldn't decide between the two and wanted more evidence. In the end, Louis XVI was sent to the guillotine by a one-vote majority—288 members of the Convention voted for immediate execution, 287 for imprisonment or a delay.

The guillotine itself was an instrument of the revolution, and perversely, a manifestation of Enlightenment thinking. Dr Joseph-Ignace Guillotin had proposed a machine which would give all those condemned to death a quick, humane execution by beheading. No longer would execution by decapitation be a privilege of the aristocracy requiring the services of a skilled swordsman, and the brutal executions of the *Ancien Regime* would be confined to a darker past.

The ultimate demonstration of the Guillotine's democratic character came on 23 January 1793, when the tumbril took the deposed King to his fate at the Place de la Révolution. Louis XVI—or as he now was, plain Citizen Louis Capet—struggled not to shiver in the cold winter air and so give an impression of fear. By all accounts, the man known for being weak and vacillating as a Monarch went to his death with courage. As his head fell into the basket, there were cries of outrage and horror from his brother and sister monarchs throughout Europe. France's revolutionary government had become isolated and despised. But this did not bother the Convention; if anything, its members embraced it. Kings and Emperors might condemn them, but surely they would find support among their poor and downtrodden subjects. Already at war with Austria and Prussia, France now declared war on Great Britain, the Dutch Republic and Spain.

But the Convention had overestimated its own support in France, let alone in the rest of Europe. There were uprisings around the country, most famously in the Vendée, a conservative and strongly Catholic rural area in western France. General Charles François Dumouriez, one of the victors at Valmy, defected to the Austrians. Faced with crises like this, the Convention decided to hand over its executive power to a new body, the nine-member Committee of Public Safety. Led by Georges Danton, a towering, intimidating Jacobin with a booming voice, it promised to quickly make the hard decisions necessary to save the Revolution.

The Committee began to search for enemies, and quickly found some in the Convention itself. From 31 May to 2 June 1793, the legislature was stormed by a mass insurrection of National Guards and Jacobin radicals. Their target was the Girondins, the moderates, who were either arrested or forced out. Robespierre looked on the purge of the Girondins with approval:

> There must be one will. It must be either republican or royalist. For it to be republican, there must be republican ministers, republican newspapers, republican deputies, a republican government. Whilst the body politic suffers from revolutionary sickness and a divided will, the foreign war is a mortal illness. The internal dangers come from the bourgeois. To defeat the bourgeois, it is necessary to rally the people.

In July, he was appointed to the Committee of Public Safety. His goal was continuous revolution.

5 September 1793, the Convention, directed by the Committee of Public Safety, issued a new proclamation: 'It is time that equality bore its scythe above all heads. It is time to horrify all the conspirators. So legislators, place Terror on the order of the day! Let us be in revolution, because everywhere counter-revolution is being woven by our enemies. The blade of the law should hover over all the guilty.'[177] The next month, deposed queen Marie Antionette and twenty-two leading Girondins were condemned for high treason and sent to the guillotine. The Convention drafted a new constitution, with even better guarantees of human rights, then put it aside until some unspecified future date. A new criminal court was established, the Revolutionary Tribunal, and freed from the demands of due process.

In the winter of 1793–1794, as the French Revolutionary Armies held back the Coalition in Flanders, the Pyrenees and the Alps, the Committee of Public Safety concentrated power into its hands. The internal rebellions were suppressed with extreme violence, and when the guillotine proved too slow or inefficient, Revolutionary commanders turned to new means of mass killing. Thousands were drowned in the Loire on the orders of Jean-Baptiste Carrier, while in Lyon, General Parein had actual or suspected counter-revolutionaries herded together and massacred with cannon fire. On 5 February 1794, Robespierre gave a speech where he defended the Committee's actions:

> If virtue be the spring of a popular government in times of peace, the spring of that government during a revolution is virtue combined with terror: virtue, without which terror is destructive; terror, without which virtue is impotent. Terror is only justice prompt, severe and inflexible; it is then an emanation of virtue; it is less a distinct principle than a natural consequence of the general principle of democracy, applied to the most pressing wants of the country.
>
> It has been said that terror is the spring of despotic government. Does yours then resemble despotism? Yes, as the steel that glistens in the hands of the heroes of liberty resembles the sword with which the satellites of tyranny are armed. Let the despot govern by terror his debased subjects; he is right as a despot: conquer by terror the enemies of liberty and you will be right as founders of the republic. The government in a revolution is the despotism of liberty against tyranny. Is force only intended to protect crime? Is not the lightning of heaven made to blast vice exalted?

The next target of the lightning of heaven was Robespierre's old mentor, Jacobin leader Georges Danton, and his associates. Convicted of financial irregularity and leniency to the enemies of the Revolution, they were sent to the guillotine in March. Robespierre's power was now approaching its zenith. Not satisfied to transform France physically, he also set out to transform it spiritually. In the place of Christianity, he established a new deist religion, the Cult of the Supreme Being. In four years, France had gone from having an absolute Catholic monarch to an absolutist deist dictator.

***

As blood-soaked terror descended on France and war consumed Europe, the advocates of the Enlightenment found themselves beset by doubts. Was this what Enlightenment in practice looked like? The rise and fall of the blade of the guillotine, the jeering mob, tyranny and gunfire? Was this the natural destination of the road which had been walked by Spinoza, Locke, Hume, Smith, Kant and the *philosophes*?

By then, most of the key figures of the Enlightenment were dead. David Hume had died in 1776, Lord Kames in 1782, Voltaire in 1778, Denis Diderot in 1784 and Adam Smith in 1790. At least fifty-six *Encyclopédists* were still alive in 1789, but most were elderly and kept a low profile. Some were politically active, usually in support of the Gironde.

Alexandre Deleyre (1726–1796) was the author of the article on the pin, one of the symbols of the Enlightenment's merger of learning and craft, as well as, ironically as events would later show, the article on fanaticism. Elected to the National Convention as a Girondin, he advocated for mass education and voted for the execution of Louis XVI. Caught up in the purge of the Girondins, he fled and was able to avoid arrest. Antoine Allut, author of an article on glass production, was not so lucky. A supporter of the Gironde and opponent of the Jacobins, he was executed in June 1794.

The Marquis de Condorcet (1743–1794) was another Enlightenment figure who was swept up in the Revolution and fell afoul of the Jacobins. A mathematician, liberal political thinker and advocate of free markets and equal rights for women and non-Europeans, he became an early supporter of the Revolutionary government and was elected to the Revolutionary Legislative Assembly in 1791. Pushing for reforms of the education system and women's suffrage, he rose to become the Secretary of the Assembly. Opposing the death penalty, he voted to spare Louis XVI's life. Denounced by Robespierre during the purge of the Girondins, a warrant was issued for his arrest in October 1793. In March 1794, on the run from the Revolutionary authorities, he stopped at an inn. Feeling particularly hungry, he ordered a twelve-egg omelette. It was a fatal error—only a nobleman would eat so many eggs at once. He was arrested, and a few days later, found dead in his cell. Whether his death was murder or suicide remains unknown.

Guillaume-Chrétien de Lamoignon de Malesherbes, aristocrat and lawyer of liberal ideas, was similarly unlucky. As the minister responsible for censorship in the government of Louis XV, he allowed the *Encyclopédie* to be published, and so made a critical contribution to the spread of Enlightenment thought. He acted as Louis XVI's defence counsel before the National Convention, but failed to save his client. Subsequently, he was unable to save himself. On 23 April 1794, in a particularly vile act of Jacobin brutality, he was sent to the guillotine with his daughter and grand-daughter.

Across the Atlantic, Washington's cabinet discussed the alarming situation in France in April 1793. They decided to keep their alliance with France, but not go to war for its sake and remain neutral. Jefferson remained sympathetic to the cause of the Revolution, but was horrified by its violence, for which he blamed (oddly) Marie Antionette. Otherwise the American Founding Fathers had their suspicions of mass democracy confirmed. In Federalist Paper 10, James Madison had written that pure democracies '… have ever been spectacles of turbulence and contention; have ever been found incompatible with personal security or the rights of property; and have in general been as short in their lives as they have been violent in their deaths'.[178] This was such an example.

***

Unsurprisingly, the brutality of the revolution turned public opinion against the Enlightenment. Catherine the Great of Russia had been a friend of the *philosophes*, but in 1794 she had come around to the view 'that the aim of the *philosophes* was to overturn all thrones, and that the *Encyclopédie* was written with no other end in view than to destroy all kings and all religions'.[179] In a debate in the House of Lords in 1793, Lord Lansdowne implied that Adam Smith's *Wealth of Nations* had helped promote the ideas which led to the French Revolution.[180]

Just as the conservative critics of the Enlightenment were emboldened, its advocates were fractured. The Revolution was famously savaged by the Anglo-Irish Whig MP Edmund Burke (1729–1797) in his *Reflections on the Revolution in France* (1790). A classical liberal and advocate for the self-government of the American colonies, Burke nonetheless saw almost nothing to like in what had happened in France. Compared to the orderly English Revolution of 1688, the French Revolution had been little more than an exercise in brigandry.

As he wrote in *An Appeal from the New to the Old Whigs* (1791):

> What was done in France was a wild attempt to methodize anarchy; to perpetuate and fix disorder. That it was a foul, impious, monstrous thing, wholly out of the course of moral nature. He undertook to prove, that it was generated in treachery, fraud, falsehood, hypocrisy, and unprovoked murder. ... That by the terror of assassination they had driven away a very great number of the members, so as to produce a false appearance of a majority.—That this fictitious majority had fabricated a constitution, which as now it stands, is a tyranny far beyond any example that can be found in the civilized European world of our age.[181]

Burke, in turn, was savaged by American Revolutionary Thomas Paine (1736–1809). Paine was born in England but migrated to the American colonies in time to join the Revolution there, and his pamphlet *Common Sense* (1776) became a best-seller in support of the American cause. Returning to England, he wrote *The Rights of Man* (1791) in defence of the French Revolution and as a direct response to Burke. His criticisms were so sharp he was prosecuted for seditious libel, and so left England for France.

Paine was initially successful. Despite not being able to speak French, he was elected to the Assembly in September 1792 as a Girondist. But he, like the rest of his party, ended up as a target of the Jacobins. In December

1793, he was arrested. He escaped execution in the purges of early 1794 by a lucky chance. Each night, the gaoler moved through the prison and made a chalk mark on the door of those who were to be taken to the guillotine the following morning. Paine had been condemned to die, but in the darkness the gaoler did not notice that his cell door was open and made the chalk mark on the inside. Paine survived.

In the end, Robespierre went the way of his enemies. Denounced by the Convention and condemned by the Revolutionary Tribunal, he went to the guillotine with his close associates on 28 July 1794. The Terror died with him. Paine was released in November, and returned to the United States. There, he wrote *The Age of Reason*, a defence of deism and an attack on organised religion. He became an early advocate for social welfare programs such as public health and education, although his irreligion made him something of an outsider in early America. Today, the two sides of the Whig tradition, represented by Burke and Paine, are reflected in the modern mainstream political right and left respectively.

***

By the time of Robespierre's Fall, thousands had died on the guillotine, and many times more had fallen to the bullet or bayonet. After another decade of political upheaval, Napoleon Bonaparte was crowned Emperor by Pope Pius VII in 1804. And so the Revolution, which had begun to deliver the people of France from an absolute monarchy, an oppressive church and an unfairly-privileged aristocracy ended with an Emperor being crowned by the Pope. It was a sad story, but one to be repeated many times in the twentieth century. George Orwell wrote *Animal Farm* with the Russian Revolution in mind, but it applies equally well to the French.

The Napoleonic Wars ended in 1815, leaving Europe's major powers deeply hostile to further change. Thanks to a volcanic eruption in Indonesia filling the atmosphere with clouds of ash 1815 was an unusually cold year, and the terms of peace settled at Vienna created a political freeze across the continent to match the meteorological one. Napoleon had barely been shipped off to Saint Helena before Austria, Prussia and Russia entered into the Holy Alliance, declaring their intention to uphold the status quo and restrain the spread of liberal, secular, democratic or revolutionary ideas. Conservative statesmen such as Klemens von Metternich in Austria and Lord Liverpool in Britain began lengthy terms in office. Further pushes for social reform were met with violence, such as the Peterloo Massacre of protestors in Manchester in 1819.

New thinkers rose to prominence. Joseph de Maistre (1753–1821), a nobleman of Savoy, knew exactly why Europe had gone through a generation of violence. Mankind, he wrote, was naturally savage, and only a strong monarchy and strong church would restrain his worst instincts. No constitution written by men would be legitimate; the only legitimate constitution would come from God. Men never respect what they have made, and so they would only follow a hereditary sovereign holding all the power necessary to maintain social order. In *Considerations on France* (1797), he snidely dismissed the 1795 French Constitution as completely impractical, and rejected the Enlightenment idea of universality in the process. 'In the course of my life, I have seen Frenchmen, Italians, Russians, etc.; I am even aware, thanks to Montesquieu, that one can be a Persian' he wrote. 'But, as for Man, I declare that I have never met him in my life. If he exists, I certainly have no knowledge of him ... This constitution is capable of being applied to all human communities from China to Geneva. But a constitution which is made for all nations is made for none.'[182]

When Denis Diderot was imprisoned at the Château Vincennes, his father had told him he would have kept himself out of trouble if he prayed to God and obeyed the King. This was the advice men like Liverpool, Metternich and de Maistre now gave to everyone in Europe.

***

Others rejected the Enlightenment for philosophical or aesthetic reasons. A number of nineteenth-century writers, artists and philosophers argued that science and reason alone could not lead to a fulfilling life, and there was much to the human experience which was emotional, inexplicable or supernatural. They looked to the past, particularly to the Middle Ages and the pre-Christian traditions of pagan northern Europe. Today, we refer to them as the Romantic Movement. Romantic works of art and literature include the *Ivanhoe*, *Rob Roy* and *The Lady of the Lake* by Scottish novelist Sir Walter Scott (1771–1832) and the operas of Richard Wagner (1813–1883). Many Romantic writers were suspicious of the Enlightenment idea of progress. In *Frankenstein*, an 1818 novel by Mary Shelley, science gone wrong produces a supernatural monster. American writer Henry David Thoreau (1817–1862) took to living in a cabin in the woods to simplify his life as much as possible, and wrote about his experience in *Walden* (1854).

The Romantic movement was closely tied to nineteenth-century nationalism. While the Enlightenment had emphasised the universality of man, the nationalists argued there was some connection between people of the same country and the land they lived in which could not be explained only with reason. The rightful place of an Italian was in an Italian state in Italy, the rightful place of a German in a unified German state in Germany, and so on. These connections between history, land and people couldn't be explained; they just were.

Along with Romanticism came a renewed interest in religion, and the early nineteenth century saw a series of religious revivals in Europe and America. For example, the Second Great Awakening in the United States. In a changing world, there was more of a desire to hold onto things which did not change. Biblical literalism spread within various Protestant denominations.

The Romantic movement had its wellspring in the works of Jean-Jacques Rousseau (1712–1778), the *Encyclopédist* and friend of Denis Diderot. Rousseau was a *philosophe* and is often called an Enlightenment figure, but he broke sharply with the others and his writing became fiercely-critical of the ideas behind the Enlightenment.

Rousseau is a difficult man to come to terms with. He led a very irregular life, which appears even more shocking in posterity as he played up his manifold sins in his colourful (and perhaps not entirely factual) autobiography *Confessions*. Like a modern celebrity, he made himself sound as bad as possible to shock his audience.

He came from a Calvinist family in Geneva. But having little enthusiasm for any of the trades he was apprenticed in he left his native city, and took various jobs over his life, often as a secretary to wealthy and aristocratic men and women (or in the case of at least one of his female employers, probably more than a secretary). In Paris, he fell in with Diderot and the *philosophes*. Among other entries, he wrote the article on 'political economy' for *Encyclopédie*. In Paris, he took up with a plain and ignorant seamstress named Thérèse Levasseur, and seemed to take some perverse delight in foisting her society on his intellectual friends and visa-versa. She bore him five children, all of whom he abandoned at the foundling hospital. He maintained affairs with other women.

In his *Discourse on the Arts and Sciences* (1750), he argued that the arts and sciences corrupt human morality and we would be better off living in the forest naked like savages. This essay attracted a lot of controversy and made him famous. In his *Discourse on the Origin and Basis of Inequality Among Men* (1754) he claimed that humans were naturally good but corrupted by institutions, and in particular, private property was responsible for most of society's ills. His argument is a direct attack on Locke:

> The first man who, having enclosed off a piece of land, got the idea of saying 'This is mine' and found people simple enough to believe him was the true founder of civil society. What crimes, what wars, what murders, what miseries and horrors would someone have spared the human race who, pulling out the stakes or filling in the ditch, had cried out to his fellows, 'Stop listening to this imposter. You are lost if you forget that the fruits belong to everyone and the earth belongs to no one.'[183]

If this could be resolved, Rousseau argued, we would need few laws, and common sense would suffice to govern human affairs. He sent a copy of the book to Voltaire in his semi-exile at Ferney near the Swiss border. Voltaire's response is an exemplar of Enlightenment criticism of Romanticism:

> I have received, sir, your new book against the human race, and I thank you for it. You will please people by your manner of telling them the truth about themselves, but you will not alter them. The horrors of that human society—from which in our feebleness and ignorance we expect so many consolations—have never been painted in more striking colours: no one has ever been so witty as you are in trying to turn us into brutes: to read your book makes one long to go about on all fours. Since, however, it is now some sixty years since I gave up the practice, I feel that it is unfortunately impossible for me to resume it: I leave this natural habit to those more fit for it than are you and I. Nor can I set sail to discover the aborigines of Canada, in the first place because my ill-health ties me to the side of the greatest doctor in Europe, and I should not find the same professional assistance among the Missouris: and secondly because war is going on in that country, and the example of the civilised nations has made the barbarians almost as wicked as we are ourselves.[184]

Rousseau had unusual beliefs about religion. He insisted that he believed in God, but said no evidence was needed. But he also said all religions were equally good, which got his books banned. He was, as we might say today, spiritual rather than religious. He could be loyal to his friends, as his efforts to get Diderot out of prison show. But he could be wild and unpredictable, and openly boasted that he acted out of passion regardless of whatever society expected of him. This naturally made him challenging company, and by the end of his life he had exhausted the patience of his friends. David Hume was the last to stick by him.

Over the nineteenth and twentieth centuries, Romantic ideas worked their way into both left- and right-wing politics. On the left, they manifested themselves as criticism of progress, an idolisation of peoples living in pre-modern societies, a quasi-religious attitude to protecting the environment, and a belief in smashing unjust and exploitative systems to return people to natural egalitarian and co-operative state. Rousseau became a hero to the Jacobins in the French Revolution. On the right, they brought a rose-tinted longing for some mythical past, nationalism, masculinism and an appeal to religion and spiritualism. On both sides, Romantic thinking promoted scepticism of the Enlightenment project and enthusiasm for charismatic leaders embodying the 'national will' (a term invented by Rousseau).

In the end, though, neither the throne-and-altar conservatism of the counter-Enlightenment nor the Romantic movement and the religious revival was able to kill off the Enlightenment project. There was another Revolution in France in 1830, one which made Metternich despair of his life's work. And then, in 1848, Revolutions swept across Europe. But not in Britain, which had expanded its electoral franchise with the *Reform Act* of 1832. The lessons were clear; Europe could not go back to 1789. And over the nineteenth century, the practical effects of the Enlightenment became clear to all.

CHAPTER XIV

ESCAPING THE MALTHUSIAN TRAP

In 1836, Richard Dillingham, a convict transported from England to Tasmania for rioting, wrote a letter to his parents. In contrast to his earlier fears, he assured them, his situation was actually very good. He had been assigned to work on the farm of a prominent settler, his master was a humane man, and he now enjoyed far more material prosperity than he had known in rural Bedfordshire. He wrote:

> ... as for tea and sugar I could almost swim in it. I am allowed 2 pound of sugar and ¼ pound of tea per week and plenty of tobacco and good white bread and sometimes beef sometimes mutton and sometimes pork. This I have every day. Plenty of fruit puddings in the season of all sorts and I have two suits of cloths a year and three pairs of shoes in a year.[185]

Dillingham's letter is a stark reminder that, to most people in pre-modern societies, eating meat every day and getting new clothes twice a year were seen as luxuries. Our images of medieval and renaissance feasts with fur-wearing nobles dining from tables groaning beneath roast boar and stuffed swan applied only to the very top sliver of society. Having cheap and plentiful food and consumer goods is by far the starkest difference between the everyday lives of ordinary people in modern western countries and those in every other human society which had ever existed.

Prior to the nineteenth century, the daily wage of a labourer in most places and at most times was enough to buy between five and twenty pounds of wheat or rice.[186] In a richer society, like ancient Athens during the golden age, it pushed thirty pounds, but didn't much exceed it.

By comparison, someone in modern Australia today working a full day at minimum wage could buy 125 pounds of rice with their daily earnings.[187] This is obviously a crude measure, as people need to buy things to survive other than grain, and different societies have had different tax rates. But the basic point is that, in relative terms, we produce far more of everything now for the same amount of work than we have for most of our history.

In his 1798 *Essay on the Principle of Population*, Thomas Malthus (1766–1834) noted that more resources would enable population growth, but a bigger population would take up more resources. And as population increased exponentially whereas production increased arithmetically, the demand for food and other goods would quickly outstrip supply and people would starve. Today, this is called the Malthusian trap. And ironically, Malthus was writing just as his country was on the verge of becoming the first human society in history to break out of it.

Today, we use Gross Domestic Product (GDP) as a measure of how much an economy produces. And by extension, how much is available for people to consume, be it food, clothing, housing, medicine, education, recreation, or any other good or service they can buy themselves or is paid for through their taxes. Measuring GDP in pre-modern times is difficult, but from the data we do have, it appears that GDP per capita has been fairly level for most of human history before turning upwards suddenly in Britain sometime between 1760 and 1830, and following soon after in the United States, the British colonies, and the rest of northern and western Europe.[188] Richard Dillingham was starting to see the effects of this change when he wrote his 1836 letter.

Let's look a bit deeper at the difference in living standards between people before this improvement in living standards and after it. According to Liza Picard's study of everyday life in eighteenth-century London, a skilled labourer would make about twenty shillings a week, while an unskilled would make nine.[189] A loaf of bread cost a penny (one-twelfth of a shilling), a dinner of cold meat, bread and beer cost sixpence (six pennies), a second-hand workman's coat cost five shillings, and a stout pair of shoes seven shillings. In other words, buying a second-hand coat would cost an unskilled labourer more than half a week's earnings, and a pair of shoes would cost nearly the entire week's wage. Choosing between food and clothing was a reality in pre-industrial societies. In 1842 Ukrainian author Nikolai Gogol published a short story called 'The Overcoat', about a man who needs to get used to going hungry in the evenings so he can afford a new coat to keep himself from freezing in the St Petersburg winter—it is hardly far-fetched. The only big expense significantly cheaper in the eighteenth century than now is housing—a furnished room could be rented for two shillings a week. But our houses are far better in every way, from their insulation to their safety to their electricity and running water.

Let's imagine Dillingham was sent to Australia today, and got a job making the current statutory minimum wage of $18.26 per hour. After tax, about $629 for a forty-hour week. As an assigned convict, he wouldn't have been paid, but we can consider how much he could get for his forty hours of labour.

From my local Coles, he could buy his two pounds (or one kilogram) of sugar for $1.80. A 250-gram box of leaf tea (half a pound) costs $4.50. A loaf of plain white bread costs $1.80, or, if we take 'good white bread' to mean a better-than-basic loaf, a cobb loaf costs $2.50. Lamb sells for $12.00 to $25.00 a kilogram, and tinned meat is much cheaper. As for fruit puddings, he could have a 700-gram Christmas pudding for $4.00 (season permitting), or a 900-gram 'luxury pudding' for $12.00. Or if it's not the holiday season, 375 grams of mixed dried fruit for $2.30. From the Kmart next door to my Coles, he could buy jeans for $20 and cotton

T-shirts for $10. Or, as he needs to be equipped to work on a farm, he could buy work trousers for $25, and a long-sleeve work shirt for $25, work boots for $49 and a hat for $7. How about a second-hand coat? Across the road from Kmart and Coles is a large shop selling second-hand clothes—men's coats go for about $30. For about a third of a week's after-tax pay, Dillingham could get an entire new outfit of work clothes. Back in his time, he would need to save half a week's pay just to buy the coat.

Economic growth was not new in 1800—Europe's economies had been slowly but steadily growing since the Middle Ages. But the growth northern and western Europe and the United States experienced after about 1830 was entirely new and unprecedented. Great Britain led, becoming the first society in human history to break out of the Malthusian Trap. The growth of the economy made the necessities of life far cheaper, and by the turn of the twentieth century, allowed for the funding of systems of social security such as disability and old-age pensions, which would have been unaffordable to any society before then. In the U.K., GDP per capita went from £2,500 in 1815 to £6,000 in 1914.[190]

Raising the living standards of everyone in a society is extremely difficult, and the time it took for the economy to really start growing shows just how much groundwork was needed. The Industrial Revolution had started in Britain in 1760, but for six decades ordinary British people saw little change to their lives, unless they were directly hired into the mills and factories or lost their land and jobs through the fencing of commons and the decline of cottage industries. According to economic historian Joel Mokyr, the growth rested on two pillars—one was empiricism, the other improved institutions (as he put it, the removal of the 'predators, pirates and parasites' who had previously held sway over society).[191] In other words, the ideas of the Enlightenment applied in practice.

***

In Europe, from the second half of the nineteenth century, life expectancy began to improve dramatically.[192] Economic growth was a cause of this, but modern medicine was another. Medicine represented a real and tangible triumph of empirical thinking. In 1798, Edward Jenner discovered that cowpox could be used to vaccinate against the far more deadly smallpox. It had been known since ancient times that someone who survived infection by a deadly disease was much less likely to catch it again, but this knowledge had little practical value. There was no point deliberately infecting yourself with a disease likely to kill you to make it less likely to kill you next time you caught it. Now, with his *An Inquiry into the Causes and Effects of the Variolae Vacciniae*, Jenner had found a means of reducing the death toll of a deadly disease. In 1842 American physician Crawford Long performed an operation using diethyl ether as an anaesthetic. And in 1867, building on work by Louis Pasteur, British surgeon Joseph Lister published the results of his research on sterilisation. These three discoveries—vaccination, anaesthesia and sterilisation—completely revolutionised medicine and saved hundreds of millions from suffering and death. By the end of the nineteenth century, life expectancy had reached around sixty years in northern Europe, North America, Australia and New Zealand, an unprecedented climb. In the same countries, infant mortality had fallen to 10%.

The western world was also becoming more peaceful still. From 1815 to 1914, there were only six years in which there was a major-power war in western Europe—the Italian Wars of 1848–1849, 1859 and 1866; the Austro-Prussian War of 1866, and the Franco-Prussian War of 1870–1871. Generations passed from childhood to middle age without seeing the march of armies; something unimaginable to those who lived before 1648.

It is important not to ignore the real horrors of the nineteenth century—the workhouses, the children in factories, the abject poverty of the industrial cities, slavery, or the violence of colonisation. And while Europe was becoming more peaceful, European armies were certainly responsible for huge-scale violence outside of Europe. Wars of Independence throughout Latin America in the early nineteenth century killed upwards of half a million people. But many of these miseries were eventually mitigated within the framework the Enlightenment had created. By 1900, the world of 1512 had been left behind, at least in the western world.

The twentieth century posed even more significant challenges for the Enlightenment project. The World Wars, the Great Depression, the rise of Fascist and Communist totalitarianism and the death and enslavement of millions and, above all, the unimaginable inhumanity of the Holocaust. But it also gave us the United Nations Declaration of Human Rights, the liberation of women, the civil rights movement, penicillin, organ transplants and public healthcare. The seedling planted by the ideas of Bacon, Spinoza, Locke, Newton, Smith, the *Philosophes* and the other thinkers of the Enlightenment had borne fruit. Humanity had been shown an escape from the Malthusian trap, and the limitations imposed by the violent and oppressive instincts in our own nature.

CHAPTER XV

THE DIVERGENCE

Sometime between the year 1600 and 1800, northern and western Europe pulled decisively ahead of the rest of the world on technological knowledge and economic power. By 1900, these improvements translated into massive and unprecedented improvements in the living standards of ordinary people. In 1683, the Ottomans laid siege to Vienna. In 1798, a French Army decisively defeated a Mamluk Ottoman force in Egypt. And in 1918, British and French troops marched into the Ottoman capital of Constantinople. This advantage has continued today. The United States, the nations of northern and western Europe, Canada, Australia and New Zealand remain the world's richest countries.

Other civilisations at other times in history had overtaken their competitors, but none had done so as decisively as post-Enlightenment Europe. This jump—called the 'European Miracle' by Eric Jones or 'The Great Divergence' by Kenneth Pomeranz—was completely unprecedented and remains one of the most important single events in human history.

Historians have debated exactly when the divergence began and what caused it. Some have argued that Europe's advantages date from before 1600, perhaps stretching back to improved farming techniques and technology developed in the Middle Ages.[193] Others have argued that the divergence only came around 1800, and may have been due to a fortuitous combination of small factors rather than any single large one.[194] Pomeranz argued there was little to suggest western Europe had a decisive economic advantage before 1800, and its success was due to 'a combination of inventiveness, markets, coercion, and fortunate global conjunctures'.[195]

My view is that the divergence was due mostly to the ideas of the Enlightenment, and the economic revolution which followed it. It explains both the great divergence, but also the 'little divergence' between northern and southern Europe which saw Britain, the Netherlands and Germany leap ahead of Spain and Italy. Italy was Europe's richest and most technologically-advanced region for two centuries prior to the Enlightenment, and Spain its superpower. By 1700, both had been decisively overtaken.

First, I will look at other explanations for the divergence, and why I think they fall short. And second, I will look through other parts of the world, and explore why they did not experience the same success as northern and western Europe did.

***

The first alternative explanation is that something culturally intrinsic to Europe led to the divergence. In this view, the flourishing of western civilisation in modern times can be traced in an unbroken line back to Greco-Roman times and the adoption of Christianity in Europe. As British journalist Daniel Johnson wrote:

> ... the West is also the culmination of aeons of shared endeavour, and the site of collective memories reaching back deep into the origins of human society. Western civilisation is the cathedral of historical consciousness, the temple of time past and time future, the destination of a journey that began in the land we still call holy, with Abraham and Moses. The Bible, in both its Jewish and Christian versions, is both the repository and summation of this civilisation; its stories still speak to us across the ages in a way that no myth or epic can.[196]

In *The Politically-Incorrect Guide to Western Civilization* Anthony Esolen likewise argues that the High Middle Ages from the crowning of Otto the Great as Holy Roman Emperor in 962 to the death of Dante in 1321 were 'the bright ages', and the long-term development of Christian theology and Scholastic philosophy was necessary for the eventual breakthrough.[197] Samuel Gregg, writing for the Acton Institute, argued that the two pillars of western civilisation are reason and Christianity, with their ultimate fusion in the Christian idea of a reasonable God.[198] Under this argument, political freedom and the scientific method had their origin in the ideas of the Greeks and Romans, and Christian values such as meekness, charity, and the recognition that all people were created by God in his image that allowed them to grow and thrive.

Another more recent argument in a similar vein was made by conservative commentator Ben Shapiro in *The Right Side of History: How Reason and Moral Purpose Made the West Great* (2019). Shapiro argues that the West managed to reconcile revealed religion (embodied by Jerusalem) with reason (embodied by Athens). He argues that revealed religion without reason leads to the violence of Islamic extremism, whereas reason without moral purpose leads to the atrocities of Stalinist repression.

There is some truth to these claims. We can see in Athenian democracy and the Roman Republic some predecessors to modern liberal democracy. We still study the maths of Euclid and the physics of Archimedes, many of Europe's legal systems are based in Roman law, and European languages are filled with Latin and Greek. But we also need to avoid looking at the past with rose-coloured glasses. Much of the Greco-Roman inheritance, arguably most of it, was simply bad. Athenian democracy killed Socrates for dissenting from its established ideas. Plato's political ideas justified totalitarianism. Aristotle developed a justification for slavery and devotion to his natural philosophy left western science in chains for a millennium and a half. The Scientific Revolution was as much a rejection of the Greco-Roman tradition as a continuation of it. If we continue with Shapiro's terminology, the Enlightenment was fiercely critical of both Athens and Jerusalem, and it was only after it that the West really showed any advantage.

I have written about Christianity in Chapter II, and how I believe its formal separation of religious and secular authority was a critical factor in the Enlightenment. But I think it is much harder to argue that elements intrinsic to Christianity were the drivers behind the west's success. Christianity became the official religion of the Roman Empire in 380 AD, yet the west enjoyed no real advantage, and was often at a disadvantage, for the next twelve hundred years. In 1600, outside of small areas such as the Dutch Republic, Europe still had no real edge over the Islamic world or China in wealth, living standards, or technology. If we were to be having this discussion in the tenth century rather than the twenty-first, we'd have to conclude that Islam, Buddhism or Confucianism were all better for a society's long-term success than Christianity. Throughout history, most Christian societies have been unfree, hostile to original thought, supportive of a rigid social hierarchy, accepting of slavery, and quite happy to inflict violence on both their own members and outsiders alike.

Ultimately, this argument can explain why the scientific and industrial revolutions happened in northern and western Europe, but fails to explain why they did not happen sooner. Consider this analogy. I have never showed much athletic ability—I was picked last for the soccer team at school, when I tried to throw a discus on sports day it somehow went backwards, and anyone who has ever watched me try to play cricket quickly finds themselves somewhere between laughter and tears. So if, in my early thirties, I suddenly became faster, stronger, and more co-ordinated than I'd ever been before, and ended up as a professional athlete, it would be absurd to suggest this was just my natural talent showing through. Those who argue that western civilisation must have intrinsic advantages which have been visible all through its history are making a similar argument.

***

Secondly, some historians—and many casual commentators—have argued that the European miracle came from wealth plundered from Europe's colonial empires.[199] On the face of it, the argument looks sound. The divergence came shortly after the Age of Discovery, which is usually held to have begun in 1492 with the beginning of the Spanish colonisation of the Americas. European countries certainly gained tremendous advantages from their colonial empires. South American silver allowed the Spanish to trade on a huge scale in east Asia. Slavery in the Americas provided Britain, France and the United States with free labour worth billions (possibly trillions) of dollars in today's terms. The slave trade was integral to the growth of ports like Glasgow.

But conquest and colonialism has only rarely led to large-scale economic and technological progress, nor was having a colonial empire a pre-condition for such progress in European countries in the seventeenth century. Alexander the Great conquered an enormous empire between 336 and 323 BC, gaining mastery of centres of ancient civilisation such as Egypt, Persia and parts of India. Yet Greek civilisation did not see material progress beyond the Golden Age of Athens. Likewise, between 1206 and 1259, the Mongols conquered the largest contiguous empire the world had ever seen, gaining control of the vast wealth and technological knowledge of China and Persia. Yet there was no Mongolian miracle; no industrial revolution in Mongolia. Arab control of Indian Ocean trade routes throughout the Middle Ages did not lead to an Industrial Revolution in the Middle East. Spain and Portugal, the two European powers to seize the largest empires at the start of the Age of Discovery, were not the wealthiest or most powerful states in Europe by 1800. If slavery provided Britain with the wealth necessary for the Industrial Revolution, we still need to explain why it didn't do the same for Spain or the Ottoman Empire.

Correlation does not necessarily flow the other way, either. The Netherlands was already the wealthiest country in Europe when it began colonial expansion with the formation of the Dutch East India Company in 1602. The North German states and Scandinavian countries had few, if any, colonies, but still became rich. Germany was already one of the wealthiest and most technologically-advanced states in Europe well before the founding of the first German overseas colonies in 1884.

Similarly, some of the world's most successful countries today are former colonies of others. Finland was part of the Russian Empire from 1809 to 1917, yet today enjoys a higher GDP per capita than Russia. Taiwan (the Republic of China) and South Korea were Japanese colonies from 1895 and 1910 respectively until Japan's defeat in the Second World War in 1945. Today, both are first-world countries.

From the sixteenth to the twentieth centuries, wealth from Africa, Asia and the Americas did flow to Europe on a titanic scale. As I argued in the previous section, any explanation as to the European miracle needs to answer two questions—why did it happen in north-western Europe, and why did it in the seventeenth and eighteenth centuries. Crediting Europe's success entirely, or even largely, to colonialism fails to answer the first question, just as crediting it to some intrinsic European advantage fails to answer the second. Ironically, it's a Eurocentric explanation for Europe's rise.

***

There are a handful of other specific factors some writers have pointed at. Pomeranz highlighted that Britain had large coal deposits within a small, compact island, whereas China's largest coal deposits were in the north-west far from major coastal cities. However, while we associate the Industrial Revolution with coal, it was only required for the steam engine and metallurgy, and had no impact on the agricultural revolution or textile manufacturing.[200] Any part of the world with abundant running water could have still built waterwheel-powered factories like those which began the Industrial Revolution in Manchester in the 1760s. On the flipside, Britain's abundant and easy-to-access coal deposits didn't lead to an Industrial Revolution until after the Enlightenment. The coal was there in 1000, or 1400, or 1600, yet nobody dug it up and used it to power steam engines. Nor did the steam engine simply drop from the sky.

A much better explanation—in my view—is a decisive shift in northern Europe in the seventeenth and eighteenth centuries. In other words, the Enlightenment. Economic historian Joel Mokyr credited empiricism and good institutions for the rapid economic growth of the nineteenth century.[201] Jack Goldstone, critical of the idea of innate western superiority, credits cultural developments in seventeenth-century England, the rise of Newtonianism and the Glorious Revolution.[202] Niall Ferguson credited the 'six killer apps' of competition, science, property rights, modern medicine, consumerism and work ethic for the success of the modern west.[203] These explanations all hinge on the Enlightenment.

***

So far in this book I have focused on Europe. But to properly answer the question of why Europe had a divergence, we need to look at the rest of the world. Why was there an Enlightenment in Europe, and not elsewhere? And can we say that the failure of an Enlightenment outside northern and western Europe held back these societies?

During the period when the Enlightenment began, European civilisation had four big rivals—the three Islamic 'Gunpowder Empires' of the Ottomans (Turks), Safavids (Persians) and Mughals (Indians), as well as China under the Ming Dynasty. In 1600, any would have been a reasonable contender for the future position of global superpower.

Let's start by considering the three Islamic empires together. In terms of scientific knowledge, prosperity and power, the Islamic world was ahead of Europe for much of the Middle Ages. During the Reign of Harun al-Rashid (786–809) the centre of the world's intellectual life was in Baghdad, where scholars in the House of Wisdom were put to work translating the collected works of the Greek and Roman writers into Arabic.

Islam and Christianity were rivals for control of the territory of the erstwhile Roman Empire for the millennium from Islam's rise to the beginning of the Enlightenment. In that time, one and then the other had gained a temporary advantage. The Enlightenment gave Christian civilisation an advantage which it has never since relinquished. Islam came close to conquering Europe on two occasions. Firstly, when Islam first arose and Europe was in the Dark Ages, Islamic armies overran North Africa and Spain and were only halted in northern France by Charles Martel at the

Battle of Tours in 732. Soon after, the rise of the Carolingian Empire in France and the Carolingian Renaissance on one hand and the fracturing of the Abbasid Caliphate on the other gave Christendom the advantage in Western Europe and over the next seven centuries Spain was gradually re-conquered by 1492. Secondly, the Ottoman Empire advanced far into Eastern Europe in the seventeenth and eighteenth centuries, conquering Hungary in 1526 and laying siege to Vienna several times, most recently in 1683. At some point not long after that, though, the Islamic world fell behind Europe and never caught up.

The beginning of the West's eventual dominance could be nicely summed up in the story of three observatories. In the 1420s astronomer Ulugh Beg built an observatory in the city of Samarkand, which quickly gained a reputation as one of the great observatories in the Islamic world. It was destroyed by religious fundamentalists in 1448. In 1570, Turkish astronomer and inventor Taqī ad-Dīn, the developer of an early prototype steam engine mentioned earlier, built a similarly impressive observatory in Constantinople. Faced with concerns Taqī would be prosecuted for heresy, the Sultan closed it in 1579. In 1576, financial support from the King of Denmark allowed Tycho Brahe to begin building an observatory at Uraniborg. It was ultimately Brahe and his assistant, Johannes Kepler, who built the heliocentric model of the solar system with the aid of the telescope, invented in the Netherlands.

Why wasn't there an Enlightenment in the Islamic empires? Arguably for many of the same reasons there wasn't one in the Catholic states of southern Europe. The Ottoman Empire had adopted a formal policy of religious toleration of Christians and Jews. Provided they paid the *jizya* tax (*cizye* in Turkish), they would be left alone to practise their religions. Parts of the Empire, particularly in Europe, had non-Muslim majorities, and in some cases they were able to negotiate a very low *jizya* with the Ottoman authorities. The Empire had a very different attitude, though, towards Muslims who preached unorthodox interpretations of Islam, and a number of prominent scholars were executed for heresy, including Mollah Qabiz, Hakim Ishak and Melami Oglan Sheikh.[204] A series of destructive wars with Shi'ite Safavid Persia pushed the Sultans to cast themselves as the defenders of orthodox Sunni Islam. Historians still debate the nature and extent of the Ottoman Empire's decline, but it's clear that by the nineteenth century it was well behind Europe's great powers, the 'Sick Man of Europe'.

From the founding of the Safavid Dynasty in Persia in 1501, the Safavids set about establishing Shia Islam as the state religion and suppressing Sunnism. The Safavids were less-tolerant of non-Muslims than the Ottomans, at times persecuting Christians and Jews and forcing them to convert. But their chief targets were Sunni Muslims, as well as Sufi Muslims and the Naqtawi sect.[205] The religious wars with the Ottoman Empire made them less tolerant, along with their enemies.

India is often overlooked by historians, yet there is a good argument that India actually had the most potential of any centre of civilisation in the sixteenth century. The Mughal Empire, which ruled most of the subcontinent from 1526 to 1857, had a varied but often tolerant religious policy. Some Mughal Sultans, such as Akbar the Great (reigned 1556–1605), allowed relative freedom of religion in order to maintain harmony between his Muslim, Hindu and Sikh subjects. The subcontinent was an economic powerhouse, accounting for about a quarter of the world's GDP in 1600.[206] At least two states, Mysore and Gujarat, were as commercially vibrant as many parts of Europe.[207] In fields such as shipbuilding and metallurgy, India was ahead of, or at least equal to, Europe into the eighteenth century. However, in the early eighteenth century, the Mughal Empire went into sharp decline. Historians still debate the reasons—military defeat by the Maratha Confederacy, religious strife between Hindus and Muslims, the central government becoming oppressive and isolated, or some combination of them all. Ultimately, the Empire's political institutions proved inadequate to governing it over the long term.

China is probably the most widely-studied alternative centre of civilisation to Europe. China accounted for a quarter of the world's population and nearly 30% of its GDP in 1600.[208] China had unquestionably been the world's most technologically-advanced state for much of recorded history. The world's largest cities, including Beijing, Nanjing and Hangzhou, were in China. Gunpowder, the magnetic compass and paper, all critical to the West's own rise, were invented in China. In the early fifteenth century, Chinese treasure fleets consisting of the largest ships then afloat had undertaken voyages as far as East Africa. If there was one nation which seemed on-track to become the global superpower, it was China. Yet at some point during the Ming Dynasty (1368–1644) or Qing Dynasty (1644–1912) China was left in Europe's wake.

The question of why Europe was able to overtake China is called the Needham Puzzle, after it was originally proposed by Joseph Needham (1900–1995), a British chemist who made an extensive study of Chinese science and history. What's the solution?

There are a few related reasons why there was never a Chinese Enlightenment and Industrial Revolution. One was the centralised nature of the Chinese state. For reasons not entirely clear, the Ming Dynasty imposed a series of restrictions on ship-building and international trade in the fourteenth and fifteenth centuries called the *Haijin* or 'Sea-Ban', and the voyages of the treasure fleets ended after 1433. In competitive Europe, such a policy would have quickly led to disaster for any country which pursued it. But China was self-sufficient and secure enough not to feel its effects until it was far too late.

This centralised state was run by a famed civil service with a rigorous entry exam. But passing the exam involved memorising the Confucian classics and commentaries rather than learning any practical knowledge. Applicants would need to spend six years memorising a total of 431,286 Chinese characters.[209] This created a huge drain on society's intellectual energy, left the best young minds in the Middle Kingdom doing nothing but memorising rows and rows of text, and naturally promoted an extremely conservative style of thinking.

Perhaps for this reason, China never managed to apply its technological knowledge in the way Europe did. Chinese printing never led to an outpouring of books. The famed water clock was not reproduced throughout towns and villages nor used widely to measure scientific experiments. And while China in 1500 had all the components it needed to build a Manchester of the East—canals with locks, water power, coal and metal foundries—it never did.[210] Chinese technological knowledge remained fractured. Historian David S. Landes wrote: 'Chinese industrial history offers a number of examples of technological regression and oblivion. The machine to spin hemp was never adapted to the manufacture of cotton; cotton spinning was never mechanized; and coal/coke smelting was allowed to fall into disuse, along with the iron industry.'[211] We don't know at which point we can say for certain that Europe overtook China, but by the time of the end of the First Opium War in 1842 the imbalance was clear.

***

In his book on the Enlightenment, Anthony Pagden proposes a hypothetical scenario where the Enlightenment never happened.[212] Europe gains no advantage over the Ottoman Empire, and in the face of Ottoman power becomes even more insular and hostile to new ideas. It falls into a vicious cycle of decline and reaction—similar to the atrophy which did afflict the Ottoman Empire in reality. Finally, the story ends with Turkish troops marching into Paris.

In his *Decline and Fall of the Roman Empire*, Edward Gibbon speculated on what would have happened had Frankish king Charles Martel been defeated by invading Muslim armies at Tours in 732. 'Perhaps the interpretation of the Koran would now be taught in the schools of Oxford, and her pulpits might demonstrate to a circumcised people the sanctity and truth of the revelation of Mahomat' he wrote.[213] This, according to Pagden, could have become a reality in Gibbon's own lifetime.

It's an interesting counter-factual, and it isn't fanciful. At the start of this book I warned against the danger of assuming things couldn't have turned out any differently to how they have. In 1512, when this book begins, a future with British troops marching into Constantinople wasn't any more likely than one in which Turkish troops marched into London. The causes of Europe's rise and the great divergence are complex, and no one explanation is likely to fully account for them all. But in my view, the best explanation is the recognition of the limits of reason, empirical thinking, the toleration of dissent, universality and progress—the ideas of the Enlightenment.

CONCLUSION

The Enlightenment project continues, bringing further successes but facing challenges. From 1990 to 2015, the number of people living on less than one dollar a day dropped by over a billion.[214] Over the past twenty years, the internet has made the entirety of human knowledge available to anyone with access to a device with an internet connection. But these developments haven't been universally positive. As farming jobs disappeared men moved into manufacturing. And as these jobs disappear in the face of automation and outsourcing, some of the people who did them can find new jobs in the service industry, but many cannot. In the United States since 1985, manufacturing productivity has nearly doubled while the number of manufacturing jobs have halved.[215] But as the service jobs shrink in the face of the growth of tech giants like Amazon, where will the workers who depended on them go next? The western world now has large areas of long-term underemployment, with all the social problems this brings with it. Many poor American states, like West Virginia, are in the grip of a wave of opioid abuse. In 2017 50,000 Americans died from drug overdoses, mostly opioids.[216] More Americans under fifty now die from drugs than any other cause.

The benefits of the globalised economy have not been felt equally, and over the last fifty years, wealth inequality has grown markedly. Not just inequality of income, but inequality of total wealth owned. The share of global wealth held by the top 0.1% went from 7% in 1979 to 22% in

2012.[217] According to an analysis by the UK House of Commons Library, on current trends the top 1% will control two-thirds of global wealth by 2030.[218] It is true that the poor have grown richer, and consumer goods like televisions which were formerly luxuries are now seen as necessities. And it is also true that, in a globalised world, one creator can reach far more customers and hence make far more money from the same work and same idea. But none of these are of much comfort to unemployed blue-collar workers in towns from Ontario to Picardy who turn on their TVs of a night to see investment bankers draped in Armani stepping into cabs on Wall Street on their way to meetings with politicians in London or Tokyo.

In my early twenties I spent two years working as a farm labourer in rural British Columbia, where I met teenaged boys whose fathers and grandfathers had worked in the local mill, but who now faced no guarantee those jobs would still exist in ten years. And even if they did, they were unlikely to pay enough to buy a house in the overheated B.C. property market and raise a family of their own.

When I first moved to Melbourne, I got a job with a multinational company specialising in commercial data. There I met people whose previous job had been in Brussels and whose next job could have easily been in Hong Kong. They were in some ways the culmination of Enlightenment thinking—they benefitted from personal and economic freedom, lived well on the surplus of technology and free trade, were used to having humanity's collective knowledge at their fingertips, and treated international borders as a small inconvenience. They donated to Amnesty International and signed petitions against abuses of human rights in Myanmar. These were two very different worlds, and needless to say, the benefits of the Enlightenment were far more visible in the second.

***

There are deeper and more philosophical questions about the Enlightenment's legacy and the basis for modern western society. For a start, there's the question of whether our conception of property rights is just. Morally, it's possible to make a good argument that entrepreneurs like Bill Gates and Elon Musk are entitled to their millions. After all, they produced something which their customers willingly bought. You can also make an argument that someone who inherits wealth has inherited it through the free choice of their parent. However, what if the wealth was originally acquired by force? In some cases, we can say for certain when this happened. The current (eighteenth) Duke of Norfolk owns estates totalling 46,000 acres. The land was originally seized by William the Conqueror in the Norman Conquest of England, and after being held by different families, was given to the First Duke in 1483 by Richard III as a reward for backing his seizure of the throne. This is hardly an example of appropriating property by mixing it with your labour, as in Locke's state of nature, even though the Duke himself is not responsible for the legal system under which he inherited his title and his fortune. At the other end of the scale, almost every African-American today is the descendant of generations of men and women who had their labour stolen from them through slavery. Many indigenous peoples are descended from ancestors who had their land taken by force. Of course, it's impossible to calculate what would be the just outcome to these injustices. But the philosophical question remains, and it is an acute one for historically-disadvantaged indigenous peoples in countries like mine. Enlightenment values have been a boon to minorities in western countries in the twentieth century. Martin Luther King Jr was able to draw upon the language of the Declaration of Independence in support of the African-American Civil Rights Movement of the 1960s. But as we saw in the introduction, the Enlightenment has a mixed legacy on race. The effects of two centuries of scientific racism cannot quickly be undone, particularly when some minority groups have historically had more restrictions on their ability to succeed and fewer opportunities to learn marketable skills and accumulate wealth.

Then it's questionable whether the assumption of rational self-interest behind Adam Smith's political and economic thinking holds up in practice. People can, and do, choose things which are not rationally in their interest. Around the world in 2017, people spent some $5.7 billion on homeopathic remedies, most of which are indistinguishable from water.[219] In 2016, Americans spent $73.5 billion on lottery tickets.[220] In my country, Australia, twenty-five million people manage to spend over twelve billion dollars every year on electronic gambling machines.[221] These are games of pure chance, where few people ever make a profit, and if people made purely rational decisions, neither lotteries nor gaming machines would exist. Across the western world, people do things which are damaging to their health in the long run, like eat calorie-dense processed foods and guzzle gallons of sugary drinks. Around two-thirds of American adults are overweight; many other countries are not too far behind. Hundreds of millions of people still smoke cigarettes regularly, even though it's incontrovertible that up to half of regular smokers will die of tobacco-related illness. Lest anyone accuse me of being smugly superior to these people, I can think of many irrational choices I've made in my life which had long-term consequences. And often, I made the worst decisions in those times when I was short of money and struggling to pay the bills month-by-month.

And there are problems to which the Enlightenment project has no answer. Take the toleration of intolerance, a real puzzle for liberalism. What do we do about minority religious groups which restrict women's rights? What do we do if those women tell us that they're quite happy to remain part of the group and accept the role they've been given? Is it ever right for the state to restrict free speech when the speech promotes profoundly anti-liberal ideas, like, paradoxically, calls to restrict the free speech of others? What about ideas based on outright falsehoods? On YouTube, it's fairly easy to find videos promoting conspiracy theories, and these can sometimes lead to violence. On 27 October 2018, eleven worshippers at the Tree of Life Synagogue in Pittsburgh were massacred by a white nationalist who had spent years stewing in a toxic online environment of anti-Semitic conspiracy theories and white supremacism. But is the censoring of such speech even possible in today's interconnected world?

Some of these ideas are simply bizarre. The Flat Earth movement has gained growing support over the past few years, and in November 2017 an international conference was held in Raleigh, North Carolina.

Flat Earthers claim to be upholding the Enlightenment principles of free scientific inquiry and treating the claims of established authority with scepticism. The assumption that the Earth is flat falls apart very quickly with the slightest analysis—if the Earth was flat there would be no horizon, going higher wouldn't allow us to see further, at night the same stars would be visible from everywhere at once, it would not be possible for the sun to be on the horizon somewhere and overhead somewhere else, among dozens of other problems. Many Flat Earthers are undoubtedly joking, but enough of them are serious enough to show just how easily absurd ideas can catch on and spread. The Flat Earth movement might seem harmless, but the assumption that the modern scientific community is engaged in a conspiracy to defraud the public is not.

***

I am finishing this book in a café in Footscray, about five kilometres to the west of central Melbourne. Melbourne's west used to be one of Australia's industrial heartlands, with factories, working-class Irish-Australians living in rows of little cottages, Catholic churches and Irish pubs. Things are very different now. The factories are mostly gone, and many of Footscray's residents now commute daily into central Melbourne to work white-collar jobs. Following the Second World War, new waves of immigrants came— first the Greeks and Italians, then the Vietnamese in the 1970s, and more recently, Chinese, Indians and Africans. The census data from the Australian Bureau of Statistics tells the story.[222] In the city of Maribyrnong (which includes Footscray) 46.3% of residents were born overseas and fewer than half of households are exclusively English-speaking. The top alternative languages are (in order) Vietnamese, Italian, Greek, Cantonese and Mandarin. Footscray is now a minority-majority area. The café I am sitting in is owned and worked by Vietnamese-Australians. Among the customers are a Vietnamese couple, some elderly men speaking in slow and sonorous Italian, and two very tall African men in strikingly-bright shirts and sport coats. Looking out the window across the road, I can see a supermarket with its name written in English, Vietnamese and Chinese.

Footscray is more educated and has more white-collar workers than it used to, but the City of Maribyrnong is poorer than average for the Melbourne metropolitan area. Average weekly income is $592, compared to $644 for the state of Victoria and $662 for Australia overall. Unemployment is 7.9%, compared to a Victorian average of 6.6%. Education-wise, the area is about average—24% of residents have been to university, compared to the Victorian average of 24.3%. It is gentrifying, but it is not rich yet.

Why should I finish a book about the Enlightenment in a café in Melbourne's inner west? Because it's here, for me, that the benefits of the Enlightenment are real. When we hear 'The Enlightenment', we think of thick and inaccessible books written by long-dead philosophers sketched in profile. But even though most of the people with me in this café would have never heard of John Locke, Baruch Spinoza, Adam Smith, or Immanuel Kant, they have benefitted tremendously from the spread of the systems of ideas they promoted. Footscray is a poor area with its fair share of social problems—poverty, crime, substance abuse—but it is also an area where most residents live productive and peaceful lives. People from all parts of the world, following all sorts of religions, live together mostly in harmony. Former refugees now own and manage successful businesses. People who were considered expendable back in Cambodia or South Sudan are now citizens who vote in elections and send their children to school. Given humanity's troubled history, Footscray is a remarkable achievement.

At the start of this book, I emphasised that the life I have now is not the natural state of humanity but an aberration. Poverty, oppression and violence are the norm—my neighbourhood, and western countries generally, are an exception. Asking how this exception came about, and how it might continue, improve and spread to all of the world's human beings was what led me to write this book. 'What crazy projects people have!' Denis Diderot comments in the article on 'Project' in *Encyclopédie*.

In this book, I have written about how the breakdown of Scholastic philosophy and central religious authority in north-western Europe in the sixteenth century allowed for new ideas to take hold—the recognition of the limits of reason, empirical thinking, the toleration of dissent, universality and progress. I have then written about how these ideas led to the scientific method, constitutional government, human rights, the free market economy and a society which is richer, more peaceful and less painful. The Enlightenment project is far from complete, and we cannot rely on an understanding of the past to fix the problems of the future. But an understanding of the past certainly helps.

Fortunately, defending the Enlightenment doesn't require us to read and memorise the books of Spinoza, Locke, Hume or Voltaire. We can be sceptical but persuadable, acknowledging the limits of our own reason. We can recognise Bacon's idols, and when we read contentious claims about science we can follow them to see if they lead back to a study published in a reputable journal. We can accept that suppressing bad ideas might not make them go away, although, sadly, people who wholeheartedly believe them may not be amenable to persuasion. We can distrust systems of thinking which divide us into arbitrary categories. Like Spinoza, we can wish for the same good we would like for ourselves for all others. Like the *Encyclopédists*, we can gather up useful knowledge about the world around us. As Kant implores us, we can dare to know.

'What is Enlightenment?' asked Immanuel Kant in 1784. Ultimately, the Enlightenment was when we took our fate into our own hands. We did not simply pray for divine intervention or hope for a better world in the afterlife; we were able to make genuine improvements to our lives in the here and now. The Enlightenment meant liberation from the brutal constraints of the world we were born into and from some of the worst excesses of our own nature. It was unexpected and remarkable, but also the best thing that ever happened to those of us fortunate enough to live in countries where Enlightenment thinking has taken hold. It is not perfection, but it is improvement. It is the cause of the success of the world's most successful countries. Sitting here in a café in Footscray, typing on a laptop and eating a croissant, I am its beneficiary. So are hundreds of millions of others.

NOTES

1 The account of Servetus' trial and execution is from Philip Schaff, 'Servetus: His life. Opinions, Trial, and Execution' in *History of the Christian Church*, 8 vols. (Hagenau: Simon & Schuster Inc., 1910), vol. 8, [page number], Christian Classics Ethereal Library <http://www.ccel.org/s/schaff/history/8_ch16.htm> and Gabriel Sánchez Veláquez, 'Servetus and the Unity of God', in Juan Naya and Marian Hillar (eds), *Michael Servetus, Heartfelt: Proceedings of the International Servetus Congress, Barcelona, 20–21 October 2006* (United States: University Press of America, 2011), p. 38.
2 Thomas Paine, *The Age of Reason*, eBook edn. (Adelaide: University of Adelaide, 2014), Part I <https://ebooks.adelaide.edu.au/p/paine/thomas/p147a/part1.html>.
3 David Garber, 'Physics and Foundations' in Katherine Park and Lorraine Datson (eds), *The Cambridge History of Science—Volume III: Early Modern Science* (United Kingdom: Cambridge University Press, 2006), p. 21.
4 Baruch Spinoza, *Ethics*, Part IV.
5 Justin E.H. Smith, 'The Enlightenment's Race Problem, and Ours', *The New York Times* [website], (updated 10 Feb. 2013) <https://opinionator.blogs.nytimes.com/2013/02/10/why-has-race-survived/?ref=opinion>.
6 Immanuel Kant, *Lectures on Physical Geography*, 9:316, cited from Pauline Kleingeld 'Kant's Second Thoughts on Race' *The Philosophical Quarterly*, Vol 57, No 229, October 2017, p. 574.
7 King K Holmes et al., 'Chapter 1: Major Infectious Diseases: Key Messages from Disease Control Priorities', 3rd edn., *The World Bank* [website], (updated 3 Nov. 2017) <https://www.ncbi.nlm.nih.gov/books/NBK525197/>.
8 Daniel Stadlbauer, et al., 'Repeated cross-sectional sero-monitoring of SARS-CoV-2 in New York City', *Nature*, vol. 590 (2021), p. 146–150 <https://doi.org/10.1038/s41586-020-2912-6>.

9   Alex Woodward, 'Coronavirus: Televangelist Kenneth Copeland "blows wind of God" at Covid-19 to "destroy" pandemic', *The Independent* [website], (updated 6 Apr. 2020) <https://www.independent.co.uk/news/world/americas/kenneth-copeland-blow-coronavirus-pray-sermon-trump-televangelist-a9448561.html>.

10 'France teacher attack: Seven charged over Samuel Paty's killing', *BBC News* [website], (updated 22 Oct. 2020) <https://www.bbc.com/news/world-europe-54632353>.

11 Ahmet T. Kuru, 'Execution for a Facebook post? Why blasphemy is a capital offense in some Muslim countries', *The Conversation* [website], (updated 21 Feb. 2020) <https://theconversation.com/execution-for-a-facebook-post-why-blasphemy-is-a-capital-offense-in-some-muslim-countries-129685>.

12 Katherine Brown, '2020 Tied for Warmest Year on Record, NASA Analysis Shows', *NASA* [website], (updated 15 January 2021) <https://www.nasa.gov/press-release/2020-tied-for-warmest-year-on-record-nasa-analysis-shows>.

13 'Antarctica logs highest temperature on record of 18.3C', *BBC* [website], (updated 7 February 2020) <https://www.bbc.com/news/world-51420681>.

14 'Reported new record temperature of 38°C north of Arctic Circle', *World Metrological Organisation* [website], (updated 23 Jun. 2020) <https://public.wmo.int/en/media/news/reported-new-record-temperature-of-38%C2%B0c-north-of-arctic-circle>.

15 Jeff Masters, 'Death Valley, California, may have recorded the hottest temperature in world history', *Yale Climate Connections* [website], (updated 17 Aug. 2020) <https://yaleclimateconnections.org/2020/08/death-valley-california-may-have-recorded-hottest-temp-in-world-history/>.

16 Christopher C. Burt, 'An Investigation of Death Valley's 134°F World Temperature Record', *Weather Underground* [website], (updated 24 October 2016) <https://www.wunderground.com/blog/weatherhistorian/an-investigation-of-death-valleys-134f-world-temperature-record.html>.

17 See, for example, NASA climate resources at <https://climate.nasa.gov/> the collected reports of the Intergovernmental Panel for Climate Change (IPCC) at <https://www.ipcc.ch/reports/>.

18 'Attribution of the Australian bushfire risk to anthropogenic climate change', *World Weather Attribution* [website], (updated 10 January 2020) <https://www.worldweatherattribution.org/bushfires-in-australia-2019-2020/>; 'The Royal Commission into National Natural Disaster Arrangements Report', *Royal Commission into National Natural Disaster Arrangements* [website], (updated 28 Oct. 2020), p. 55 <https://naturaldisaster.royalcommission.gov.au/>.

19 Max Roser, Hannah Ritchie and Bernadeta Dadonaite, 'Child and Infant Mortality', *Our World in Data* [website], (updated Nov. 2019), <https://ourworldindata.org/child-mortality>.
20 Max Roser, 'Ethnographic and Archaeological Evidence on Violent Deaths', *Our World in Data* [website], (updated 2 Aug. 2013) <https://ourworldindata.org/ethnographic-and-archaeological-evidence-on-violent-deaths>.
21 Paul E. Lovejoy, 'Slavery in Africa' in eGad Heuman and Trevor Burnard (eds), *The Routledge History of Slavery* (United States: Routledge, 2011) page number.
22 Peter H. Wilson, *Europe's Tragedy: A History of the Thirty Years' War* (United Kingdom: Allen Lane, 2009), p. 790.
23 Gómez Moreno and de Mata Carriazo, 1962, 516 ff, cited in Perez Moreda, 'Spain' in eds Guido Alfani and Cormac Ó Gráda, *Famines in European History* (United Kingdom: Cambridge University Press, 2017), p. 52.
24 J. N. Hays, *The burdens of disease: epidemics and human response in western history* (United States: Rutgers University Press, 2003), p. 58.
25 Paul Heyman, Leopold Simons, and Christel Cochez, 'Were the English sweating sickness and the Picardy sweat caused by hantaviruses?', *National Library of Medicine*, vol. 6, issue 1 (2014), p. 151–171, at p. 157.
26 Raphael Holinshed, *Chronicles of England, Scotland, and Ireland*, 6 vols (London: J Johnson, 1807–1808), vol 3, p. 735–6.
27 John Hostettler, *A History of Criminal Justice in England and Wales* (United Kingdom: Waterside Press, 2009), p. 69.
28 S.H. Burke, *The Men and Women of the English Reformation* (London: R. Washbourne, 1870), p. 240.
29 Terrateig, Baron de., *Politica en Italia del Rey Catolico, 1507–1516: correspondencia inedita con el embajador Vich*. 2 vols. Madrid, 1963, p. 182, Cited from Stephen Bowd, 'Mass Murder in the Italian Wars', 10 November 2016, <http://research.shca.ed.ac.uk/mass-murder/2016/11/10/the-machiavellian-massacre/>.
30 Joyce Appleby, *Shores of Knowledge: New World Discoveries and the Scientific Imagination* (United States: W. W. Norton and Company, 2013), p. 25.
31 Eltjo Buringh, Jan Luiten Van Zanden, 'Charting the "Rise of the West": Manuscripts and Printed Books in Europe, A Long-Term Perspective from the Sixth through Eighteenth Centuries', *The Journal of Economic History*, vol. 69, issue 2 (2009), p. 417.
32 Thomas Aquinas, *Summa Theologica* I–II, questions 90–96.
33 David Garber, 'Physics and Foundations', *The Cambridge History of Science—Volume III: Early Modern Science*, ed. Katherine Park and Lorraine Datson (United Kingdom: Cambridge University Press, 2006), p. 26.
34 Immanuel Kant, *Answering the Question: What is Enlightenment*, trans. Mary C. Smith (United States: Columbia University, 1784) <http://www.columbia.edu/acis/ets/CCREAD/etscc/kant.html>.

35 Matthew 22:15-22, Mark 12:13-17, Luke 20:20-26.
36 John Knox, *The Liturgy of John Knox: Received by the Church of Scotland in 1564* (Glasgow: University Press, 1886), p. 243–244.
37 Peter H. Wilson, *Europe's Tragedy: A History of the Thirty Years' War* (United Kingdom: Allen Lane, 2009), p. 465.
38 Ibid, p. 787–789.
39 Ibid, p. 789.
40 Zack Beauchamp, '600 years of war and peace, in one amazing chart', *Vox* [website], (updated 24 Jun. 2015) <https://www.vox.com/2015/6/23/8832311/war-casualties-600-years>.
41 Gerhard von Glahn and James Larry Taulbee, *The Law of Nations: An Introduction to Public International Law* (New York: Routledge, 2017), p. 96.
42 Arthur Herman, *The Scottish Enlightenment: The Scots' Invention of the Modern World* (London: Fourth Estate, 2003), p. 23.
43 John Walsh, 'Austen power: 200 years of Pride and Prejudice', *The Independent* [website] (updated Jan. 2013) <https://www.independent.co.uk/arts-entertainment/books/features/austen-power-200-years-of-pride-and-prejudice-8454448.html> and currency calculation from <https://www.measuringworth.com>.
44 Gordon Marshall, *Presbyteries and Profits: Calvinism And the Development of Capitalism In Scotland, 1560–1707* (Oxford: Clarendon Press, 1980), p. 118–119.
45 Ibid, p. 225.
46 Plato, *Apology*, trans. Benjamin Jowett [(place, year)] available at <http://classics.mit.edu/Plato/apology.html>.
47 Thomas Aquinas, *Summa Theologica*, Treatise on the Theological Virtues, Question 11, Of Heresy, trans. the Fathers of the English Dominican Province (1947).
48 Cyril Glassé and Huston Smith, *The New Encyclopedia of Islam* (United States: Rottman & Littlefield Publishers Inc, 1989), p. 491–492.
49 See, for example, John B. Henderson, *The Construction of Orthodoxy and Heresy: Neo-Confucian, Islamic, Jewish and Early Christian Patterns* (United States: State University of New York Press, 1998), p. 5.
50 John Foster, *The Church of the T'ang Dynasty* (United Kingdom: SPCK, 1939), p. 40, cited from <http://www.religion-online.org/book-chapter/chapter-5-christianity-in-china/>.
51 From the Sanskrit text, Tattvasaṃgraha and Tibetan text Jñānasamuccayasāra, cited in the *Encyclopedia of Buddhism*, ed. Damien Keown and Charles S. Prebish (United Kingdom: Routledge, 2009), p. 151.
52 This was Cayetano Ripoll, a schoolteacher prosecuted for rejecting the teachings of the Catholic Church and promoting deism. The Inquisition wanted him burned at the stake, but the secular authorities opted to hang him.

53 Jonathan I. Israel, *The Dutch Republic: Its Rise, Greatness and Fall 1477–1806 (The Oxford History of Early Modern Europe)*, (Oxford: Clarendon Press, 1995), p. 4.
54 Ibid, p. 4.
55 Ibid, p. 106.
56 James Madison, Federalist Paper 20, 11 December 1787.
57 Jonathan I. Israel, *The Dutch Republic: Its Rise, Greatness and Fall 1477–1806 (The Oxford History of Early Modern Europe)*, (Oxford: Clarendon Press, 1995), p. 307, 308, 328.
58 Ibid, p. 309.
59 Ibid, p. 648.
60 Ibid, p. 678.
61 <http://web.mnstate.edu/mouch/spinoza/excomm.html>.
62 Baruch Spinoza, *Theologico-Political Treatise*, trans. Robert Wills (London: Trübner & Co., 1862).
63 Stephen Nadler, *A Book Forged in Hell: Spinoza's Scandalous Treatise and the Birth of the Secular Age* (United States: Princeton University Press, 2011), p. 222.
64 Margaret Bald, *Literature Suppressed on Religious Grounds* (New York: Facts on File, 2006), p. 102.
65 See the articles on 'Liberty of the Press' and 'Atheism'.
66 Harriet Sherwood, 'Albert Einstein's "God letter" reflecting on religion auctioned for $3m', *The Guardian* [website], (updated 5 December 2018) <https://www.theguardian.com/science/2018/dec/04/physicist-albert-einstein-god-letter-reflecting-on-religion-up-for-auction-christies>.
67 Jutta Bolt and Jan Luiten Van Zanden, 'The First Update of the Maddison Project Re-Estimating Growth Before 1820', Maddison-Project Working Paper WP-4, January 2013, <https://www.rug.nl/ggdc/historicaldevelopment/maddison/publications/wp4.pdf>, p. 12.
68 *Summa Theologica*, 2.2, question 104.
69 King James I, *The True Law of Free Monarchies: or The Reciprocal and Mutual Duty Betwixt a Free King and His Natural Subjects*, ed. Daniel Fischlin and Mark Fortier ([place], 1598; 1603; 1616) available at <http://www.wwnorton.com/college/english/nael/17century/topic_3/truelaw.htm> James was solely king of Scotland when he wrote the first edition of the tract.
70 Romans 13:1-5.
71 Descartes, R., 1643, Letter to Father ****, in J. Cottingham, R. Stoothoff, and D. Murdoch (eds), *The Philosophical Writings of Descartes* (Cambridge: Cambridge University Press, 1984), 3.230–1.
72 House of Commons Journal Vol 8: 17 October 1666, p. 636–637, at <http://www.british-history.ac.uk/commons-jrnl/vol8/pp636-637>.
73 Cited from <https://www.british-history.ac.uk/commons-jrnl/vol10/p14>.

74 Thomas Babington Macaulay, 'Chapter X', in *The History of England from the Accession of James II* (Cambridge: Cambridge University Press, 1849), p. 554–670.
75 I have cited in this book the University of Adelaide eBook edition, 2014, translated from the Latin by William Popple, at <https://ebooks.adelaide.edu.au/l/locke/john/l81t/>.
76 Arthur Herman, *The Scottish Enlightenment: The Scots' Invention of the Modern World* (London: Fourth Estate, 2003), p. 2–8.
77 Bill of Rights, 1 Wm and Mary Session 2, <http://www.legislation.gov.uk/aep/WillandMarSess2/1/2>.
78 Section 87.
79 Bertrand Russell, *History of Western Philosophy* (United Kingdom: Routledge Classics, 2004, first published 1946), p. 588.
80 François Marie Arouet de Voltaire (1694–1778). Letters on the English, The Harvard Classics, 1909–14, Letter VI.
81 Adam Smith, 'Chapter 1' in *The Wealth of Nations: Book V* [(place: publisher, date)], [page number] https://ebooks.adelaide.edu.au/s/smith/adam/s64w/chapter30.html.
82 Kenneth D. Stern, 'John Locke and the Declaration of Independence', *Cleveland State Law Review*, vol. 15 (1966), p. 193.
83 Willard Sterne Randall, *Thomas Jefferson: A Life* (United States: Harper Perennial Modern Classics, 2014), [page number], eBook Location 878, 3287.
84 Letter from Thomas Jefferson to James Madison, 30 August 1823, at <https://founders.archives.gov/documents/Jefferson/98-01-02-3728>.
85 Stanley Jevons, *The principles of science: a treatise on logic and scientific metho* (London: Macmillan & Co, 1874), p. iii.
86 Sydney Ross, 'Scientist: The story of a word', *Annals of Science*, vol. 18, issue 2 (1962), p. 65-85, <https://www.tandfonline.com/doi/pdf/10.1080/00033796200202722>.
87 Ibid, p. 71.
88 David Garber, 'Physics and Foundations' in Katherine Park and Lorraine Datson (eds), *The Cambridge History of Science—Volume III: Early Modern Science* (United Kingdom: Cambridge University Press, 2006), p. 33.
89 Lyn S. Joy, 'Scientific Explanation From Formal Causes to the Laws of Nature' in Katherine Park and Lorraine Datson (eds), *The Cambridge History of Science—Volume III: Early Modern Science* (United Kingdom: Cambridge University Press, 2006).
90 First edition: Philosophical Transactions, *May 30, 1665; 1 (1)* <http://rstl.royalsocietypublishing.org/content/1/1.toc>.
91 Noah Moxham and Aileen Fyfe, 'The Royal Society and the Prehistory of Peer Review, 1665–1965', *The Historical Journal*, vol. 61, issue 4 (December 2018), p. 863–889.

92 Cited from the Newton Project at <http://www.newtonproject.ox.ac.uk/view/texts/normalized/ALCH00069>.
93 1693 letter to John Locke, cited from David Brewster, *Memoirs of the Life, Writings, and Discoveries of Sir Isaac Newton*, vol. 2 (2009) (Edinburgh: 1855), p. 148–149 at <http://www.newtonproject.ox.ac.uk/view/texts/normalized/OTHE00078?start=par79&end=par97>.
94 Archimedes, *The Sand Reckoner*, trans. Thomas L. Heath (Cambridge, Cambridge University Press Edition, 1897).
95 Cited in Owen Gingerich, 'The Astronomy and Cosmology of Copernicus', in G. Contopoulos (ed.), *Highlights in Astronomy: Volume 3*, 1973, International Astronomical Union, p. 82.
96 Arthur Koestler, *The Sleepwalkers: A history of man's changing vision of the universe* (United Kingdom: Penguin, 1990), p. 325.
97 Richard Pogge, *Religious Objections to Copernicus* (Ohio: Ohio State University, 2005), [page number] at <http://www.astronomy.ohio-state.edu/~pogge/Ast161/Unit3/response.html>.
98 Consultant's Report on Copernicanism, 24 February 1616, at <http://shipseducation.net/galileo/library/1616docs.htm>.
99 Cited from <https://physics.info/gravitation/>.
100 Bertrand Russell, *History of Western Philosophy* (United Kingdom: Routledge Classics, 2004, first published 1946), p. 493.
101 Quote from *Cosmos*, Episode III, *The Harmony of the Worlds*.
102 Arthur Herman, *The Scottish Enlightenment: The Scots' Invention of the Modern World* (London: Fourth Estate, 2003), p. 58.
103 Adam Smith, 'Chapter II' in *Wealth of Nations*, Book V [(place: publisher, date)], [page number].
104 Irene Maver, '18th-century Glasgow', *BBC* [website], (updated 17 Feb. 2011) <https://www.bbc.co.uk/history/british/civil_war_revolution/scotland_glasgow_01.shtml>.
105 Ibid.
106 John Rae, *Life of Adam Smith* (London: Macmillan & Co, 1895), p. 10.
107 Francis Hutcheson, *A System of Moral Philosophy, in Three Books*, Book II, vol. I, R. & A. , (London: Foulis Press, 1755), p. 294.
108 Rae, *Life of Adam Smith*, p. 20.
109 Ibid, p. 31.
110 David Hume, *My Own Life*, [(place: publisher, date), page number] cited from <http://web.mnstate.edu/gracyk/courses/web%20publishing/hume%27slife.htm>.
111 Ibid.
112 *Treatise on Human Nature*, 2.3.3.
113 E. C. Mossner, *The Life of David Hume* (Oxford: Clarendon Press, 1980), p. 311.
114 *Discourse of the Common Weal of this Realm of England*, 1549, cited from

Fernand Braudel, *The Wheels of Commerce, Civilization and Capitalism 15th–18th Century* (United States: University of California Press, 1979), p. 204.
115 Paolo Malanima, *The Italian Renaissance Economy (1250–1600)* paper presented to International Conference at Villa La Pietra, Florence, 10–12 May 2008, Europe in the Late Middle Ages: Patterns of Economic Growth and Crisis; Paolo Malanima 'Italy in the Renaissance: a leading economy in the European context, 1350–1550' *The Economic History Review* Volume 71, Issue 1, February 2018, p. 3–30.
116 Cited from <http://www.vatican.va/archive/ccc_css/archive/catechism/p3s2c2a0.htm>.
117 *Summa Theologica*, question 77.
118 Aristotle, *Politics*, trans. Benjamin Jowett, (Adelaide: [year]) University of Adelaide eBook edition, Book I.
119 *Summa Theologica*, question 78.
120 Vermeersch, Arthur 'Usury' in Charles Herbermann (ed.), *The Catholic Encyclopedia* (New York: Robert Appleton Company, 1913), [page number].
121 John Munro, *Usury, Calvinism, and Credit in Protestant England: from the Sixteenth Century to the Industrial Revolution* Working Paper 439, Department of Economics, University of Toronto, 28 June 2011.
122 Renée Lettow Lerner, Enlightenment Economics and the Framing of the U.S. Constitution, 35 Harvard Journal of Law and Public Policy 37 (2012), p. 1–10, at p. 2.
123 Samuel Johnson, *The Works of Samuel Johnson, Vol 1–2* (New York: George Dearborn, 1837), p. 619.
124 Rae, p. 42.
125 Ibid, p. 56–57.
126 Book I, Chapter II, https://ebooks.adelaide.edu.au/s/smith/adam/s64w/chapter2.html.
127 Book I, Chapter IV, https://ebooks.adelaide.edu.au/s/smith/adam/s64w/chapter4.html.
128 Book IV, Chapter I, https://ebooks.adelaide.edu.au/s/smith/adam/s64w/chapter21.html.
129 Book IV, Chapter II.
130 Book V, Chapter II.
131 Book V, Chapter I.
132 Rae, p. 286.
133 Ibid, p. 290–291.
134 Immanuel Kant, *Answering the Question: What is Enlightenment*, trans. Mary C. Smith (Columbia, 1784), Columbia University edition, at <http://www.columbia.edu/acis/ets/CCREAD/etscc/kant.html>.
135 Philipp Blom, *Enlightening the World: Encyclopédie, the Book that Changed the Course of History* (United States: Palgrave Macmillan, 2005), p. xiii.

136 Voltaire, 'Christianity' in *Philosophical Dictionary* (Adelaide: University of Adelaide, [year]) University of Adelaide eBook edition, <https://ebooks.adelaide.edu.au/v/voltaire/dictionary/chapter115.html>.
137 Denis Diderot, *Jacques le Fataliste*, cited in Blom, p. 18.
138 Pagden, p. 84–86, from *La Religion de Voltaire*, Réné Pomeau, 1956, Librairie Nizet, Paris.
139 Voltaire, 'Christianity', *Philosophical Dictionary* (Adelaide: University of Adelaide, [year]) University of Adelaide eBook edition, <https://ebooks.adelaide.edu.au/v/voltaire/dictionary/chapter115.html>.
140 P. Bonnefon, 'Diderot prisionnier à Vincennes' in *Revue d'Histoire Littéraire de la France*, vi, 1899, p. 203, cited in Blom, p. 42.
141 Blom, p. 98–99.
142 Voltaire, 'Torture', *Philosophical Dictionary* <https://ebooks.adelaide.edu.au/v/voltaire/dictionary/chapter454.html>.
143 Micheline R. Ishay, *The History of Human Rights From Ancient Times to the Globalization Era* (United States: University of California Press, 2008), p. 7.
144 All quotations from the Qur'an are from the 1938 translation by Mohammed Marmaduke Pickthall, now in the public domain in Australia.
145 <https://ebooks.adelaide.edu.au/p/paine/thomas/p147r/chapter1.html>.
146 Act 3, Scene 6.
147 Act 3, Scene 3.
148 Act 4, Scene 7.
149 Hugo Grotius, *Hugo Grotius on the Law of War and Peace, Student Edition* ed. Stephen C. Neff (United Kingdom: Cambridge University Press, 2012), p. 8.
150 Ibid at p. 323.
151 Ibid at p. 325.
152 Prolegomena, section 11.
153 Lynn, John A. II, 'Honourable Surrender in Early Modern European History, 1500–1789' in Holger Afflerbach and Hew Strachan (eds), *How Fighting Ends: A History of Surrender*, (United Kingdom: Oxford University Press, 2012), p. 99–110, p. 103; Sibley, N. W. and Smith, F. E., *International Law as Interpreted During the Russo-Japanese War* (United Kingdom: T. Fisher Unwin & William Blackwood and Sons, 1905), p. 71.
154 Zack Beauchamp, '600 years of war and peace, in one amazing chart', *Vox* [website] (updated 24 Jun. 2015) <https://www.vox.com/2015/6/23/8832311/war-casualties-600-years>; using data from Max Roser.
155 Matthew White, 'Statistics of Wars, Oppression and Atrocities of the Nineteenth Century', *Necrometrics* [website] (updated Jan. 2014) <http://necrometrics.com/wars19dc.htm>.

156 James Heath and John Phillips, *A Chronicle of the Late Intestine War in the Three Kingdoms of England, Scotland and Ireland* (London: James Heath, 1675), p. 466.
157 Cited from <https://www.pepysdiary.com/diary/1660/10/20/>.
158 Cesare Bonesana di Beccaria, *An Essay on Crimes and Punishments. By the Marquis Beccaria of Milan. With a Commentary by M. de Voltaire. A New Edition Corrected.* (Albany: W.C. Little & Co., 1872). 12/8/2018. Originally 1764 At <https://oll.libertyfund.org/titles/beccaria-an-essay-on-crimes-and-punishments>.
159 Ibid, at 99–100.
160 Cited from <https://ebooks.adelaide.edu.au/v/voltaire/dictionary/chapter454.html>.
161 Shaw, A. G. L., *The Reasons for the Foundation of a British Settlement at Botany Bay in 1788*, ARTS, vol. 4, ([place: publisher], 1984), p. 83, available at <http://openjournals.library.usyd.edu.au/index.php/ART/article/viewFile/5505/6176>, p. 84; Robert Hughes states that the equivalent numbers were two-thirds of felons condemned to death actually executed in 1760 and one-sixth in 1808, see *The Fatal Shore: The Epic of Australia's Founding*, p. 35. Regardless of the exact numbers, it is certain that more and more people sentenced to death were being reprieved as the eighteenth century progressed.
162 Aristotle, Politics, Book I, Part VI.
163 M'bokolo, Elikia 'The Impact of the Slave Trade on Africa' in *Le Monde Diplomatique*, ([place: publisher], April 1998), available at <http://mondediplo.com/1998/04/02africa>.
164 Blackstone, William, *Commentaries on the Laws of England, Vol. I* (United Kingdom: Clarendon Press, 1769), p. 124.
165 Cited in Joel Mokyr, 'The Great Synergy: the European Enlightenment as a factor in Modern Economic growth', ([place: publisher], April 2005), p. 9 available at <https://pdfs.semanticscholar.org/cff8/3056fab568f5085024a918df813a7661a28a.pdf>.
166 Ibid, p. 11.
167 Apostolides, Alexander; 'English Agricultural Output And Labour Productivity, 1250–1850: Some Preliminary Estimates', ([place: publisher], 26 November 2008), p. 36.
168 Joel Mokyr, *The Enlightened Economy: An Economic History of Britain 1700–1850* (United States: Yale University Press, 2012), p. 86.
169 Ibid, p. 84.
170 Andrew Carnegie, *James Watt* (New York: Doubleday, Page and Company, 1905), p. 12.
171 Eric Hopkins, *The Rise of the Manufacturing Town: Birmingham and the Industrial Revolution* (United Kingdom: Sutton Publishing Ltd, 1998), p. 7.

172 Roll, Erich, *An Early Experiment in Industrial Organisation: being a History of the Firm of Boulton & Watt. 1775–1805* (United Kingdom: Longmans, Green and Co., 1930), p. 20.
173 John Workman, 'James Watt and his historical 1776 Parliament Engine', *Black Country Bugle*, [vol/issue] (13 March 2019), [page number].
174 Hay, Douglas, 'Property, Authority and the Criminal Law' in *Albion's Fatal Tree: Crime and Society in Eighteenth-Century England* (United Kingdom: Penguin, 1975), p. 22.
175 *Somerset v Stewart* (1772) 98 ER 499, cited from <http://www.commonlii.org/int/cases/EngR/1772/57.pdf>.
176 Jefferson to Washington, December 4, 1788, in PTJ, 14:330, Jefferson to Madison, July 31, 1788, in PTJ, 13:442, cited from Nancy Verell, 'French Revolution', 11 August 2018, at <https://www.monticello.org/site/research-and-collections/french-revolution>.
177 Andress, David, *The Terror: The Merciless War for Freedom in Revolutionary France* (New York: [publisher], 2005), 178–179. .
178 Federalist Paper 10, <http://avalon.law.yale.edu/18th_century/fed10.asp>.
179 Paul Hyland, Olga Gomez, and Francesca Greensides (eds), *The Enlightenment: A Sourcebook and Reader* (United Kingdom: Routledge, 2003), p. 171.
180 Rae, p. 291.
181 Edmund Burke, *The Works of Edmund Burke*, vol. 4 (United States: Jazzybee Verlag, [year]), p. 35.
182 Joseph de Maistre, *Considérations sur la France* (Lyon: J. P. Pélaguad, 1880), p. 88–89.
183 <https://ebooks.adelaide.edu.au/r/rousseau/jean_jacques/inequality/complete.html>.
184 Voltaire to Rousseau, 30 August 1755, cited from <http://courses.washington.edu/hsteu302/Voltaire%20Letter%20to%20Rousseau.htm>.
185 Richard Dillingham, letter to his parents, 29 September 1836, Dillingham Papers, Ms-CRT, 150:24, Bedfordshire County Records Office, cited in Hughes, Robert (2004) *The Fatal Shore* Vintage, United Kingdom (first published 1987), p. 315–316.
186 Clark, Gregory, *A Farewell to Alms: A Brief Economic History of the World* (Princeton: Princeton University Press, 2007), table 3.4 at p. 50.
187 The current Australian minimum wage as at 1 July 2018 is $18.93 per hour. Someone working 7.5 hours would therefore make $141.98, enough by buy 56 kilograms of rice at $2.50 per kilogram at my local supermarket.
188 Kanguole. Gross domestic product (at purchasing power parity) per capita between 1500 and 1950 in 1990 International Dollars for selected nations, depicting data excerpted from Contours of the World Econo-

my, 1–2030 AD. Essays in Macro-Economic History by Angus Maddison, Oxford University Press, 2007, ISBN 978-0-19-922721-1, p. 382, Table A.7, 2010. CC 3.0 Unreported; Joel Mokyr 'The Great Synergy: the European Enlightenment as a factor in Modern Economic growth', April 2005, available at <https://pdfs.semanticscholar.org/cff8/3056fab-568f5085024a918df813a7661a28a.pdf>, p. 11.

189 All numbers from Liza Picard, *Dr Johnson's London: Everyday Life in London in the Mid 18th Century* (United Kingdom: W&N, 2004) [page number].

190 Max Roser <https://ourworldindata.org/life-expectancy , <https://ourworldindata.org/child-mortality>, <https://ourworldindata.org/economic-growth>.

191 Joel Mokyr, *The Enlightened Economy: An Economic History of Britain 1700–1850* (United States: Yale University Press, 2012), p. 7, 122.

192 Max Roser, Esteban Ortiz-Ospina and Hannah Ritchie, 'Life Expectancy', *Our World in Data* [website], (updated Oct. 2019) <https://ourworldindata.org/life-expectancy>.

193 For example, Lynn White in *Medieval Technology and Social Change* (1962), Alfred Crosby in *The Measure of Reality: Quantification and Western Society, 1250–1600* (1997) and Eric Jones in *The European Miracle: Environments, Economies and Geopolitics in the History of Europe and Asia* (1981).

194 Jack A. Goldstone, 'The Rise of the West—or Not? A Revision to Socio-economic History', *Sociological Theory*, vol. 18, issue 2 (2000), p. 175–194.

195 Kenneth Pomeranz, *The Great Divergence: China, Europe, and the Making of the Modern World Economy* (Princeton: Princeton University Press, 2000), p. 16, 23.

196 Daniel Johnson, 'The Fate of the West', *Standpoint Magazine*, [vol/issue] (July/August 2017), [page extent] <http://www.standpointmag.co.uk/node/6888/full>.

197 Anthony Esolen, *The Politically-Incorrect Guide to Western Civilization* (United States: Regnery Publishing Inc, 2008), p. 131.

198 Samuel Greg, 'Reason, faith, and the struggle for the future of Western civilization', *Acton Institute*, [vol/issue] (30 August 2017), <https://acton.org/publications/transatlantic/2017/08/30/reason-faith-and-struggle-western-civilization>.

199 For example, Blaut, J. M., 'Political geography debates no. 3: On the significance of 1492: I. Fourteen ninety-two', *Political Geography*, vol. 11 issue 4 (1992), p. 355–385.

200 Joel Mokyr, *The Enlightened Economy: An Economic History of Britain 1700–1850* (United States: Yale University Press, 2012), p. 100.

201 Ibid, p. 122.

202 Jack A. Goldstone, 'The Rise of the West—or Not? A Revision to Socio-economic History', *Sociological Theory,* vol. 18, issue 2 (July 1, 2000), p. 175–194.
203 Niall Ferguson, *Civilization: The Six Killer Apps of Western Power* ([place: publisher], 2012) [page extent].
204 Ismail Safa Ustun, *Heresy and Legitimacy in the Ottoman Empire in the Sixteenth Century* (United Kingdom: University of Manchester, 1991) [page extent]; Hakan Köni, 'Politics of Religion and Secularism in the Ottoman Empire; 14th to 20th Century: A Study', *International Journal of Research In Social Sciences* vol. 2, issue 1 (May 2013), p. 11–20; Edip Golbasi, 'Turning the "Heretics" into Loyal Muslim Subjects: Imperial Anxieties, the Politics of Religious Conversion, and the Yezidis in the Hamidian Era', *The Muslim World*, vol. 103, issue 1 (2013), p. 3–23; Ramazan Biçer, 'A Belief Crime In The Ottoman In Point of Socia-Cultural: Being a Zindiq (Heresy)', Paper presented to Crime and Punishment Within the Culture: Past and Present conference, Samara, Russia, 2003.
205 Vera B. Moreen, 'The Status of Religious Minorities in Safavid Iran 1617–61', *Journal of Near Eastern Studies,* vol. 40, issue 2 (April 1981), p. 119–134.
206 1600, 24% of the world's GDP, Angus Maddison, *The World Economy: Historical Statistics* OECD, ([place: publisher], 2003), p. 261.
207 Kenneth Pomeranz, *The Great Divergence: China, Europe, and the Making of the Modern World Economy* (Princeton: Princeton University Press, 2000), p. 16.
208 Angus Maddison, *The World Economy: Historical Statistics,* OECD, ([place: publisher], 2003), p. 261.
209 Justin Yifu Lin, 'The Needham Puzzle: Why the Industrial Revolution Did Not Originate in China', *Economic Development and Cultural Change*, vol. 43, issue 2 (January 1995), p. 269–292.
210 Joel Mokyr, *The Lever of Riches: Technological Creativity and Economic Progress* (United States: Oxford University Press, 1990), p. 57.
211 David S. Landes, 'Why Europe and the West? Why Not China?', *Journal of Economic Perspectives*, vol. 20, issue 2 (Spring 2006), p. 3–22, 6.
212 Pagden, p. 346.
213 Edward Gibbon, *The History of the Decline and Fall of the Roman Empire*, 6 vols. (London: T. Cadell, 1837), vol. 5, p. 932.
214 'World Bank Poverty Overview', *World Bank Poverty* [website], (updated 26 Apr. 2022) <https://www.worldbank.org/en/topic/poverty/overview>.
215 Elena Holody, 'China isn't the only reason Americans are losing manufacturing jobs', *Business Insider* [website], (updated 10 Dec. 2016) <https://www.businessinsider.com.au/manufacturing-output-versus-employment-chart-2016-12?r=US&IR=T>.

216 'Overdoes Death Rates', *National Institute on Drug Abuse* [website], (updated 20 Jan. 2022) <https://www.drugabuse.gov/related-topics/trends-statistics/overdose-death-rates>.
217 Lisa Keister et al., 'Rising Wealth Inequality: Causes, Consequences and Potential Responses', *University of Michigan Poverty Solutions* [website], (updated May 2015) <http://www.npc.umich.edu/publications/policy_briefs/brief40/.
218 Michael Savage, 'Richest 1% on target to own two-thirds of all wealth by 2030', *The Guardian* [website], (updated 7 Apr. 2018) <https://www.theguardian.com/business/2018/apr/07/global-inequality-tipping-point-2030>.
219 'Homeopathy Products Market', *Zion Market Research* [website], (updated 26 Oct. 2018) <https://www.zionmarketresearch.com/report/homeopathy-products-market>.
220 Chris Isidore, 'We spend billions on lottery tickets: here's where all that money goes', *CNN Money* [website], (updated 24 Aug. 2017) <https://money.cnn.com/2017/08/24/news/economy/lottery-spending/index.html>.
221 'Latest edition of the Australian Gambling Statistics', *Victorian Responsible Gambling Foundation* [website], (3 Oct. 2018) <https://responsiblegambling.vic.gov.au/about-us/news-and-media/latest-edition-australian-gambling-statistics/>.
222 'Maribyrnong 2016 Census All persons QuickStats', *Australian Bureau of Statistics* [website], (updated 2016) <http://quickstats.censusdata.abs.gov.au/census_services/getproduct/census/2016/quickstat/CED228>

INDEX

Abbé Mallet, 177
Abbé Martin de Prades, 185
Act Against Usury, 157, 158
Act of Toleration, 90
Acts of Supremacy and Uniformity, 68, 91
Adolphus, Gustavus, 41
Africa, 21, 26, 28
   Chinese voyages to, 35, 252
   European voyages around, 20, 35
   Islamic conquests in, 249
   slavery in, 22, 205, 248
Agricultural Revolution, 209, 230
Aikenhead, Thomas, 91, 133
Al-Biruni, 111
Allut, Antoine, 228
Anabaptism, 40, 44, 46
anaesthesia, 5, 241
Ancient Greece, 6, 8, 19, 29, 34
   innovation in, 36, 131
   politics in, 65
   science in, 111, 121, 131
   slavery in, 203

Anglican Church, 40, 68, 69, 78, 114
   bishops of, 69
   in Scotland, 136, 143
   monopoly in England, 68, 90
   relationship with the monarchy, 70, 79
Anglo-Dutch Wars, 64, 80, 166
antibiotics, 14, 21, 106
Aquinas, Thomas, 29, 119, 198, 203
   influence by Aristotle, 30, 31
   natural law, 30, 88, 94
   political philosophy, 65, 66
   Summa Theologica, 29, 47, 65, 155
   views on economics, 119, 156
   views on heresy, 47
   views on usury, 156
Archimedes, 111, 120, 128, 245
Arian Heresy, 37, 48
Aristarchus, 120
Aristotle, 8, 29, 66, 245
   astronomy, 8, 121, 127
   influence on Scholastic

philosophy, 29, 31,
logic, 109
On the Heavens, 108
political philosophy, 65, 66, 74, 75
science, 66, 108, 109, 111, 119, 121, 130
views on slavery, 203
views on usury, 156
astronomy, 107, 119, 121, 125, 127, 220
atheism, 59, 76, 90, 150, 151, 160, 172, 175, 181
Avicenna, 111
Ayala, Balthasar, 196
Aztecs, 28

Bacon, Francis, 112, 119, 150, 242
Novum Organum, 112
Bakewell, Robert, 209
Baptist Church, 41
Barre, Chevalier François-Jean de la Barre, 189
Battle of Culloden, 147, 221
Battle of Valmy, 224
Bayle, Pierre, 172
Beccaria, Cesare, 200
Bible, 1, 8, 29, 38, 44, 60, 91, 92, 111, 116, 135, 177, 244
Criticism from the *philosophes*, 180
German translation, 38
King James version, 69
Old Testament, 50, 60, 185, 192, 199
science in, 8, 125, 127

Bill of Rights (English), 96, 201
Bill of Rights (American), 97, 104, 193, 220
Bishops' War, 71
Black Death, 21, 28, 50
Black, Joseph, 216
blasphemy, 15, 60, 76, 91, 133, 189
Bonnie Prince Charlie, *see* Charles Edward Stuart (Bonnie Prince Charlie)
Book of Common Prayer, 68
Boulton, Matthew, 217
Boyle, Robert, 112, 114, 119
The Sceptical Chymist, 114
Brahe, Tycho, 123, 250
Britain, *see* Great Britain
Bubonic Plague, 23, 221
Buddhism, 49, 246
Burke, Edmund, 230
Reflections on the Revolution in France, 205

Calvin, John, 2, 15, 39, 44
Calvinism, 2, 40, 43, 45, 234
In Scotland, 45, 69, 84, 142, 157
In the Netherlands, 52, 79, 196
Link to economics, 45, 157
capital punishment, 21, 25, 103, 197
decline, 202, 221
capitalism, 7, 46, 154
Casas, Bartolomé de las Casas, 27, 204
Castellio, Sebastian, 4

Catholic Church
  banned books, 58, 61
  emancipation, 91
  in England, 68, 77, 79, 83, 91, 101
  in France, 172, 189, 225
  in Scotland, 83
  in the Netherlands, 55
  liturgy, 31
  persecution of, 44, 68, 70, 78, 83, 85, 90, 101, 137
  Protestant criticism of, 38, 44, 76, 77
  religious monopoly, 19, 29, 33, 37, 43
  schism with Eastern Orthodox Church, 36
  theology, 156
  views on commerce, 44
  views on science, 127,
  views on usury, 156
Charles Edward Stuart (Bonnie Prince Charlie), 145
Charles I of England and Scotland, 70, 79, 86, 87, 119
Charles II of England and Scotland, 64, 72, 77, 87, 114
Charles V, Holy Roman Emperor, 41, 52, 203
Châtelet, Madame du Châtelet, 180, 183, 186
China
  decline relative to Europe, 13, 212, 246, 248, 249, 252
  economy of, 251
  government of, 35, 36
  religion in, 6, 36, 48, 49
  science in, 8, 11, 132, 209, 252
  technological innovation in, 21, 24, 35, 212, 252
Civil Rights Movement, 14, 242, 257
Columbus, Christopher, 111
Committee of Public Safety, 225
Common Law of England, 134, 191, 199, 207
Condorcet, Marquis de Condorcet, 228
Confucianism, 6, 48, 246, 252
Constantine the Great, 37
Cook, James, 213
Copernicus, Nicolaus, 20, 112, 120, 123, 126, 127, 128
  On the Revolution of the Celestial Spheres, 123
cottage industries, 23, 210, 240
cotton mill, 210, 217
Covenanters, 71, 214
Cranmer, Thomas, 40, 67, 68
criminology, 200
Cromwell, Oliver, 42, 71
crop rotation, 209, 212

D'Alembert, Jean-Baptiste Le Rond, 173, 177, 187
D'Epinay, Louise, 175
Damiens, Robert-François, 186, 221
Danton, Georges, 225, 227
Darwin, Charles, 212
de Witt, Johann, 53, 60, 61, 62
Declaration of the Rights of Man and the Citizen, 193, 222
Deleyre, Alexandre, 228

Denmark, 26, 32, 250
Descartes, Réné, 55, 59, 76, 107, 108
The Principles of Philosophy, 56, 107
Dickens, Charles, 211
Diderot, Denis
  arrest and imprisonment, 182, 232
  biography, 173, 228
  contributions to *Encyclopédie*, 174, 187, 260
  Letter on the Blind, 179, 181
  Philosophical Thoughts, 179
  friendship with Rousseau, 183, 233, 235
  relationship with Voltaire, 181, 186
  Skeptics' Walk, 179
  The Indiscreet Jewels, 179
  views on race, 176
  views on religion, 177
Diggers, 72
Disease, 5, 11, 14, 23, 24, 28, 115, 201, 221, 241
Doctrine of the Trinity Act, 91
Dutch East India Company, 63, 247
Dutch Reformed Church, 52, 54, 55, 61, 79, 196

Eastern Orthodox Church, 36, 46
  schism with Catholic Church, 36
Edict of Fontainebleau, 54
Edict of Nantes, 43, 54, 171
Edward VI, 67
Eighty Years' War, 42, 43, 52

Elizabeth I, 68, 70
empiricism, 6, 8, 10, 12, 57, 66, 73, 86, 108, 114, 150, 167, 172, 176, 200, 209, 212, 219, 240, 248, 254, 261
  link to scientific method, 106, 109, 121, 142
Encyclopædia Britannica, 169, 170
Encyclopédie
  contributors, 175, 184, 234, 260
  editorial position, 176, 178, 207
  government censorship of, 184, 187, 229
  Jesuit criticism of, 184, 187
  origin, 172
  religion in, 177
  size and scale, 170, 188
England,
  colonial empire, 136
  criminal justice system of, 24, 44, 191, 201, 237
  economy of, 86, 139, 143, 157, 158, 162, 209, 211
  government of, 66, 81, 82, 84, 85, 257
  monarchy of, 24, 26, 67, 69, 71, 78, 80, 93
  Reformation in, 40, 52, 67
  religion in, 38, 44, 68, 69, 72, 86, 91, 99, 157
  slavery in, 206, 222
  warfare, 64, 80, 84
English Civil War, 71, 72, 79, 87, 92, 115, 217
European colonisation of the Americas, 27, 70, 99, 111, 136, 147, 203, 205, 247

famine, 11, 23, 135
Farel, William, 2
feudalism, 22, 25, 27, 29, 51, 134, 153, 217
Filmer, Robert, 93
France
   criminal justice system of, 187, 189, 221
   economy of, 158, 162
   government of, 154, 162, 222, 224, 230, 231, 232
   monarchy of, 52, 56, 58, 77, 78, 87, 154, 171, 222
   Reformation in, 40
   revolution of 1789, *see* French Revolution
   revolution of 1830, 236
   religion in, 42, 172, 189, 227, 231
   science in, 118
   slavery in, 206, 207, 221, 247
   warfare, 64, 80, 114, 146, 171, 182, 186, 187, 194, 221, 223, 249
   Wars of Religion in, 42
Francisco de Vitoria, 196
Frederick the Great, 180, 186, 187, 220
free trade, 55, 154, 160, 166, 176, 256
French Revolution, 11, 162, 172, 220, 223, 225
French Revolutionary War, 199, 224

Galileo Galilei, 108, 112, 119, 120, 125
   Sidereus Nuncius, 126

GDP (Gross Domestic Product), 21, 63, 158, 212, 238, 240, 248, 251
Geneva, 1, 39, 187, 232, 234
Geocentrism, 121, 126, 128, 131
George I, 137, 138, 147
George II, 145,
germ theory of disease, 5
Germany
   colonial empire, 247
   economy of, 154, 157
   government of, 32, 36, 233
   innovation in, 29, 116, 118, 128, 213
   Reformation in, 33, 38
   religion in, 39, 45, 157
   success of, 244
   warfare, 42, 84
Girondins, 223, 224, 226, 228
Glasgow, 134, 141, 146, 152, 159, 215, 247
Glorious Revolution, 85, 90, 92, 96, 102, 137, 247
Gnosticism, 58
Great Britain
   creation, 136
   criminal justice system, 166, 221
   colonial empire, 221, 247
   economy of, 154, 162, 167, 206, 209, 240, 248
   government of, 139, 220, 232, 236
   monarchy of, 137, 139
   slavery in, 206, 207, 221, 247
   success of, 101, 244, 247, 248

warfare, 144, 145, 182, 186, 225
great divergence, 243, 253
Grimm, Friedrich Melchior, Baron von Grimm, 175
Grotius, Hugo, 196
    On the Law of War and Peace, 196
guilds, 52, 154, 158, 209, 215
guillotine, 225, 228, 229, 231
Gutenberg, Johannes, 29

habeas corpus, 191, 192
Harrison, Thomas, 199, 202
Heliocentrism, 121, 131
Henry VII, 24, 26, 67
Henry VIII, 24, 26, 40, 67
heresy,
    arguments for suppression, 47, 50, 127
    capital punishment for, 2, 25, 36, 44, 50, 68, 201
    in China, 48
    in Islam, 48, 250
Hinduism, 155, 191, 209, 251
Hobbes, Thomas, 72, 92, 93, 95, 98, 108
    The Leviathan, 73, 76
Holbach, Paul-Henri Thiry, Baron d'Holbach, 175
Holy Roman Empire, 20, 22, 32, 36, 38, 42, 203
Hooke, Robert, 115, 130
House of Commons, 66, 76, 82, 84, 87, 167, 256
House of Lords, 66, 84, 230
Huguenots, 54, 171, 172

human rights, 6, 8, 10, 13, 97, 176, 190, 194, 204, 207, 221, 226, 242, 256, 261
Hume, David, 9, 12, 143, 149, 160, 167, 172, 175, 228, 261
    Treatise on Human Nature, 143, 149
Hutcheson, Francis, 141, 151, 160

Ibn al-Haytham, 111
Ibn al-Nafis, 1
Ibn Sina, *see* Avicenna
India, 34, 247
    European colonisation of, 20, 63, 155
    technological advancement in, 7, 251
Industrial Revolution, 7, 10, 209, 211, 219, 240, 246, 252,
infant mortality, 12, 221, 241
infection, *see* Germ Theory of Disease
Inquisition, 36, 58, 127
Ireland
    Cromwellian conquest of, 42
    universities of, 135,
    Williamite War in, 85
Islam
    Golden Age of, 246, 249
    heresy in, 48, 58, 250
    relationship with Greek Philosophy, 29, 122
    relationship with Scholastic Philosophy, 29, 108, 111
    theology, 6, 9, 36
    usury in, 155

Italy
  economy of, 63, 154, 157, 158, 244
  Renaissance in, 7, 11, 19, 22, 27, 35, 36, 154, 244

Jacobins, 223, 226, 235
Jacobite uprising of 1689, 84
Jacobite uprising of 1715, 138, 145
Jacobite uprising of 1745, 145, 149, 161
Jacobites, 84, 137, 138, 143, 151, 161
James Francis Edward Stuart (Old Pretender), 79, 137, 138, 145
James II and VII, 77, 78, 80, 84, 91, 98, 137, 147
James VI and I, 69, 70, 72
Jefferson, Thomas, 12, 103, 104, 223, 229
Jeffrys, George, First Baron Jeffrys, 78, 102
Jesuit Order, 8, 31, 49, 83, 172, 173, 181, 184, 187
Judaism, 9, 24, 48, 53, 58, 91, 154, 157, 177, 191, 244, 250, 251
just war theory, 196

Kames, Henry Home, Lord Kames, 148, 152, 161, 207, 228
Kant, Immanuel, 9, 13, 34, 170, 220, 223, 228, 260
  What is Enlightenment? 170, 220, 261
Kepler, Johannes, 124, 127, 131, 250,
  Astronomia Nova, 125

Knox, John, 40, 69, 135

Leibniz, Gottfried Wilhelm, 116
Libertinism, 41
Locke, John
  A Letter Concerning Toleration, 86, 88, 92, 103, 109
  An Essay on Human Understanding, 86, 108
  argument for toleration, 6, 10, 88, 92, 151
  biography, 87, 90, 105
  criticism of, 100, 234
  empiricism, 108
  First Treatise on Government, 93
  friendship with Isaac Newton, 117
  influence on Hutcheson, 141
  influence on Voltaire, 180
  influence on the United States, 103
  political thought, 12, 92, 95, 98, 176, 192, 257
  Second Treatise on Government, 93, 97, 101, 103
  state of nature, 93, 98
  views on atheism, 90
  views on Catholicism, 90
Lollardy, 38
Louis XII, 26
Louis XIV, 54, 58, 64, 78, 85, 87, 105, 154, 171
Louis XVI, 222, 225, 228, 229
  execution, 225, 228, 229
Luther, Martin, 33, 38, 44, 46
  Ninety-Five Theses, 33, 38

Views on astronomy, 127
Views on usury, 157
Lutheranism, 2, 39, 40, 43, 46

Madison, James, 48, 91, 199, 205, 236, 239
Maistre, Joseph de Maistre, 232,
Malesherbes, Guillaume-Chrétien de Lamoignon de Malesherbes, 184, 229
Malthus, Thomas, 238, 240, 242
Mar, John Erskine, Earl of Mar, 137, 145
Marie Antionette, 226, 229
Mary I, 68
  Marian persecutions, 68, 79
Mary II, 80, 91, 105, 135, 137
Maskelyne, Nevil, 213
Maximilian I, 26
Mercantilism, 153, 166
mercenaries, 19, 27, 42, 158
Metternich, Klemens von Metternich, 232, 236
Mohammed, 15, 36
Mongols, 49, 50, 247
Monmouth's Rebellion, 78
Montesquieu, Charles Louis de Secondat, Baron de Montesquieu, 96, 105, 187, 192, 206, 209, 232
Mosaic Law, 192, 193

Napoleon Bonaparte, 199, 231
Napoleonic Wars, 11, 200, 231
natural law, 30, 74, 77, 88, 94, 197, 198, 204
Netherlands

colonial empire, 64, 247
economy, 54, 63, 157, 158, 209
government, 25, 32, 52, 79
independence, 43
innovation in, 209
Reformation in, 40, 52
religion, 53, 55, 196
science, 128, 250
success of, 51, 54, 63, 158, 244
warfare, 26, 42, 80, 225
Newcomen's steam engine, 214, 215, 219
Newton, Isaac
  as a Member of Parliament, 82
  biography, 115
  friendship with Locke, 117
  law of universal gravitation, 116, 129, 130, 132
  laws of motion, 130
  membership of the Royal Society, 115
  Principia, 117, 128, 132, 180
  rules for reasoning, 117

Oresme, Nicole, 122
Ottoman Empire, 21, 26
  decline, 243, 247, 250
  rivalry with Europe, 249, 253

paganism, 8, 20, 30, 37, 233
Paine, Thomas, 9, 10, 207, 231
  The Age of Reason, 9,
  The Rights of Man, 193, 230
Parlement of Paris, 171, 187, 189
Parliament (Britain), 101, 136, 139, 167, 201, 218

Parliament (England), 66, 67, 70, 77, 82, 86, 87, 90, 96, 136, 159, 192

Parliament (Scotland), 44, 84, 136, *see also* House of Commons and House of Lords

patents, 158, 213, 216, 218

Patrizi, Francesco, 111

Pepys, Samuel, 116, 200

Persia, 13, 21, 35, 48, 111, 232, 247, 249, 251

Phillip II, 52,

philosophes, 149, 162, 172, 189, 228, 234, 242

Philosophical Transactions of the Royal Society, 115

Plato
- political views, 65, 74, 208, 245
- reasoning, 109
- rediscovery in the Renaissance, 19, 111
- science, 122

Portugal, 20, 26, 35, 27, 53, 205, 247

Presbyterianism, 69, 143, 146, 160, 161, 214

printing press, 29, 38, 121, 170

Protestant Reformation, 39, 41, 44, 45, 128, 157, 158, 170

Ptolemy of Alexandra, 122

Puritanism, 41, 42, 68, 69, 70, 71

Putney Debates, 71

Pythagoreans, 121

Quakerism, 41, 44, 207

racism against non-Europeans, 12, 13, 176, 206, 257

Reform Act, 236

religious toleration, 37, 43, 46, 48, 50, 53, 55, 71, 77, 79, 86, 135, 136, 151, 172, 190, 196, 250, 254

Restoration of the monarchy in England and Scotland, 72, 77

revolutions of 1848, 236

Robespierre, Maximilien, 12, 223, 226, 227, 231

Roebuck, John, 216

Roman Empire, 21, 34, 36, 37, 46, 59, 70, 89, 180, 190, 245, 246, 249

Romantic Movement, 233, 236

Rousseau, Jean-Jacques
- biography, 233
- *Confessions*, 233
- contributions to *Encyclopédie*, 175
- *Discourse on the Arts and Sciences*, 234
- *Discourse on the Origin and Basis of Inequality Among Men*, 234
- friendship with Diderot, 174, 183
- religious views, 235

Russell, Bertrand, 100, 110, 131, 161
- views on induction, 110

Rye House Plot, 87

Savery's steam engine, 213, 214

Scholastic philosophy, 29
- criticism of, 38, 45, 74, 76, 260
- Greek influence, 31, 127, 156
- political philosophy, 64

reasoning, 110
religious influence, 31, 181, 184
science, 107, 111, 127
usury, 156
scientific method, 6, 8, 10, 106, 111, 118, 220, 245, 261
Scientific Revolution, 7, 106, 119, 121, 123, 131, 133, 245
Scotland
  economy of, 139, 141, 159
  literacy in, 44
  government of, 71, 85, 86, 136, 139, 144
  monarchy of, 69, 70, 78, 84
  Reformation in, 40, 44
  religion in, 44, 69, 71, 86, 92, 136
  union with England, 136
  universities of, 134, 139, 141, 144, 149, 160, 162, 215
Select Society of Edinburgh, 161, 217
Seleucus of Seleucia, 122
separation of church and state, 36, 37, 86, 104
separation of powers, 96, 104
Sepúlveda, Juan Gines de Sepúlveda, 203, 204
Servetus, Michael, 1, 17, 40, 44, 151
Seven Years' War, 221, 182, 188, 199
Shaftesbury, Anthony Ashley Cooper, First Earl of Shaftesbury, 87, 99
Shakespeare, William, 28, 194, 195
slave trade, 22, 141, 205, 247

slavery
  abolition, 183, 206, 221
  in Africa, 22, 205
  in Ancient Greece, 245
  in European colonies, 12, 101, 241, 247
  in the United States, 101, 105, 241, 247
  religious arguments for, 192, 203, 246
  religious arguments against, 94, 205, 207
  wealth gained from, 247, 257
Smith, Adam
  argument for toleration, 101
  biography, 139, 228
  criticism of mercantilism, 165
  criticism of slavery, 207
  friendship with David Hume, 149
  political views, 166
  The Wealth of Nations, 133, 139, 161, 163, 140, 167, 209, 230
  Theory of Moral Sentiments, 161
  time at Oxford University, 143
  time in Glasgow, 159, 215
  time in Paris, 162, 175
Socrates, 47, 110
Spain
  colonial empire, 20, 27, 35, 64, 203, 247
  economy of, 20, 23, 158
  Islamic rule over, 49
  monarchy of, 41, 77
  reconquest by Christians, 250
  religion in, 50, 53

warfare, 26, 85, 138, 144, 199, 225
Spinoza, Baruch
  biography, 58
  condemnation of, 61, 76
  Ethics, 59
  humanism, 10,
  Theologico-Political Treatise, 59
  state of nature, 73, 93, 98, 257
storming of the Bastille, 222
Suárez, Francisco, 196
Sweating Sickness, 24, 28
Sweden, 26, 41, 42, 57, 85, 176

Taoism, 49
Telesio, Bernardino, 111
Ten Commandments, 30, 40, 192
Thirty Years' War, 41, 42, 50, 56, 194, 198,
Tories, 77, 78, 82, 87, 92, 136, 137, 138, 143, 147, 151
Townshend, Charles, 209
Treason Act 1695, 102
Treason Act 1790, 201

Union of England and Scotland, 136
Unitarianism, 41, 90, 91
United States of America
  Bill of Rights, 220
  Constitution, 193, 220
  Declaration of Independence, 103, 190, 191, 257
  economy, 238, 240, 243
  government of, 52, 105
  religion in, 233
  slavery in, 12, 247

universities
  Cambridge, 82
  in France, 185
  in Germany, 35
  in Scotland, 91, 134, 139, 141, 144, 149, 160, 162, 215
  in the Netherlands, 196
  Oxford, 143
  scholastic philosophy in, 158, 209
usury, 31, 45, 155, 156
vaccination, 5, 14, 241

Valladolid debate, 203
Voltaire, François-Marie Arouet
  biography, 179, 228
  condemnation of torture, 189, 200
  contribution to *Encyclopédie*, 186
  criticism of Rousseau, 234
  Philosophical Dictionary, 62, 181, 189
  views on religion, 101, 172, 181, 189
  visit to England, 101

War of the Austrian Succession, 144, 145, 182, 221
War of the League of Cambrai, 27
War of the Spanish Succession, 198, 221
Wars of Religion, 41, 42, 67
Washington, George, 215, 223, 229
Watt, James, 213
  steam engine, 218

Whigs, 77, 82, 85, 87, 137, 144, 151, 220, 230
William II, Dutch Stadtholder, 53, 79
William III and II of England and Scotland, *see* William of Orange
William of Ockham, 111
William of Orange, 53, 79, 84, 91, 96, 135, 137, 141, 146
Wollstonecraft, Mary, 221

www.ingramcontent.com/pod-product-compliance
Lightning Source LLC
Chambersburg PA
CBHW021349300426
44114CB00012B/1136